Postcapitalist cities

Towards a common urban future

Oli Mould

MANCHESTER UNIVERSITY PRESS

The right of Oli Mould to be identified as the author of this work has been asserted in accordance with the Copyright, Designs and Patents Act 1988.

Published by Manchester University Press
Oxford Road, Manchester, M13 9PL

www.manchesteruniversitypress.co.uk

British Library Cataloguing-in-Publication Data
A catalogue record for this book is available from the British Library

ISBN   978 1 5261 6728 6   hardback
ISBN   978 1 5261 6729 3   paperback

First published 2025

The publisher has no responsibility for the persistence or accuracy of URLs for any external or third-party internet websites referred to in this book, and does not guarantee that any content on such websites is, or will remain, accurate or appropriate.

EU authorised representative for GPSR:
Easy Access System Europe, Mustamäe tee 50, 10621 Tallinn, Estonia
gpsr.requests@easproject.com

Typeset
by New Best-set Typesetters Ltd

Contents

Figures

Introduction
What's your perfect city?

Imagine your *perfect* city. What does it look like to you? How tall are the buildings and what kind of architectural styles do they have? How many trees do you see? Is there a river? How big are the roads? Are there are roads at all? What are the sounds of the streets like? How does it smell? How do you get around from one place to another? How is it governed? Do you have a say in how it is run? Do you go to work or simply enjoy a life of leisure and cultural pursuits? What is your home like? Who do you live with? Is it your family or a commune? Do you rent it, or own it yourself or collectively? Given that, according to the UN, 56 per cent of the human population of the planet live in urban areas; the kinds of city that the majority of us already live in will undoubtedly shape the answer to those questions. That is because in trying to dream up utopias, we inevitably (and automatically) fall onto the realities of the present.

But dream we must because our urban centres are at somewhat of a crossroads. The 'model' of development that has ubiquitously characterised urbanity over the last two centuries – namely, one based on the ideology of capitalism with its relentless pursuit of profit and that nebulous yet seemingly sacrosanct notion of 'growth' – has led to a mix of planetary-wide ills including environmental degradation, social inequality, famine, genocide, political unrest, fascist governments, and a climate crisis of unprecedented scale: this is a mix that is toxic, and if radical change is not forthcoming, is likely to prove even more catastrophic than it already has.

Yet, as these crises unfold in the cities that we inhabit – within the cracks of the capitalist city's facade, between the glistening offices of financial might and the informal settlements that carpet the fringes, underneath the surfaces of the street and above the endless forests of concrete and glass – lie the seeds of an urban transformation beyond capitalism that promises what dreaming of utopia can only envisage. Cities have always been epicentres of human ingenuity and creativity, and today is no different in that they are the sites of the concretisation of a potential *post*capitalist city: places where sustainability, equity, community and justice – all those tangible socio-economic goals that capitalism destroys – are not only fought for, but realised. This book is my attempt to look for, analyse and celebrate these postcapitalist cities, wherever they are, however long they last.

But what exactly is a postcapitalist city? Do any research on the topic and you'll undoubtedly come across the same artistic pieces, architects' utopias, soaring narrative prose, and historical accounts that I did. As enlightening and exciting as some of them are, they are largely unsatisfactory when it comes to fully grounding – both empirically and conceptually – what a postcapitalist city is and how it can be achieved in sufficient detail. This book is an attempt to address this lacuna, but to do so it's important (both in terms of an academic narrative but also simply to frame the picture I wish to paint in your mind as this book unfurls) to initially define what a postcapitalist city is in simple terms.

Ultimately, this book rests on the recognition that a postcapitalist city is not an urban provision that is bestowed from above by institutions, governments and corporations; it is won and built from below by citizens, communities and activists. More specifically, that means a city – or more precisely, an urbanised society – that is democratically structured, maintained and *alive* (in radically different ways to the current dominant forms of governance that litter the world), and one that stretches those organising principles across space to encompass a diverse, multifaceted and kaleidoscopic urbanism. Too often, cities that 'work well' (often in service of wealth generation for the elite) are quick to be recast as urban models that can be scaled up beyond the level of the local, neighbourhood level at which their experience is most intimately felt, into homogenous, replicable and ultimately profitable enterprises. A postcapitalist city rejects such scaling and is manifested instead through a heterogenous connectivity into a planetary form of lived urban experience that may be wildly varied experientially, culturally and aesthetically, but shares the same common democratic ideals. As such a postcapitalist city is one built, maintained and enjoyed by its citizens. All the systems that make a city tick – from its economy, transportation, leisure facilities, utilities and systems of care – are controlled by and for the people they serve. As such, a postcapitalist city is one that is fundamentally held in common. This theoretical position will be reinforced as this book progresses with empirical detail, but first, to frame 'postcapitalist cities' more coherently, I need (perhaps rather paradoxically) to take those words in reverse order.

Framing the postcapitalist city

A 'city' can be defined easily if all you're after is a definition for governance and administrative purposes. Indeed, 104 countries of the world use only one or more of three criteria for city status: either population size, the presence of national administrative functions, or specific characteristics (UN Habitat, 2018). In Denmark, for example, a city is any settlement with over 200 people, but in Japan, that number is 50,000. In the United States of America, a city is defined purely by what administrative functions have been devolved to it by the State or Federal government. For example, Maza, in North Dakota was a city with a population of just five people (before its status was dissolved in 2002). In the UK, contrary to popular belief that the presence of a cathedral is all that is needed, city status is actually bestowed by the reigning monarch, and therefore can be lobbied and campaigned for. Indeed, David Amess, the Conversative MP for Southend, spent much of his political career lobbying for the coastal town to be granted city status, arguing that it would boost trade and tourism. After his murder at the hands of a terrorist in 2021, Southend was granted city status in his honour.

The UN also uses the category of 'megacity' to designate cities with populations of over ten million, but given that many of the world's cities, particularly in the global majority, lack official counts of the vast suburban sprawl of informal settlements, the figures are often, at best, vague estimates (Hoole *et al.*, 2019). In addition, variations in national definitional methods mean that, for example, the population of Chinese cities includes vast rural hinterlands of inhabitants that would never set foot on concrete, whereas in some other parts of the world, the entire country *is* the city (i.e. Vatican City, Singapore and Monaco).

What 'makes' a city, then – purely from an official perspective – is fairly straightforward. But all those legal definitions are couched in overtly national frameworks and don't allow for any sort of commensurability across the planetary fabric of urbanity: not that I have been able to visit it, but I would surmise that visiting Maza (pre-2002, of course) would entail a vastly different experience of urbanity than visiting Tokyo at the same time. Southend may be a city now, but could you really argue that it is on a par with Singapore (indeed, would you want to argue that, and if so, why?)? What makes a city is hence far more than estimates by the UN, decrees from kings, or the stroke of a pen from officers in a national statistics agency.

For some, the notion of the city itself is redundant, given that the world is an interlocking mesh of networked people, money, things and ideas that create a 'planetary urbanisation' (Brenner and Schmid, 2011). This concept is a proclamation that there has been an 'emergence of qualitatively new, genuinely planetary forms of urbanization' (Brenner *et al.*, 2012: 237) and it has ignited a wide range of contestations and counter-contestations about the nature of urban theory and how to define 'the city'.[1] It is not within the scope of this book to reiterate those arguments; suffice to say they are positioned as a corrective to the idea (purported by the UN and other supranational governance bodies) that cities can be defined purely by a single administrative or statistical motif. So, taking this more relational approach to the term 'city', this book will use it to speak to the relative *intensities* of those relational urban processes, rather than any rigidly defined boundaries. Of course, that process is ambiguous, debated and conflicting, but the more intense those processes are, the more a city is experienced. For example, the darkest depths of the Mariana Trench, if using traditional definitions, are as far as you can possibly imagine from being urban. But look closer and there's an Internet cable on the ocean floor that carries digital information animating the trading-room floors of Wall Street and Canary Wharf. Hence, while being surrounded by salt water and aquatic life hitherto unrecorded by science, it is still part of the urban.

Therefore, this book is built on the premise that cities are the *spatialisation* of our social relations. As such, how we relate to one another as human beings and the non-human things around us will be how our cities will form. And it will come as no surprise to anyone reading this book that those relations in the twenty-first century can only really be described as 'capitalist', which brings us to the second term: 'post*capitalist*'. The first part of this book will analyse how the contemporary city can be empirically and theoretically considered capitalist, but first, it is useful to explore that most controversial of ideologies – capitalism – on its own terms.

There is little point in trying to cover the centuries of analysis and scholarship on the nuances of capitalism and how it has developed over time since Marx scrutinised it so meticulously back at the end of the nineteenth century; there are a myriad of scholars whose sole aim is to do just that (e.g. Fisher, 2008; Picketty, 2014; Mazzucato, 2018; Blakeley, 2024, to reference just a few of those I've found useful). Suffice to say that, as far as this book is concerned, capitalism refers to the fundamental (and increasingly violent) process of extraction of surplus value from the working class (broadly defined) by a profit-seeking capitalist class (of people, institutions and govern-ments). This ranges from the simple act of casual employment, through the rapaciousness of real-estate gentrification, to the extraction of fossil fuels and the related planetary ecocide their burning entails. Beyond this kernel of truth, though, the nuances of capitalism – its application, its theorising, its empirical hues and spatial variations – are seemingly infinite. Arguably, the most important theoretical impetus capitalism has had in the last few decades has been that of neoliberalism – again, a term that has garnered entire libraries full of scholarship. Fundamentally, neoliberalism, as described by Davies (2016), is an attempt to replace political and social judgement with economic evaluation, where self-interested competition is seen as the cornerstone of social liberty (see also Brown, 2015). Neoliberalism as a political philosophy extends this competitive market-centric view to all aspects of life, and purports that everything, including human emotions and relationships, can be commodified and subjected to market principles, as that is the pathway to liberty. Hence capitalism in the contemporary world, yoked as it is to a neoliberal guiding philosophy (cemented in the Global North by its most ardent of political champions, Margaret Thatcher and Ronald Reagan), permeates into the very recesses of human life. From the intense competition between corporations with their global supply chains ensnaring millions of labourers and tonnes of raw materials, to the marketisation of our most basic human desire for intimate companionship via social media dating apps, capitalism defines social relations and the spaces they create. From an urban perspective, we see this most readily in the corporatisation of 'urban governance' and the rise of city metrics that, along with the concept of the 'global city' (Sassen, 2001; Acuto, 2022), have fuelled a race to the top among cities. However, this process is not uniform; Peck *et al.* (2013) argue that neoliberalism mutates across different places and cities, influencing urban policy and management practices in varied ways that displace, marginalise and immiserate the urban poor most acutely, but end up homogenising cities in the image of capital.

It is also worth framing capitalism in the broader suite of social ideologies that are caricatured by political discourse. There are those who will make a very hard and reductive distinction between capitalism and communism, nominally those who are still mired in the Cold War rhetoric that saw the USA pitted against the USSR and the stereotypical motifs that entailed. Then there is socialism, an oft-misunderstood term which, in the UK at least, is often erroneously used to label any politician that has the temerity to be positioned politically to the left of the Conservative Party. Anarchism also plays an important role in the narrative around the definition of capitalism, given that it is used as a catch-all term for chaos, disorder and the actions of anyone who partakes in even the slightest form of protest against the ruling class. Of course, none of these stereotypes are true. Communism, socialism and anarchism (and many other 'isms' that can be identified in relation to capitalism) each have their own particularities and modes of operating within an urban setting that aim to undo the injustices of capitalism. Again, this is not a discussion of the nuances of these terms, but they will be alluded to throughout this book as part of the broader analysis of postcapitalism. That is because these ideologies seek to redefine what urban life could and should be. More often than not, the challenges this presents are for a different future; these ideologies are attempting to enact a '*post-*capitalist' city. But rather than being limited to a temporal rigidity for the prefix 'post' (from the Latin, *post*, meaning after, but also behind), I prefer to broaden its definitional field beyond just time. It can be used spatially, emotionally and philosophically, to mean beyond, within, in between, outside, marbled through, hidden, diffuse or even completely absent and not yet conceived of.

With that in mind, the concept of the capitalist city ultimately revolves around the notion of power, with a central question being: who has the right to the city? This is a question that has been asked by communists, socialists and anarchists throughout the course of the history of the capitalist city, but it was Lefebvre, in his seminal work in 1968, *Le Droit à la ville*, who first posited this question (at least in the written, published form) as a way to probe the fundamentals of who possesses the right to not only create the city, but to be a part of urban life. This question was, and still is, crucial in understanding the power dynamics of cities increasingly shaped by capitalist processes in the twenty-first century. In urban environments that are becoming squeezed by the profit motive of capitalism and the governments that genuflect to it, the very everyday use of space and access to it becomes a highly contentious issue, reflecting broader questions of equity, power distribution, public, and social justice. Hence, the claim of the 'right to the city' has fuelled decades of anti-capitalist critiques and movements (some of which are discussed throughout Part II of this book). From this claim, multiple practices of postcapitalism emerge which contribute to 'cityness': there are the protests and activist tactics of resistance, of course, but also acts of urban living revolving around reciprocity, care, mutual aid, democratic housing models, shared infrastructures, and many others that will be evidenced throughout this book.

So, in envisioning a postcapitalist city, the framework for this book diverges significantly from the other ideologies such as the purely economic analysis of Mason (2016), who posits a temporal trajectory characterised by technological reinvention which he labelled as 'postcapitalism'. Similarly, while there is a great deal to be gleaned from Varoufakis's (2024) notion of 'techno-feudalism', the insistence that capitalism has been usurped is wide of the mark. Instead, the conceptualisation of postcapitalist cities in this book aligns more closely with the theoretical framework that Lefebvre (1968) proposed when detailing the right to the city (and as will be become a recurring theme in this book, the year 1968 is critical and one of the reasons for leaning on his work). Foreshadowing the planetary urbanisation debate (and its unease at supranational definitions of the city as outlined above), Lefebvre distinguished between the 'city' and 'urban society', arguing that the contemporary city aspires to become an abstract entity, an easily replicable model propagated by corporate and governmental actors seeking to maximise profits globally. Conversely, an 'urban society' embodies a city liberated from centralised control, promoting a radical, heterogeneous and self-managed urbanist paradigm. This view of the city as a more or less intense, messy coagulation of people and things has been built on and adapted over the decades with post-colonial (Roy, 2011), feminist (Kern, 2020), queer (Oswin, 2015), anti-racist (Danewid, 2020), disability (Jaffe, 2021), crip (Ehrenspreger, 2022) and other theories, all highlighting the tensions, contradictions, resistances and 'radical undecidability' (Roy, 2011: 235) that are bounded up in the conceptualisations of a city postcapitalism. Essentially, the postcapitalist city of this book is one that foregrounds democratic control that spreads outwards via federal connections of solidarity, rather than scales up to formulate models that end up homogenising urban space. It is not envisaged as an ultimate state but as a foundational premise for reimagining urban life beyond the confines of capitalism. This resonates (and in many ways connects) with commensurate analyses of a postcapitalist politics articulated by many scholars (but perhaps more persuasively and presciently by Gibson-Graham (2006)), emphasising a continuous effort to mitigate the pervasive urban injustices exacerbated by climate-catastrophe-inducing, inequality-exacerbating, socially homogenising and politically polarising capitalism.

Postcapitalist cities prioritise a Lefebvre-inspired urban society that is about inclusivity, democracy and sustainability. They actively dismantle the dominant (white, male, able-bodied and cis) hierarchical structures; they plan infrastructure and urban form that is ecologically sustainable and regenerative; politically, they attempt to create democratically run urban environments; crucially, they do not scale upwards homogenously but stretch outwards, increasing their heterogeneity as they touch other cultures and social make-ups. These cities – which as this book will evidence, *do* exist within the 'gaps' of the capitalist urban fabric – offer a transformative vision for urban life that seeks to benefit all citizens, underscoring the necessity of a political and social commitment to sustainability, democracy and justice.

Why now?

The urgency of this transformation cannot be overstated, for two main and interrelated reasons. First, climate-related disasters are escalating in both frequency and severity across the globe, a phenomenon extensively documented in scientific literature (IPCC, 2021). Coastal metropolises are increasingly vulnerable to rising sea levels (Goh, 2021), while urban areas are experiencing intensifying heatwaves that render densely built environments, often disparagingly referred to as 'concrete jungles', nearly uninhabitable (Dawson, 2017). These climatic shifts expose the inadequacies of traditional and often ageing urban infrastructures, which were designed for a bygone era characterised by industrial expansion and are now glaringly ill-equipped – materially, socially and culturally – to meet and overcome contemporary climate challenges and injustices. The critical nature of this transformation is underscored by the growing body of planetary research advocating for systemic changes in urban planning and policy. Indeed, Stone, Jr. (2024) has argued for a total paradigm shift towards sustainable urbanism, emphasising the need for infrastructures that are community-based, adaptive, resilient and designed to mitigate the adverse effects of climate catastrophe; in short there is a call to 'unlearn' how to plan sustainable cities and start from scratch.

Second, the social fabric of our cities is fraying under the mounting pressures of economic inequality. The wealth disparity between an affluent elite and the impoverished masses has reached unprecedented levels, creating stark contrasts within urban landscapes (Piketty, 2014; Dorling, 2019). Luxury skyscrapers, symbols of opulence and economic power, overshadow dilapidated neighbourhoods, starkly illustrating this divide that manifests in quotidian issues such as housing, cost of living, and the access (or lack thereof) to public space (Harvey, 2012). This spatial and economic binary extremism is not merely a matter of social injustice; it fundamentally undermines the sustainability of urban life in an era increasingly defined by rampant neoliberal capitalism. In the same way that total urban transformation has been noted as required to mitigate climate catastrophe (Stone, Jr., 2024), total socio-economic urban transformation will be required to combat the furthering of inequality that the climate crisis will engender.

This book will focus less on the first transformation needed for climate emergency, and more on the second one. They are, of course, interrelated and one change will necessarily require the other, but purely from the point of view of my expertise and research, I have focused more on the social transformation that postcapitalist cities envision rather than the ecological. The latter requires (among other things) an intricate understanding of infrastructural engineering, hydrology, and/or climate science that is well beyond my capabilities as a critical urban social scientist. But this understanding of the social and political transformation of cities from capitalist to postcapitalist cities will absolutely inform and relate to how cities will need to transform to adapt to the climate catastrophe; after all, the climate crisis is a crisis of capitalism and our over-consumption. Therefore, to cleave urban transformation into distinct areas is ultimately a fool's errand; we need to always keep in mind that while analysis and critique requires a narrow focus to unearth empirical means of actualising transformative action, the name of that barrier to emancipatory justice in all its forms remains the same: capitalism.

Despite this universal truth, it is important to acknowledge that postcapitalist cities won't emerge in a spatially bounded vacuum. As much as local residents, communities and urbanites have the innate power to democratically shape the future urbanisms of their city, their ultimate longevity will depend upon their connectivity with others. The 'success' of a postcapitalist city will rest just as much on an internationalism that extends beyond the city's boundaries, and even the country's borders, as it will on the democratic impulses of its residents. Indeed, a viable sense of internationalism is a key ingredient of postcapitalist praxis (Gibson-Graham, 2006). In the Marxist tradition of advancing from a capitalist society towards the communist horizon, a stateless, borderless world is essential (in other work, I have articulated this as a 'planetary commons' (Mould, 2021)). Collaboration (and conspiring) of the urban proletariat and the marginalised from *all* parts of the world in forging the vision for a fairer city will ensure the availability of vital resources against the inevitable revanchist violence of the capitalist city. Hence, while this book will touch down in various parts of the globe to narrate how postcapitalist cities are emerging and thriving in the cracks and blind spots of a suffocating urban racial capitalism, it will also emphasise – both empirically and conceptually – that such postcapitalism will not and cannot be realised, conceptualised and sustained without an accompanying postcapitalist planetary commoning ethics (Mould, 2021).

That said, this book stems from research conducted from where I have been able and lucky enough to travel. With ongoing COVID-19 restrictions limiting travel in between 2020 and 2022, and the other (mostly financial but also temporal) restrictions that come from being an academic in the hyper-neoliberalised UK sector, there is a clear global-north bias to the empirics of this book (particularly to my home city-region of Greater London). This bias is further intensified by me being anglophone, white, European and able-bodied. The positionality (and associated research reflexivity) of 'professionalised' academic research has been the focus of a great deal of important critique (see Crossa, 2012 and Beebeejaun, 2022). In short, 'positionality is not only an epistemological matter that shapes how we see and know the world, but also an ontological matter in terms of *what we see*' (Crossa, 2012: 126, emphasis added). As such, dear reader, it is vital that you take on board that the text of this book will be a culmination of what I have seen of, and thought about, postcapitalist cities, but refracted through all those identities I embody. It will therefore be incomplete, skewed and twisted by the books I have read, the education I have received, the languages I (cannot) speak and the resources I have access to. But by now (and if you have read this far), this *problématique* will be no doubt familiar as it is a structural characteristic of academic work; the problem comes when such issues of positionality are not declared, or worse, assumed to be incidental.

With all that in mind, the book's case for postcapitalist cities proceeds as a three-step exponential model: problem, reaction, solution. Each step is larger than the one before and consists of an analytical chapter(s) and a more nuanced, specific and perhaps polemic narrative around a single event or idea. As such, while the book hasn't been as bold as those of some authors in producing a 'fragmented narrative' that expertly mirrors the conceptualisation of the 'fragmented city' (à la McFarlane, 2021), there is still an attempt to vary the prose and styles of text to elucidate different emotions that, for me, a postcapitalist reading demands.[2]

Part I briefly identifies the *problems* of the capitalist city, first though a catch-all overview of gentrification and racial capitalism, and a discussion of the social murder at Grenfell, and how the disaster can be thought of as a microcosm of the fatal symptoms of the capitalist city. This will no doubt be familiar to readers (hence the brevity) but is necessary in positioning the deleterious issues of the racialised capitalist city that need to be tackled by postcapitalist urban imaginaries.

Part II concentrates on the *reactions* to the capitalist city and how postcapitalist urbanism emerges. It first historicises this with a focus on the year 1968, which stands out in the twentieth century as a pivotal time in resistance, protest and planetary awakening. The second chapter of Part II theorises postcapitalist urbanity through the aesthetic and political lens of psychedelia, to evidence the 'how' of postcapitalism on an everyday and artistic level. Part II's closing narrative considers the fare strikes in Santiago in 2019 that mushroomed into protests, causing national political change.

Part III evidences the *solutions* of postcapitalist cities and is the largest part, given that it houses the evidence, analysis and exposition of what a postcapitalist city entails (and as such, houses much of the empirics of the book). The first chapter outlines how that most fundamental of provisions within postcapitalism, care, is conceptualised as a radical break from capitalist readings to create a *careful* city that helps to regenerate its residents to become active participatory citizens. The second chapter posits some of the existing alternative housing models presented as a means of enacting social transformation in cities. The third chapter focuses on three site visits to 'concrete' cities that exemplify the different ideological hues of postcapitalism. Finally, there is an analysis of the emergent movement of solarpunk, and how it has the potential to radically shift the discussion of postcapitalist cities.

All in all, this book is about envisioning a 'future' (that can exist in the present) where our cities transcend the contradictions of the capitalist model and embrace a paradigm grounded in equity, sustainability and communal well-being. So, as I asked you to do at the outset, imagine your perfect city. Does it look, sound, smell and feel like the ones that we already inhabit, or is it radically different? The good news is that the postcapitalist cities our current catastrophic times require do exist, and this book attempts to highlight, analyse and celebrate them as a collective endeavour. This book is an invitation to imagine, to critique and to build these new urban realities, drawing inspiration from the seeds of transformation already sprouting within our midst.

Part I

Problems

Chapter 1

The gentrification of everything
The ideologies of the racial capitalist city

Gentrification, at its heart, is just what the capitalist city does. It may have different characteristics, actors and processes to align with the different politics, culture and social geographies, but capitalist cities *demand* that places become 'capitalised'. In other words, capitalism requires urban space to bend to its will; it extracts value from the often common and/or public fabric of the city (or soon-to-be-urban land) and converts that into value that can be exchanged and profited from. Gentrification is the very process by which this happens. With all the nebulous definitional and geographical nuances it has to offer, gentrification is an identifiable and analysable process that highlights and narrates the capitalisation and privatisation of *our* urban realm.

As the aim of this book, then, is to envisage and articulate a postcapitalist city, first there is a need to fully grasp how gentrification has become so embedded in the process of urban change. I have no doubt that, as a reader of this book, you will be very familiar with the gentrification story and the racism therein imbued, but to know what we're up against, it's worth briefly visiting the key ideas.

Defining gentrification

'Ruth Glass, it's all about class' is the rhyming phrase that I get my students to chant during my lectures, to instil in them the underlying and foundational kernel of truth to all gentrification studies: that you cannot talk about gentrification without first going back to the crucial concept of class. That is because for the urban sociologist Ruth Glass (and her peers, writing in the mid-1960s) London was being commandeered by the elitist classes as per the historical situation in rural environments with the landed gentry – *gentri*fication. But of course, in the sixty-odd years since the term was first coined, the term has taken on all sorts of new meanings. It has been the subject of fierce debate around the world, in the pages of academic books and journals, broadsheet and tabloid newspapers, blog posts, op-eds, dedicated social media accounts, artistic exhibitions, videogames, pop songs, and even Pixar films. It has been used in conjunction with a myriad of social processes and therefore cuts cross gender (Van den Berg, 2018), race (more of which is detailed in the next chapter), queer geographies (Christafore and Leguizamon, 2016), and has also been related to labour movements (Gourzis *et al.*, 2019), environmental issues (Checker, 2011), social media (Boy and Uitermark, 2017) and rurality and the global majority world (Lees and Philips, 2018; López-Morales, 2015). Moreover, the financial levels involved dwarf the kind of spending power of individuals and families that Glass was analysing. Today, billionaires have replaced millionaires as the emblems of urban inequality, and rather than individual houses or flats, they talk of 'portfolios' of assets, and they are welcomed into the city by the elite supposedly because of their job-making potential. The overbearing sense in all the debates is that gentrification is just what contemporary cities do. They change all the time, and there are winners and losers in the process. The problem is, of course, that the winners invariably continue to win.

That's because the class dynamics that characterised gentrification all those years ago have themselves been transposed and mutated into the globalised form of capitalistic urban development that is so rampant in our cities in the twenty-first century. Some companies are easily identifiable as actors with massive global influence, such as Blackstone in the US (Christophers, 2022), Peel in the UK (Mould, 2015; Ward and Swyngedouw, 2018), and Evergrande in China (Yang and Ley, 2018). There are also many, many others that are smaller and more locally focused, but will nevertheless operate more or less within the same capitalist logics. The corporate interests that develop cities have commodified urban land to such a degree that it has brought about the 'financialisation' of housing and the urban stock more broadly (Fields, 2017b; Christophers and Fine, 2020). That is, houses (and increasingly retail and service provisions) are built as devices to trade: they are more akin to stocks and shares on the trading-room floor than places of shelter and rest for an overworked and exploited urban population. And the rent gap, often thought of to be a 'naturalised' phenomenon of urban-land-market-financialised logics, can and is manipulated via deliberate disinvestment to depress the present 'capitalised' value, all the while waiting for the 'potential' value to rise further (Minton, 2015; Madden and Marcuse, 2016).

And the state is in on the act too, of course. Developers, when negotiating with urban and local governments about how much of their resultant housing to give back to the city, will argue down their allocation of socially responsible provision by proving that such a development wouldn't be financially viable. And as noted by Madden and Marcuse (2016), this whole process can lead to a 'double gentrification' effect where not only does the new development increase local property values and cost of living, but the lack of contributions to affordable housing exacerbates the housing crisis, pushing lower-income residents out.

It's not just local governments that are complicit in the gentrification story. Some nation states are in and of themselves private gentrifying enterprises. Many Gulf States have invested heavily in urban space across Europe and North America to diversity their financial portfolio from volatile petrodollars into the far more stable and low-risk urban-land grab. In addition, major international global events such as the Olympics, instigated by supranational institutions such as the International Olympic Committee, are also used as catalysts for gentrification. The legacy of the London 2012 Olympiad has majorly transformed Stratford (and East London more broadly) into a landscape of high-rise new builds catering for high-income professionals, tourists, students and real-estate speculators, rather than the incumbent low-income often migrant communities that called it home pre-2012.

Gentrification therefore has come to compile a lot more of the process of global capitalism and geopolitics than when Ruth Glass first wrote about it in the 1960s. Fundamentally, class dynamics fuel gentrification's engines, but the infrastructures it utilises – social, economic, governmental – have shifted and mutated with capitalism. The victims of gentrification – those losers who continue to lose as the winners continue to win – remain obdurately resolute; overwhelmingly, it is the urban poor.

Sassen (2014) has argued that in the contemporary globalised world, economic and territorial restructurings (including all those analysed above) will often lead to the forceful removal of people from their livelihoods, homes or geographic locations; she uses the term 'expulsions'. For Sassen, expulsion occurs when individuals, groups or even entire communities are pushed to the edges of the economic system (and often to the urban fringes), rendering them invisible and irrelevant. This process is not just about the exacerbation of poverty or inequality; it's about a deeper and deliberate societal severance where the expelled become surplus to the core operations of the urban economy. The expelled are not just marginalised; they are actively defenestrated from social, economic and the associated urban orders.

In many ways then, gentrification is *domicidal*. Nowicki (2023) uses the term 'domicide' – traditionally referring to a tactic of warfare that destroys the homes of civilians – to analyse the violence that urban capitalism wreaks upon the urban poor. In the UK, for example, specific governmental policies such as the 'Removal of the Spare Room Subsidy', better known as the 'Bedroom Tax', deliberately 'unmake' home. More than simply denying someone a property to live in, this policy which reduced social-housing tenants' benefits if they were deemed not to be using all of their bedrooms, was an invasion of people's home-making practices.

An added aspect of this domicide is that neighbourhoods lose their culture and identity. Historic buildings, local shops, community centres, and public spaces that once reflected an area's heritage and hosted its collective memories are frequently demolished or repurposed to suit the preferences and needs of capital in the guise of newer, wealthier residents. In particular, racialised and ethnic communities are at risk of expulsion, given that they predominately occupy economically and geographically marginalised urban communities. Moreover, it is not just the loss of physical spaces; this cultural erasure also manifests in the disappearance of community traditions, local businesses, and artistic practices. Festivals, markets and gatherings that once drew people together and strengthened communal bonds fade away or are replaced by events catering to a very different, often professionalised demographic who may not spend as much time (and effort) in local community provisions. This bleeds into psychological impacts, as residents who manage to stay in their gentrifying neighbourhoods can often feel like strangers who experience intense disempowerment (Lees *et al.*, 2016). As decisions about the neighbourhood are increasingly made by and for new, wealthier inhabitants, long-time residents often feel they have no voice or democratic control over their lives.

One of the more obvious signifiers of gentrification is the 'look'. This will of course vary from city to city, continent to continent, but there are homogenising tendencies to gentrification as the money that catalyses it (and the ideological trends that go with it) is ultimately the same. In New York City, there has been a glut of 'super-skinny' skyscrapers built on so-called 'Billionaires Row' (i.e. the area to the immediate South of Central Park around West 57th Street). There have been three main reasons for their rapid rise. The first is that New York City has pioneered a law called 'Transfer of Development Rights' (sometimes called 'air rights') which allows developers to buy the right from their neighbours to build upwards. If a developer owns a particular 'tax lot' (the smallest unit of developable land under NYC planning law), legally they are only allowed up to a certain floor-to-area ratio. However, if any surrounding lots have 'spare' capacity with regards to this ratio, it can be sold off, thereby allowing the purchaser to go even higher on the same lot. Essentially, it is the capitalisation, or privatisation of thin air (and with the height some of these condos reach, the air is particularly thin).

The second catalyst has been the technological innovation, particularly in relation to mitigating the effects of wind on skyscrapers. New stabilising technologies and 'gaps' in the skyscrapers every twenty floors or so allow super-thin skyscrapers to withstand high winds (useful in an age of increasing extreme weather events). Thirdly, and most importantly perhaps, is demand. In the immediate aftermath of the financial crash of 2008, skyscraper development halted around the world. However, the post-crash political economic landscape of bailouts for the rich and austerity for the poor has seen the wealth of the elite skyrocket. And post-COVID, the wealth of the super-rich has further intensified due to huge government subsidies (and spurious contracting). The intense demand for multimillion dollar penthouse suites that overlook Central Park simply didn't exist, but now that the world has more billionaires than ever, it means that the exuberant construction costs become worth it because there will always be someone among the super-rich willing to pay.

This hyper-luxury 'feel', or aestheticisation, of the city breeds an overt ostentatiousness that has gone hand-in-hand with the rise of branding, social media and the general 'Instagramification' of urban life (Boy and Uitermark, 2017). Put bluntly, the super-rich flaunt their wealth more than ever. A mile or so down the western edge of Manhattan from Billionaires Row is the High Line – New York's most visited walkway – surrounded as it is by luxury condominiums. What is particularly notable about these properties, if you take a leisurely stroll down the High Line, is their floor-to-ceiling windows, lack of curtains or blinds, and a distinct absence of personal modesty. Walking the High Line these days is part-nature adventure, part-peep show. Similarly, in London, there is an ongoing and much publicised legal battle between the Tate Modern art gallery and the residents of a luxury housing block built next door. The residents' glass walls can be peered into from the gallery's viewing platform, prompting legal wrangling over privacy rights and 'overlooking'. But despite the flats being built in 2012, a good twelve years after the Tate Modern opened (so presumably knowing full well that they were being built next to a public viewing gallery), the residents' won their case in February 2023 for the platform to alter its design to stop visitors from peering into their opulent, elite but often empty flats (Pritchard-Jones, 2023).

The 'gaze' of the city, the sublime urban vistas of these glazed monoliths that come with such a high price tag, is an intoxicating image, one that is hawked by urban branding agencies just as much as it is desired by the super-rich. Hence the broader aesthetics of gentrification are a deliberate ploy to cater to the professional and creative classes that are so beloved by urban managers (Mould, 2018). Adhering to the latest trends, fashions, architectural styles, artistic trends, and marketing vernaculars is what the contemporary city does, whether that's Manhattan or Maputo. This was no more evident than with the release of a clutch of promotional videos for high-rise luxury developments in London that made the news for all the wrong reasons back in 2015. Red Row developers, in advertising their newest construction, One Commercial Street in Aldgate, created a short video which many online critics and commentators decried as crass and mirroring the disturbing aesthetics of Patrick Bateman in Mary Harron's 2000 film *American Psycho* (based on the 1991 novel by Bret Easton Ellis). In the advert, we follow a slick, affluent male as he works in a seemingly high-powered job, drinks at expensive bars and fantasises about sexually assaulting women in lifts. It shows the opulent luxury of the building's living quarters, all set to a monologue in which the protagonist bemoans, 'The doubts. The need to be different; to define yourself; to be more than individual. To stay true to what you believe' (a monologue that wouldn't be out of place in an Ayn Rand novel). Other, similar adverts came out around the same time, all showing individualistic, super-rich lifestyles and a distinct lack of authentic urban community life. The critics of these abominations were vociferous enough to get many of them taken down (and elicit an apology from those responsible). But the very appearance of them speaks to the kinds of urbanism that the contemporary branding sector surrounding London's real-estate industry is eulogising: a luxury, individualistic, hyper-commercialised, not to mention a very white and male-dominated, urban form, creating what Heiserová (2021) has very aptly described as an urban phallocracy.

Racial gentrification

This will come as no surprise to many readers who have been paying attention to debates about urban change over the years: one of the main critiques of gentrification studies is that it has been relatively single-minded on the class dynamics of the city, and has been (relatively) blind to the intricacies of race (see Kirkland, 2008; Danewid, 2020; Fallon, 2021). The painful presence of this lacuna is emphasised by the fact that capitalism goes hand-in-glove with racism. As far as the development of the city goes, capitalism and racism are reliant on each other; so much, that they are largely indistinguishable in practice. The entire history of capitalism's dominance and its development, from European mercantilism to contemporary populist and culture-war politics, has included various forms of racist ideologies. This is the basis of the theory of 'racial capitalism', as first outlined by Robinson (1983). His writings were wide-ranging from a geographical perspective, but rooted in African studies and the historical exploitation of Black bodies from Africa by European and American systems of capital accumulation. He argued that 'from its very beginnings, this European civilization, containing racial, tribal, linguistic and regional particularities, was constructed on antagonistic differences' (Robinson, 1983: 10). What this means is that for Robinson capitalism developed from the fourteenth to the sixteenth centuries via increasing networks of urban trade across the European continent and its various colonial nations. But the capitalist class that developed along with it (i.e. those merchants who got very rich via trade) did so not by breaking free from feudal structures and practices of reciprocity; they didn't somehow transcend the feudal logic of accumulation with reason and rationality that came from a more enlightened form of global capitalist trade. Instead, for Robinson, this class mutated from feudal logics to include the violent enclosure of racialised bodies from non-white European peoples, including those from Eastern Europe and North Africa: what were referred to as generally 'barbarian' peoples (a vernacular that developed in the Roman Empire). In other words, in feudal times, in a prospering Europe, slavery was *already* happening via movement of the 'barbarians' coming to Europe looking for work (Pulido, 2017). Europeans would then bring these racialised bodies – Gypsies, Romani, Slavs, but also Black bodies – into the production system as slaves. So, as capitalism developed, it brought with it these practices of feudal slavery that were already embedded. Hence, Robinson argues that capitalism developed with slavery already a part of it. As Pulido (2017: 528) has also argued, 'racial capitalism requires that we place contemporary forms of racial inequality in a materialist, ideological and historical framework'. Gilmore (2020) builds on this work by claiming that all capitalism is racial: she argues that 'capitalism requires inequality and racism enshrines it … You cannot undo racism without undoing capitalism'. As a geographer, Gilmore is specifically concerned with the spatial logics of racial capitalism as it exists now in the twenty-first century, and argues that it 'requires all kinds of scheming, including hard work by elites and their compradors in the overlapping and interlocking space-economies of the planet's surface' (Gilmore, 2022: 225).

This is evident very readily in the city networks of the past and their relation to today. Corporations such as the East India Company and the Dutch East India Company of the seventeenth century onwards formalised the trade routes between urban centres of the Old and New World that shaped the contours of the twenty-first century neo-imperialist global economy of an exploiting Global

North and an exploited Global South. So, if, as racial-capitalism theorists argue, the racist practices of the mercantile class were embedded in the development of modern forms of capitalism, then that same racism is deeply scored into the global city networks and production chains that are being analysed today. Indeed, as Danewid (2020: 17) has convincingly argued, 'Although cities such as London, New York, Cape Town, Dubai, Shanghai and Rio de Janeiro have transformed themselves over the last few decades into glitzy centres of financial capital and real-estate speculation, the cost of this transformation has predominantly been carried by racialised "surplus" people and places.'

The analysis of rampant social polarisation and spiralling inequality has long been a part of global city discourse (Mollenkopf and Castells, 1991; Greenberg, 2008; Rast, 2019). Focusing on the divide between elite and service workers, especially in the networked financial centres such as Wall Street, Canary Wharf and the like, racial issues within the global city theoretical critique remain implicit rather than explicit, although they are something which has been addressed by more recent scholarship on race in the global city (Dorries *et al.*, 2019; Phinney, 2020; Danewid, 2020, 2023). So, urbanisation – as understood as a spatial manifestation of capitalist development – is pregnant with existing racial injustices, and we can see that playing out in cities across the world.

Within gentrification studies, though, the literature has predominantly focused on class rather than race, and is too often concerned with purely economic arguments (Dantzler, 2021; Rucks-Ahidiana, 2022), and renders Black bodies as 'ungeographic' (McKittrick, 2006). Indeed, as Fallon argues:

> gentrification studies have historically highlighted gentrification as a class-based change, while including race as an epiphenomenal component of analysis and description. The result is that race is used consistently and implicitly in studies without a motivating theory or logic to define how race is expected to operate within each context. (Fallon, 2021: 19)

Hence, if gentrification is about the extraction of surplus value from a given piece of land, then it stands to reason that that value is predicated upon existing racialised structures just as much as class structures (Fallon, 2021). For instance, it is part of the established canon on gentrification that deliberate disinvestment often occurs prior to profitable reinvestment to expand the rent gap (Slater, 2011). That disinvestment process very often runs along racialised lines as much as it does along economic or class ones (indeed, we can pinpoint this historically with the process of 'redlining' that will be discussed later). Additionally, Black neighbourhoods, once gentrification is established enough to encourage the professional and creative classes (Mould, 2018), can often experience an acceleration in the value extraction and profitability of an area precisely *because* of the cultural milieu developed by Black and majority world ethnicities (Rucks-Ahidiana, 2022). To return to London, one only has to visit Brixton to see how contemporary forms of 'creative city' gentrification have embraced the areas' ethnic make-up as part of the capitalistic offerings, but only on a superficial level: murals of Black activists stand proudly on the street next to gleaming luxury skyscrapers, some of which will be occupied by white gentrifiers who gaze down upon the murals with smug satisfaction that they live in a 'culturally rich' area.

Modern urban capitalism therefore actively brings to bear on the city the spatial logics of racial erasure learned from the past, precisely because it aids in 'enshrining' inequality into the urban realm with various processes, not least for Gilmore (2022) the creation of the prison-industrial complex in the US (which will be returned to later in this chapter). That is, of course, not to exclude the European powers that formed the crucible of Empire, the expansions of which across the centuries brutalised and colonised the global majority world. Many European metropoles were themselves not only segregated racial geographies that foregrounded the contemporary 'splintered' racial urbanism of today, but architecturally, they were built from the ill-gotten resources of the Global South. For instance, the term 'ghetto' was used vociferously in the US in the 1980s and 1990s to territorially stigmatise urban centres of Black and minority people (Wacquant, 2008). Yet the term originates from the Venetian dialect, where it was first used in the early sixteenth century to describe the area of the city of Venice to which the Jewish population were restricted and segregated. Wirth (1928) famously analysed how the word was derived from the Italian word *getto* meaning foundry, as the first Jewish 'ghetto' was established in 1516 near a foundry on a swampy Venetian Island. This marked the beginning of what would become the sanctioned practice of segregating Jewish communities within cities right across Europe, justified through various social, religious and economic excuses. This *ghettoisation* of Jews in Europe was not merely a geographical separation but a manifestation of prevailing anti-Semitic sentiment and hence a mechanism institutional to racial capitalism via a form of social and economic control (Schwartz, 2019). It was a process of 'racing' people geographically within the city, laying the racist foundational blueprint for European cities throughout the centuries to be replicated across the continent, and via imperial conquest, to the global majority world.

Furthermore, the fabric of the European city itself was built on the back of violence and extraction. For example, the architectural surfaces of Brussels, the capital of the Belgian colonial empire that brutalised the people of the Congo, Rwanda and Burundi so forcefully during the late nineteenth and early twentieth century, is made from the materials gleaned from that bloody period. As the Re-Arrangements Collective (2023: 499) eloquently articulate: 'Belgium's colonial history is baked into the country's landscape ... Traces of violence and violations are extant in street names extolling colonial legacies and resound in the copper of statues and the gold of their moldings, informing the physical and cognitive architecture its residents inhabit.'

Right across Europe, urban inhabitants are reminded of the colonial legacies with statues celebrating enslavers, military leaders, and political figures that pervade public spaces. The oppression of this commonplace colonial and racist urbanism does not go unnoticed, of course, with often coordinated campaigns to remove some of the most symbolic icons, officially or not (with one of the more famous moments being the toppling of the statue of Edward Colston in Bristol and the ceremonial dumping of it in the harbour during the Black Lives Matter protests of 2020).

Another way in which racial capitalism imprints itself upon contemporary urban processes is what White (2020) calls 'hyperlocal demarcation'. Focusing on the borough of Newham in East London, she argues that this process involves four dimensions – legislation, communities, sonic landscape, and town planning – which come together to act upon young Black people in London to shape their experience of urban life: both negatively through brutal policing and discrimination in the job and rental market, but also positively through the creation of new cultural and creative art forms such as grime and drill music (more of which is analysed in Chapter 5).

Hence the racial discrimination and the systematic erasure (or co-option) of Blackness within capitalism – and its infection of state institutions such as the police, the prison-industrial complex, education, urban planning and local, regional, state and national governments – unfolds within the logic of spatial development, including cities. The theoretical analysis of racial capitalism as applied to urban development then brings into the narrative of capitalist urbanisation the racial injustices that are experienced around the world daily by people of colour.

Such ingrained racial urban capitalism manifests as violence on a variety of levels: the everyday, (infra)structural and of, course, institutional. The epicentre for this (or at least, that which has provoked the most resistance both in the pages of literature and the streets of the city) is the US, but this is not to say that other countries should not be regarded as less implicated within a racial-capitalist discourse. Europe and indeed the UK are no less susceptible to institutionalised forms of racism than the US (Wacquant, 2008; Akala, 2018; Elliott-Cooper, 2021), and many groups as well as the Black community experience racial prejudice in European countries (such as the Arabs in France, Gypsies in Eastern Europe and so on). Yet it is in the US where racism is perhaps most violently and institutionally visible in the anglophone and Global North, and perhaps (rightly or wrongly) why more of the detailed and academically nuanced studies conducted on racial capitalism have been based there so far.

Mechanisms of racial capitalism

Perhaps the most pernicious of those racist urban processes is redlining. After the Great Depression, cities in the US were carved up into 'zones' in order to facilitate mortgage applications. Highly diverse and ethnically concentrated parts of a city were subsequently designated 'hazardous' or 'high risk', and as such it became much harder to secure investment opportunities or lending within them. This laid the foundations for the next century of racial discrimination in urban planning in the US. Law enforcement follows a similar historical trajectory, in that these zones were more harshly policed.

The term 'redlining' itself derives from the red ink used by planners and financial power brokers of the time to draw lines around certain neighbourhoods on maps. This practice was then officially endorsed by the Federal Housing Administration (FHA) and the Home Owners' Loan Corporation (HOLC) in the 1930s, meaning that it became commonplace across the urban centres of North America during that decade (So, 2021). Notably though, and in concordance with the prevailing social trends and political narratives, the FHA and HOLC used subjective and discriminatory racial and ethnic criteria to determine the 'creditworthiness' of neighbourhoods, such as the race of the neighbourhood's residents or the presence of minority-owned businesses, which were deemed to be more susceptible to foreclosure (a susceptibility based on nothing other than skin colour (Rothstein, 2017)). So, of course, these predominately Black communities were denied financial investment and the socio-economic externalities that came with that investment, in contrast to predominantly white areas of cities. In all, of the $120 billion that was given out by the FHA between 1934 and 1962, only 2 per cent was given to non-white families (So, 2021).

Redlining was officially banned by the Fair Housing Act of 1968 (more on the events of this year in Chapter 4), but as is obvious, its legacy continues to impact American cities today. It further deepened the already wide disparities in economic and health between whites and non-whites and catalysed a spiral of disinvestment which is still ongoing. By 2019, 74 per cent of the neighbourhoods that the HOLC deemed hazardous in the 1930s remained in the low to moderate income bracket, and more than 60 per cent were predominantly non-white (Solomon *et al.*, 2019). These localities have lower access to public parks, grocery stores, and, in an era of climate catastrophe, are generally hotter (due to a lack of greenery, more exposed paving, and an exacerbated 'heat island' effect (Anderson, 2020)).

Another institutionalised form of violence is clearly that of the police, particularly in the US. As Gramsci (1999 [1926]) convincingly argued when detailing the modus operandi of cultural hegemony, the coercive forces of the state, the army, the courts and, notably, the police are not 'apolitical' at all, but are the enforcers of the interests of the ruling class. They exist solely to protect capital's growth, and as that growth is predicated upon the delineation of bodies that are worthy of capital and those, often Black and Brown bodies, that are not, violent policing is therefore systematic of capitalism. And, as the police are the main 'coercive force' that shapes the urban context (in that the military, at least pre-Trump's second term, acts more as an enforcer of the spaces of the nation-state internationally and geopolitically), how policing happens under capitalism is a vital part of understanding the capitalist city. Indeed, as Correia and Wall (2021: 16, original emphasis) explain, 'The *nature* of the police is to establish the necessary conditions and relations for the accumulation of capital.' Hence, the 'success' of capital accumulation relies on disciplining the urban population to contribute to it, and to criminalise those who don't. And in the US in particular, the policing of Black bodies has a long, dark, violent and nefarious history.

Due to the radical differences in racial demographics, the establishment of policing differed in northern regions of the US from the South, but both had underlying racist origins. The transformation of the North's economy into a more industrialised structure from the 1800s onwards required more and more labouring bodies. Consequently, a significant number of immigrants, predominantly from Germany and Ireland, but also from non-European countries, settled in cities like New York and Boston during the early nineteenth century. But this influx of immigrants, as is so often the case throughout history, triggered a surge in violent nationalism or 'nativism' (Denvir, 2020), characterised by the spurious belief among 'native' born (i.e. white) Americans that they were inherently superior to these immigrant newcomers, particularly those from non-European, i.e. Black, countries.

This influx of immigrants, combined with the burgeoning of a more capitalist economic system across the US, had a profound effect. Most readily, this new system demanded the forced removal of people from their land for corporate expansion, subjecting previous incumbents to destitution and segregation in unfit neighbourhoods, as we saw with the redlining process. But more generally, as the agricultural sector transitioned to industrialisation, Black workers, previously enslaved, became essential workers (but also disposable) to the capitalist economy. Despite their relative emancipation from physical chains, they remained economically yoked to their capitalist masters due to systemic discrimination, land dispossession, and limited access to education and resources (Beckert and Rockman, 2016). Consequently, many Black people were forced into low-wage jobs and confined to impoverished urban neighbourhoods, which therefore set the stage for heightened police surveillance and brutality.

After all, as Gramsci (1999 [1926]) noted, the police are first and foremost maintainers of the capitalist order, and their purpose is to make sure that the bodies that require order most are kept in check. So, as urban industrialised capitalism mushroomed and cities became the primary loci of profit-generation, policing became the primary tool to wield state violence in the service of safeguarding cities from potential rebellions and resistance (Rodríguez, 2020).

Today, the over-policing of Black communities is qualitatively and quantitatively beyond doubt. Black men are two and half times more likely to be killed by police than white men (Edwards *et al.*, 2019), Black people are nearly four times more likely to be arrested for drug offences than white people (despite similar rates of drug use) (American Civil Liberties Union, 2020), and Black people are twelves times more likely to experience 'police misconduct' than any other racial group (Wang, 2022). As well police interactions themselves being overtly racist, pre-policing is perhaps even more so. Racial profiling is a pervasive problem in American policing (as it is in Europe), which involves the specific targeting of individuals based on their race, ethnicity or national origin (Elliott-Cooper, 2021). The use of racial profiling is often spuriously justified by law enforcement as a means to identify and apprehend criminals, but this practice is highly problematic, is often based on existing prejudices, and frequently results in the unjust and sometimes violent treatment of individuals solely on the basis of their appearance. For example, Black drivers are 31 per cent more likely to be pulled over by police compared to white drivers. Additionally, Black drivers are more likely to be subjected to searches and less likely to be let off with a warning compared to white drivers, even when there is no evidence of criminal activity (Pierson *et al.*, 2020).

All this has culminated in a systemic breakdown in trust between the police and minority communities. So much so that the slogans 'All cops are bastards' (ACAB) and 'Fuck the police' (FTP) have become embedded within resistance activities to all forms of repression, notably within the Black community. Wall and McClanahan (2025) suggest that these slogans – that have worked their way into the cultural forms of hip-hop lyrics, social media trends, T-shirts and films, among others – form 'part of the necessary conditions of any revolutionary struggle against capitalism, which will always have to be a struggle against cops'.

What is also evident in much of the research is that the over-policing of Black populations occurs in locales that could be considered 'early-stage' gentrification. Beck (2020: 269), when studying New York, 'saw between 0.2 percent and 0.3 percent more discretionary arrests with every 5 percent increase in their property values'. In addition, when studying Oakland and the rampant gentrification therein (mainly caused by the development of the tech sector in the 2000s and 2010s), Ramírez (2020) identifies how Black and Latino communities were forced into specific parts of the city via police-enforced 'gang injunctions', which are analysed as carceral policies of racial urban capitalism. Indeed, the general overview of policing in US cities has been described as racist 'slow violence' that is intertwined with gentrification (Kramer and Remster, 2022).

All these processes of police brutality can be microcosmically evidenced in the controversial development of the Atlanta Public Safety Training Center, more colloquially called 'Cop City'. The proposed facility, spanning over 100 acres deep in Atlanta's South River Forest, is to include firing ranges, a mock-up city for 'scenario training', and an array of tactical training amenities for the police of Atlanta, and no doubt from further afield. The resistance to the initial development proposals was based on environmental concerns, with the fact that the development would destroy many acres of trees in what is one of the country's most forested cities. The proposal, though, soon attracted fierce opposition from community groups across the city, not least because the timing of the announcement, coming shortly after police shot and killed Rayshard Brooks in June 2020. The Atlanta police force, rather than focusing on the profound injustice of their institutionalised racism and complicity in the nationwide wave of brutalisation that spawned massive protests and riots from Black Lives Matter groups, bafflingly used the murder to justify the development of Cop City, claiming it would give their officers further training in such situations (Bethea, 2022). In addition, the police force, as well as their supporters in City Hall, gave highly spurious crime data indicating an increase in violent crime in the city as further justification that a multimillion-dollar training facility was needed (Herskind, 2022). The opposition, however, claim that Cop City is just another example of the militarisation of the police, which will of course disproportionately affect people of colour (Correia and Wall, 2021), and therefore lead to more fatalities within the Black community at the hands of those who are supposedly there to protect them.

The official sign-off of Cop City happened at a meeting at City Hall in September 2021, in which up to seventeen hours of pre-recorded objections were heard over many days. Despite the issue bringing together previously disparate (and often conflicting) groups – including prison abolitionists, environmentalists, civil-rights campaigners and neighbourhood associations, to name but a few – the city took the advice of a handful of city councillors and police chiefs and ultimately agreed the development by a vote of 10–4 (Herskind, 2022). In response to this, there were mass protests, rallies and civil disobedience across Atlanta. In January 2023, a protest camp at the site of the proposed development was set up, but clashes with police led to the fatal shooting of a twenty-six-year-old activist, Manuel Esteban Paez Terán.

The actual existence of such an idea in the first place, let alone its passing through city law, is a concretised realisation of the institutionalisation of racial urban capitalism. The investment in such a large-scale policing facility, in lieu of community development or social services that have a proven track record of being a far better process of crime alleviation (McDowell and Fernandez, 2018), reflects the prioritisation within capitalist cities of control and surveillance over community empowerment, particularly in areas predominantly inhabited by racial minorities. The development of Cop City, therefore, is not just a local issue of urban planning or environmental concern within Atlanta. It is a potent symbol of the ongoing struggle against a form of urban governance that disproportionately impacts minority communities, perpetuating a cycle of mistrust, fear and resistance.

This chapter has detailed specific processes of a gentrifying and racist urbanism in the US and across Europe, but there are many more that are untouched (or deliberately hidden) by academic discourse, and that affect the lives of billions of urbanites daily. Racialised gentrification is an institutional force held together by the everyday – and seemingly mundane – practices of politicians, technocrats, urban managers, civil servants, corporate managers, retail workers and citizens. This is not to *accuse* people of being racist; to pin the violence of racism onto the individual and to cast it as simply a defective character trait is to fall into the traps that a neoliberal framing sets. It is of course true that there are racist people in this world; people who actively promote and enact institutionalised violence against other marginalised, racialised people. But, as the scholarship detailed throughout this chapter (and much more besides) has vociferously argued, racism is first and foremost a structural and institutional force that is heavily intertwined with the structures of gentrification. Therefore, to be anti-capitalist, one must first and foremost be anti-racist. To advocate for a postcapitalist city (which is, after all, the purpose of this book), is to foreground the injustices of racial capitalism, rather than to leave them somehow implicit. Hence, as the theorising and empirical evidence unfurl in the rest of this book, the hybridised nature of racism and capitalism will be foregrounded. However, it cannot go unrecorded that a published book, by a white male academic from an anglophone Higher Education institution located in the heartlands of Empire, no less, is itself entangled within the very same institutional processes it is critiquing. But this impasse is by no means unique, and therefore I adhere to Haraway's (2016: 3) radically feminist perspective and aim to 'stay with the trouble', to 'follow the threads where they lead in order to track them and find their tangles and patterns crucial for staying with the trouble in real and particular places and times'. With that in mind, and following the threads that that the preceding pages have laid out – namely gentrification, urban inequality, neoliberal city governance, architectural homogeneity, racial capitalism, and an empirical (and indeed personal) attachment to the city of London – it leads, really, only to one place, one tower, even: Grenfell.

Chapter 2

A city on fire

On a hot summer's night in June 2017, a fridge freezer with faulty electrical wiring caught fire in flat 16 on the fourth floor of the Grenfell Tower in Kensington, West London. Within a matter of minutes, the fire spread via the highly combustible cladding on the outside of the building, and quickly erupted into a devastating and deadly conflagration that killed seventy people that night, and two more in the days and months after.

More than this, though, the fire scorched a narrative of violence, tragedy and urban catastrophe into the collective memory of a city, a nation and beyond. Because while the initial event was utterly tragic and shocking, the inferno itself was not a freak incident but rather a culmination of systemic failures deeply entrenched in the fabric of a gentrifying global city created by successive neoliberal national governments, themselves guided by the global flows of capital.

As the flames engulfed the high rise, they illuminated the stark realities of an urban system where economic disparities and social injustices are as pervasive and combustible as the cladding that enveloped the structure. Furthermore, that such a tragedy unfolded in London, supposedly one of the most advanced cities in the Global North, pinpoints how fallible the capitalist global city – and the disregard of public and community life – has become.

Grenfell Tower was originally a council-house block in the wider Lancaster West Estate, and was built in 1974, with fourteen of the 120 flats (increased to 127 after refurbishment in 2015–16) being bought in the 1980s under Thatcher's Right to Buy scheme. The estate was home to many London immigrants, including those of the Windrush generation, but like so much social housing had fallen into disrepair via neglect by the local council, in this case Kensington and Chelsea, one of the richest, but also most unequal, boroughs in London.

For example, according to the 2021 census, child poverty in the borough is around 27 per cent, roughly in line with the London average. Within the most impoverished areas of the city, this figure rises to 58 per cent. Conversely, in the affluent enclave surrounding Hyde Park (also within Kensington and Chelsea), child poverty plunges to a mere 6 per cent. Astonishing disparities persist even within proximity. For instance, while one street in Knightsbridge has a health deprivation rating of 0 per cent, two miles away and still within the remit of the council's social services, a block within the World's End council estate exhibits a staggering 65 per cent health deprivation rating.

Within the World's End estate, the average income is only £15,000 annually (well below the UK average of £34,000), a stark contrast to the £100,000 average earnings enjoyed by residents just a stone's throw away on the opposite side of the King's Road. Such disparities underscore the profound socio-economic inequalities endemic within the borough, where extreme wealth and poverty exist in stark juxtaposition, defining the lived experiences of its inhabitants based on their postcode (Gentleman, 2017). This is emblematic of the 'dual' character of contemporary global cities (Mollenkopf and Castells, 1991) where so much of the in-rushing capital centres on specific areas and concentrates in the hands of the few (Sassen, 2001).

So, the tower, once a symbol of practical housing solutions for the urban poor that was the vision of so many local urban planners and managers of the postwar period, was transformed overnight into a harrowing emblem of urban decay after many years of neglect and oversight. Yes, the fire ripped through the building, and the lives of seventy-two people and their families, in a matter of hours on the inauspicious night of 14 June 2017, but the years of neoliberal urban governance, underfunding and spending cuts, global city development and the racial capitalism that breathed life on the fire had been in place for many decades prior.

In the aftermath, political fallout was swift. The then prime minister, Theresa May, was roundly criticised for lack of compassion, the finger of blame was quickly pointed at the council and the corners they cut on the refurbishment of the building, and the residents themselves highlighted that they had raised concerns in the years prior (Grenfell Action Group, 2016). The broader community of the Lancaster West Estate and those who rose in solidarity sprang into action in the days and weeks afterwards, creating mutual aid networks that provided food and shelter for those that needed it, shaming the slow and cumbersome response by the council and national government. And to this day, silent protest walks are held regularly to remember those that lost their lives, but also to highlight the catastrophic failings of urban governance in the lead up to the tragedy, and in the aftermath. At the time of writing, the official inquest is still ongoing.

The now covered, but still charred, remains of Grenfell Tower stand as a sombre reminder of the cost of neglect and the price of apathy. The tragedy has reverberated through the streets of London and across the globe, sparking a wave of introspection, outrage and a fervent call to re-evaluate the principles that govern our urban spaces. It became painfully clear that the fire was not just an accident but an alarm bell, urging society to extinguish the long-smouldering injustices that burn in the furnace of modern urbanism, where the sanctity of human life is often sacrificed on the altar of capitalist gain.

This short chapter then evidences how the processes detailed in the preceding pages (and indeed other related practices of urban neoliberalism and governance) often culminate in tragedy for the urban poor, and, as Grenfell showed, sometimes in utter disaster. Gentrification, increasing inequality, government cuts in public expenditure, racial capitalism, accumulation by dispossession, and the privatisation of social and public urban land – they ignite fires of injustice throughout the city that have violent and, as Grenfell (by no means the only instance) so starkly highlights, deadly results.

Social murder in Kensington and Chelsea

Friedrich Engels, the nineteenth-century philosopher and political theorist, is best known for his collaboration with Karl Marx in penning *The Communist Manifesto*, published in 1848. While Marx focused primarily on the economic aspects of class struggle and capitalism, Engels contributed significantly to understanding the social and political dimensions of oppression and exploitation. One of Engels's concepts that remains relevant today – particularly in relation to Grenfell (Hamlett Films, 2018) – is his theory of 'social murder'.

Engels (2009 [1845]) examined the appalling living and working conditions experienced by the working class in industrial England. He argued that the conditions of poverty, squalor and disease endured by the working classes were not merely unfortunate accidents (or somehow the fault of the workers themselves and their lifestyle choices), but rather the result of deliberate actions and policies perpetuated by the factory owners and the ruling class more broadly. As he noted,

> When one individual inflicts bodily injury upon another such that death results, we call the deed manslaughter; when the assailant knew in advance that the injury would be fatal, we call his deed murder. But when society places hundreds of proletarians in such a position that they inevitably meet a too early and an unnatural death … when it deprives thousands of the necessaries of life, places them under conditions in which they cannot live … its deed is murder just as surely as the deed of the single individual. (Engles, 2009 [1845]: 95)

Engels wrote that the industrialised factory of a capitalist system, driven by the pursuit of profit and the accumulation of wealth by the capitalist class, *systematically* condemned large segments of the population to lives of misery and deprivation that seriously endangered their long-term health, and ultimately their lives. He coined the term 'social murder' therefore to describe the collective and systemic violence inflicted upon the working class by the ruling elite through exploitation, neglect and oppression. Given his background as the son of factory owner (and that he himself went on to co-own a textile factory in Manchester – a curious life choice that he seemed to reconcile by using his funds to bankroll the Marx family and the subsequent writings of his comrade Karl), his writings clearly come from a place of personal despair and perhaps even guilt. The concept of social murder was rooted in the specific historical context of the slum conditions within industrialised towns and cities of England, and, clearly, existed disparately to the legal scholarship of the day.

Yet, today, we can see echoes of social murder in the structural violence and systemic injustices that persist in the contemporary global city, including poverty, inequality, discrimination and environmental degradation. Indeed, the term has seen somewhat of a 're-emergence' in UK discourse, particularly in the wake of Grenfell and the national austerity programme that has been in place since the inception of the Conservative-led coalition government in 2010 (Medvedyuk *et al.*, 2021). With regards to the austerity programme, it has been linked to over 330,000 excess deaths in the UK (Walsh *et al.*, 2022) and a whole host of social ills (including, apparently, the average height of British children in comparison with their continental European counterparts (Hill, 2023)). But in relation to the Grenfell disaster, analysis claims that the event cannot be called anything other than an act of social murder.

The reports and inquiries that followed the fire unveiled a litany of systemic failures and neglect that paved the way for the tragedy (see Tombs (2020) for a detailed overview). Like many cash-strapped local councils, Kensington and Chelsea created housing associations and 'tenant management organisations', often with private involvement, to govern their stock of council housing (although one could ponder whether a more progressive tax regime could have mitigated much of their fiscal shortfall, given the number of high-income residents in their borough). The Kensington and Chelsea Tenant Management Organisation (KCTMO) were essentially the landlords of the Grenfell Tower, and formed part of a broader network of institutions, collectives, architects, planners and companies that had to work together to manage the estate. This broader system exemplifies 'urban governance': a system of smaller, networked and often privatised bodies that typify neoliberal urban management (Raco, 2009). This is in contrast to 'urban government', which describes the previous, more traditional postwar top–down and hierarchical urban management that is emblematic of a centrally planned system (Lefebvre, 1998). Such neoliberalisation of urban management was part of the broader push by the ruling and political class to implement market efficiency within the social realm, a classic Thatcherite ideology. And this is exactly what austerity represents, not least through the drastic reduction in funding for local councils from the Treasury. These decisions have gutted funding for essential public services that local councils were assigned to provide, including social housing, but also fire-safety inspections and housing-benefit and disability payments. According to a damning report by the National Audit Office (2020), funding for building safety in England was slashed by 50 per cent between 2010 and 2015, leaving crucial safety measures unaddressed and buildings like Grenfell Tower vulnerable to catastrophic events.

Indeed, the residents of the Lancaster West Estate themselves foresaw the disaster, with the now infamous blog post by the Grenfell Action Group in November 2016 – only seven months before the fire – that read: '[We] have reached the conclusion that only an incident that results in serious loss of life of KCTMO residents will allow the external scrutiny to occur that will shine a light on the practices that characterise the malign governance of this non-functioning organisation. (Grenfell Action Group, 2016). Their concerns were based upon well-documented deficiencies in provision by the KCTMO, noting their corruption but also inability to effect change given the intricate web of interlocking institutions that were part of the broader framework of urban governance. The neoliberalisation of urban management is supposedly designed to increase efficiency and innovation, but in this case (and many more besides) only served to create obfuscation and drastically reduce residents' agency in key decision-making processes (Slater, 2021).

Furthermore, Grenfell Tower was populated largely by ethnic minorities. Of the residents who lost their lives in the fire, 85 per cent were non-white. Given the wider processes of racial capitalism and domicide detailed in the previous chapter, it should come as very little surprise that the enclaves of ethnic minorities created by the neoliberal housing policies of global cities are most at risk from catastrophe. Ever since the aftermath of Hurricane Katrina in the southern US in 2005 – in which a disproportionate number of Black neighbourhoods were flooded because of a lack of sea defences, which were abundant in whiter, wealthier parts of the city – the over-vulnerability of ethnic minority communities to 'natural' disasters has been a part of racial capitalist discourse (Hartnell, 2017). Because Grenfell, and the wider Lancaster West Estate, was disproportionately (in relation to the rest of the borough) home to ethnic minorities, it was always going to be in a more vulnerable place given the systemic devaluing of these kinds of communities within a racial urban capitalist system.

Furthermore, it has been well-documented in the aftermath of the fire (Booth, 2022), including in the ongoing inquest, that the decision to clad Grenfell Tower in flammable material, despite warnings from fire-safety experts, was emblematic of a wider culture of cost-cutting and deregulation that prioritised profit over people's lives. As Tombs (2020: 127) has noted, 'in 2014, a decision was taken [by Kensington and Chelsea council] to replace fire-resistant zinc cladding in the refurbishment contract with cheaper aluminium panels to save £293,368'. The decision itself to fit cladding was based upon a recommendation by the architects commissioned to 'upgrade the look' of the building to disguise what was perceived to be its drab 1970s concrete facade, which, it was felt, contrasted with the more modern aesthetic that was to be implemented in newer buildings (Apps, 2020).

This use of cheaper, combustible cladding materials was driven by a pursuit of efficiency and cost-saving measures that under austerity became the norm. It was a chilling illustration of how neoliberal urban governance and its associated austerity policies affected vulnerable communities such as those in Grenfell Tower – in the case of Grenfell, all for the price of £293,368. As such, it is painfully clear that the Grenfell Tower fire was not merely a tragic accident but a result of systemic failures and political decisions that prioritised profit over people's lives.

In the immediate aftermath of the fire, there was also evidence of the effects of the capitalist city in the real *lack* of an official response. First-responding fire fighters and paramedics were widely praised for their efforts, but it soon became apparent that survivors were not being housed adequately, there was a lack of food and water, and that, generally, local and national politicians were distancing themselves from the disaster and lacking compassion, with the *Guardian* newspaper proclaiming Grenfell to be Prime Minister Theresa May's 'Hurricane Katrina moment' (*Guardian* Editorial, 2017). Stepping into the void left by local and national governments (and a poor response from official NGOs and charities), the local community acted quickly: food distribution centres were set up, shelter was provided by local faith centres, and people opened up their homes to survivors. Even beyond the events of the first few days after the fire, the government's response to the broader systemic issue of poor regulations around fire and building safety has been criticised for being too slow. The government's own committee reported in 2019, two-plus years after the fire, that the £200 million set aside for improvements to regulations was not enough, and that their implementation has been cumbersome and ineffective (UK Parliament, 2019).

It is clear, then, that the Grenfell disaster was the result of intersecting and conflating processes inherent to the contemporary capitalist city. The Conservative government's austerity policies, inequality, domicide, deregulation, racial urban capitalism – all directly contributed to the conditions that made the fire not only possible, but sadly inevitable. By ignoring repeated warnings and failing to address underlying social and economic inequalities, the neoliberal urban governance structures effectively committed an act of social murder.

Part II

Reactions

Chapter 3

Histories of resistance

Resistance to the capitalist city has taken many forms across multiple histories. From the Peasants' Revolt in 1381, when Britain's peasant population rose up against King Richard II and demanded an end of serfdom, through the pan-European uprisings of 1848 to the contemporary and overlapping campaigns of Occupy, the Arab Spring, Black Lives Matter, MeToo, Extinction Rebellion and the myriad of associated movements around the world, resistance to the injustices of imperialism and oppression have taken on a very *urban* form. Indeed, as Sassen (2011: 574) so forcefully argues, cities continue to be vital arenas where 'the powerless can make history'. The spatial manifestation of a viable postcapitalist society is most present (and because of its presence, the most oppressed) within the fabric of the city, but those people and communities that have championed it have done so in the face of brutal and violent oppression by the powers of the status quo. Postcapitalist cities will not, and cannot, come into being via a seamless and frictionless transition somehow granted from above; they will be realised by the powerless from below.

This chapter then will follow in the footsteps of many acute, intricate, rigorous and brilliant studies of the past to dissect the history of urban revolution, and to analyse their attempts at realising postcapitalist cities (see Lefebvre, 1970; Abu-Lughod, 2007; Harvey, 2012; Dikeç, 2017; Chenoweth, 2021, and many others). But rather than take a macro approach to the course of history, I have grounded the narrative via a forensic examination of one of the critical fulcrums of recent times: the year 1968. Earmarked by many scholars of capitalism and critique (Bolstanki and Chiapello, 2005; Kurlansky, 2005; Fisher, 2008) as a vital period of rapid shifts in the relation between capital and people, 1968 stubbornly haunts contemporary urban scholarship, standing alone outside of the nostalgia industries that continually collectivise disparate and unrelated events and cultural movements in neatly packaged decades. Yes, the radical tendencies of the 1960s – spiritual, sexual and cultural – fomented a fervour of revolutionary practice throughout the world. And yes, 1968 is still just an arbitrary label gleaned from a centuries old Eurocentric Gregorian calendar to map a full lap of the Earth around the Sun. But despite that, it provides a neat analytical frame to ground the grand history of urban revolutions, given that so many important and intersecting events took place around the world in that year.

However, while this chapter seeks to analyse the events of 1968, framing them as a critical juncture in the development of a theoretical and empirical praxis of revolution that continues to influence the evolution of postcapitalist urbanism, understanding 1968 as a culmination of revolutionary potential requires situating it within a broader historical continuum. In particular, the Haitian Revolution (1791–1804) and the European uprisings of 1848 form essential antecedents that established ideological and material trajectories later echoed in 1968. The Haitian Revolution, as the first successful nationwide revolt of the modern era against colonial slavery, not only dismantled entrenched systems of racialised exploitation but also redefined revolutionary agency by centring marginalised voices, an agency that echoes through 1968 to today. Similarly, the upheavals of 1848 challenged European monarchical and capitalist orders, forging connections between class struggle, democratic aspirations, and crucially for the conceptualisation of postcapitalist cities, urban centres across the continent. Together, these earlier revolutions provide a critical foundational framework for interrogating the dynamics of 1968, where anti-colonial resistance, labour struggles, and cultural insurgencies converged, echoing and reconfiguring these historical precedents in ways that resonate within contemporary postcapitalist urban imaginaries.

From Haiti to Hungary: Nineteenth-century revolutions

The Haitian Revolution, which historians agree spanned from 1791 to 1804, has been intricately analysed as a pivotal event in the annals of resistance against imperialism, and the capitalist system that it helped to foster (Ott, 1973). This specific rebellion, originating in Saint-Domingue, a colony of the French Empire teeming with the harsh realities of slavery, led to the establishment of Haiti, the first Black republic, and the second independent nation in the Americas.

Within the context of the late eighteenth century, Saint-Domingue was the crown jewel of the French colonial empire, and stood as a testament to the highly lucrative trade in human slavery and the genesis of racial capitalism (Koekkoek, 2020). Forming part of the 'triangular trade' that was common at the time, enslaved people form Africa were shipped to the Americas to work on plantations producing mostly sugar and coffee, which was then shipped to Europe to be enjoyed by the bourgeoise and aristocratic class. However, as the century came to close, the ongoing revolution by the proletariat back in the heartland of empire in France was beginning to send ripples of intersectional dissent to its colonies (Fick, 1990). The enslaved and raced people of Saint-Domingue began to conspire, and organised riots and revolts against the plantation owners. But it was the Toussaint L'Ouverture (sometimes called the 'Black Spartacus'), an enslaved man with immense military prowess and knowledge, who was able to marshal the rioting people into an effective revolution (James, 1938). The competing global imperial forces to the French, namely the British and the Spanish, seized on this opportunity and offered L'Ouverture support, but he was quick to repel these attempts at substituting one imperial power with another, arguing that the people of Saint-Domingue ought to govern themselves. In 1801, after bloody battles with the French Army, a Haitian constitution was established that gave the colony a degree of autonomy and independence never before seen within the French Empire. Post-1801, Napoleon came to power and was able to restore a sense of imperial rule; he imprisoned L'Ouverture. But, in a pre-echo of rhizomatic resistances that reform, remould and re-engage after a setback, a new leader emerged. Jean-Jacques Dessalines (one of L'Ouverture's lieutenants) pushed back Napoleon's army and brutally massacred any French people and imperial sympathisers that remained. On 1 January 1804, Dessalines declared the independence of Saint-Domingue, renaming it Haiti.

The Haitian Revolution is vital to the theorising of postcapitalist cities because it was a direct affront to the imperial order from a previously unthinkable source of antagonism. The revolution's success was unthinkable within the prevailing global order because the autonomy, agency and intrinsic humanity of enslaved people had previously been systematically denied by racial capitalism (Trouillot, 2015). First and foremost, it was an uprising which gave a voice to a previously voiceless and raced people, and ended the violent practice of slavery in a key colony of empire. But more than this, the uprising disrupted the global economy of slavery and plantations, and therefore posed a threat to other colonial empires and their global economic and emerging capitalistic practices. The Haitian Revolution, often marginalised in mainstream historical accounts of global resistances, evidences how race is a fundamental catalyst of revolution. As Chapter 1 outlined, race is systemically tied to the development of the capitalist city (Gilmore, 2020), and hence to resist the capitalist city is to necessarily engage with anti-racist praxis. And the Haitian Revolution provides the foundational event for this praxis: it evidenced perhaps the first (certainly the most seismic) time that Black enslaved people had a 'voice' in (geo)political discourse.

Whether the Haitian Revolution fomented discord across the Atlantic in Europe is up for debate by historians, but what is not in doubt is that in the heartland of empire, urban revolutions were stirring. This all came to a head in early 1848, a time which is collectively known as the 'Springtime of Peoples', when a series of widespread but, crucially, *coordinated* uprisings took place across urban and rural Europe. In the half a century or so prior, certainly since the Congress of Vienna of 1815 in which a post-Napoleonic Europe was being carved up by only a handful of powerful aristocrats from Great Britain, Prussia, Russia and Austria (referred to rather pompously as the 'Holy Alliance'), economic and social turmoil gripped the continent. There was high unemployment and food shortages in many of the key European cities, and discontent was growing, particularly among a population that was getting younger, more educated and thus more aware of feudal and aristocratic oppression (Sperber, 2005). Fundamentally, key revolutionary ideologies like democracy (in the form of suffrage), liberalism (including press freedom), nationalism and socialism gained prominence among the populations, and resulted in violent challenges to the traditional autocratic regimes in cities right across the continent including Paris, Berlin, Copenhagen, Buda, Pest, Stockholm, London and many others.

Despite varying degrees of success in implementing constitutional reform, they laid the groundwork for urban revolutions in the centuries to come, largely because 1848 is credited as the first set of coordinated revolutions across space (Jørgensen, 2012). Technological advances aided this (including printing and faster movement across bigger distances), but it was a systematic attempt to share resources and ideologies across different European cities to create a stronger revolutionary vanguard. This is important to consider for today's resistances to capitalist-city discourses because the same 'transurban interconnectivity' (Jørgensen, 2012: 201) exist today, in that social movements coordinate campaigns, share resources and disseminate protest tactics across national borders.

Such connectivity is an important processual catalyst of a post-capitalist city networked terrain. The events of 1848 in Europe are analytically crucial because they help to historicise the creation of a class-conscious internationalism (or at least federalised regionalism) that mirrored, and critiqued, capitalism's globalisation via trade routes and the corporate imperialism that bloated the core cities of Europe with ill-gotten wealth from the Global South. In the rest of this chapter, then, I want to paint a picture of how that form of interconnected, international, anticapitalistic and, crucially, urban process crystallised in the subsequent decades, but came to a head in 1968. Clearly, 1968 was like any other year (albeit a leap year), but the frequency and importance of urban uprisings in all populated continents of the world suggest that there was something unique about this particular year. Moreover, the internationalism foregrounded by Haiti and the uprisings of 1848 and developed through the twentieth century through two world wars arguably reached its zenith on 8 April 1968, when the astronauts of Apollo 8 took the now famous 'earthrise photo'. More than a stunning piece of photography, the image seared itself onto the collective psyche of the world, creating in effect a 'planetary' consciousness (Mould, 2023). The image of a fragile globe, marbled with various hues of blue, green and white, radically shifted the psychology of environmentalists and emboldened narratives of a collective global, delicate and life-sustaining ecosystem that requires safeguarding and protecting from the dangers of over-consumption that are international in scope, and planetary in effect. Equally, the image – coinciding with the ubiquity of television sets in the home – was said to have created a 'globalisation of consciousness' (Robertson and Buhari-Gulmez, 2017), a radical shift in the positionality of progressive activists from individuals and local collectives to a planetary body of action. When writing specifically about the countercultural movements in Germany and France, Brown (2013: 5) has stated that 'the globality of 1968 [was] not in the multiplication of individual national scenarios but in the intersection of global vectors across one local terrain'. In essence, as the rest of this chapter will argue, 1968 witnessed a marked and substantial shift not only in the urban revolutionary discourse of the world, but also on a far deeper psychological level and via one single photo it birthed a tangible collective 'spirit' of the world that was previously only hinted at (see also Kurlansky, 2005).

With this fomenting of planetary consciousness in the background, the urban uprisings, revolutions and riots of 1968 become less a surprising amount of individual events concentrated in a twelve-month period, more a connected tissue of revolutionary praxis that ignited from one continent to the next. It is in this spirit of international solidarity that I present the narrative of the remainder of this chapter, highlighting those events that garnered the most historical analysis (and those that resonate most coherently with the themes of the book). That is not to say that they are a definitive list: of course, there will be a myriad of untold stories, resistances, postcapitalist movements and revolutionary events that happened in 1968 that never made it into the history books, nor the archives I was able to scour. But focusing on the key events allows the international scope of the urban, postcapitalist revolutions to come to fore, and hopefully evidence – and further catalyse – how today in the twenty-first century we can narrate a similar internationalist, connected and revolutionary paradigm to bring about a postcapitalist urban reality.

The year that changed the world: 1968

Of course, the events of 1968 didn't happen spontaneously: there had been decades of unrest since the end of World War II, with the Cold War boiling into a very hot Vietnam War that started in the 1950s. But after the capitalist hegemony of the US officially declared war against the communist Vietnamese forces in 1964, the war's unpopularity grew rapidly among the US population, igniting many specific anti-war protests and activist responses, further adding to the general civilian unrest of 1968. The increasing poverty conditions in the US, felt acutely by the Black and ethnic minority populations of inner cities, were seemingly being ignored by President Lyndon B. Johnson's Democratic administration because of his obsession with the war. This was creating the mass ghettoisation in many US cities (Schwartz, 2019), culminating in the 'long hot summer' of 1967 in which there were race riots in over 150 American cities. Also, it would be remiss not to point out the murder of Che Guevara in October 1967 as a major event of US hegemonic violence. Guevara had been largely instrumental in the Cuban revolution and the country's recalcitrance in the face of US oppression. In 1965, before he disappeared from public life, he had criticised both the US and the USSR, championing a socialist future for the Global South. In his final public speech in Algeria, he had denounced the Soviet Union for forgetting the teachings of Marx and supported the Vietnamese in the defiance of the US. Essentially, he had become a champion of socialist values, and in rallying the stewards of the world's major resources – the global majority world population – he was causing a massive headache for the imperial hegemons of Europe and the US by whipping up anti-capitalist enthusiasm among an increasingly political aware, young and well-educated population (Löwy, 2023). His murder by a CIA-backed Bolivian militia effectively martyred Guevara to the anti-capitalist cause and set the stage for the rapid uptick in revolutionary praxis around the world in 1968.

With anti-imperialist and anti-capitalist sentiment bringing in the new year, it was not missed by the anti-Vietnam War activists in the US that, while the narrative of 'liberating' Vietnam from a communist tyranny was in full force, there were very illiberal policies of anti-Blackness and violence against the Black community being played out at home. The civil rights movement had been gathering significant momentum, resulting in the Civil Rights Act coming into force four years prior in July 1964. The law was designed to prevent economic discrimination based on a range of characteristics including gender and race. However, many leaders of the civil rights movement were vocal about how little the law changed practice on the ground, and the movement continued to produce schisms, protests and full-on riots. Ultimately, it was the bloody events of March 1965 in Selma, Alabama – when state troopers and a hastily deputised posse attacked protestors on the Edmund Pettus Bridge – that forced President Johnson to bring in the Voting Rights Act later that year. However, this was merely politically performative, and the economic injustices of racial capitalism (outlined in Chapter 1) remained rife in US society, despite these two acts being signed. Among the backdrop of the ongoing Vietnam War (itself drafting a disproportionate number of Black Americans: at the time, the US population was 12 per cent Black, but the US Vietnam draft was 16.3 per cent), economic conditions continued to deteriorate for the Black populations of inner cities. By the start of 1968, there were multiple instances of violations of the Civil Rights Act, notably in Memphis, Tennessee. In February, two sanitation workers, Echol Cole and Robert Walker, were killed. They were trying to shelter from torrential rain, but because of the still enforced (but illegal) segregation laws of the city, they were refused entry into nearby buildings and instead had to take refuge in their truck's compactor area. It accidentally activated, crushing both men. The event highlighted not only the ongoing unjust segregation laws, but served as a breaking point for Black workers, who were paid less than white employees, had no access to basic amenities at work, no sick pay nor any other of the perks enjoyed by their White counterparts. Black workers therefore went on strike, and they were visited in April 1968 by the civil rights leader (and outspoken anti-capitalist) Martin Luther King, Jr. But on 4 April 1968, King was shot dead by James Earl Ray. King's death sparked a wave of riots across the US, coined 'The Holy Week' (Levy, 2018), with Black people targeting white businesses in affluent neighbourhoods in Baltimore, Washington, DC, Chicago, New York and other major US urban centres. Clearly the death of King was the main driver of these riots, but analysis since has evidenced that the continuing economic injustices suffered by the Black population was also a major catalyst (see Laurent, 2019).

King's death only served to focus the minds of the anti-racist activists and the civil rights movement more broadly, resulting in the Poor People's Campaign (Laurent, 2019). This was a coordinated campaign, organised by King, but carried forward by Ralph Abernathy, that presented a set of demands to the US government. The campaign then established a three-thousand-people-strong protest camp called 'Resurrection City' in Washington DC in May. The protest camp was made up of wooden makeshift accommodation (Taub, 2020), and became a site of fervent political activity with civil rights activists meeting with Congress women and men to discuss their demands. There was also a university set up, with a young Jesse Jackson sermonising to other young Black people angry at King's assassination (Diamond, 2018); it even had its own zip code, 20013. Resurrection City was formed in May 1968 and only lasted for six weeks before it was dismantled by police; arrests were made after its official permit expired and the organisers were refused an extension. However, it was important (and still is) for two reasons: first is that it represents the evolution of protests tactics, and second because it was an attempt to fuse the push for economic *and* racial justice. Hence it was a manifestation of King's teachings that the two are intimately connected, and that the emancipation of Black people in America requires action against the oppressive forces of poverty on *all* peoples.

In terms of protest tactics, sit-ins were a fundamental part of the civil rights movement. From Rosa Parks's refusal to move to the back of the bus in 1955 to the sit-in movement of 1960–64 by young, predominantly Black students (Flowers, 2005), the civil rights movement utilised this non-violent tactic effectively throughout its campaign (with also more than an echo to the revolutionary practices of the Paris Commune (Ross, 2016)). Resurrection City also fore-grounded future urban encampments as a protest tactic of Occupy in 2011 and 2012, and the Capitol Hill Autonomous Zone (known as 'Chaz') in Seattle in the wake of the Black Lives Matter protests of 2020 (Mould, 2020). Moreover, Resurrection City (and the future camps it inspired) created more than simply a protest environment; it provided education, cooperation and basic needs for poor people (such as food and shelter), and a general arena in which discussions and action around postcapitalism and anti-racism can occur. These camps never last long (after all, having such open and brazen displays of anti-establishmentarianism in the heartland of the capitalist city will only be tolerated for so long (Dikeç, 2017)), but they exist as part of the *longue durée* of postcapitalist urbanism; they act as release valves against the suffocating oppression of racial urban capitalism, and evidence that despite the apparent ubiquity of capitalist realism, a radically different urban future has been, and is, available in the *past* and *present*.

In terms of the broader movement for economic justice, Resurrection City (and the Poor People's Campaign that it was the culmination of) represented a movement to link class and racial politics within the American political zeitgeist. In the lead up to 1968, the civil rights movement had rightly foregrounded racial injustice in terms of Black suffrage and economic opportunities; however, as aforementioned, King was adamant that racial justice was tied to economic justice (Jackson, 2007). Indeed, he famously said in a speech to the Southern Christian Leadership Conference a few months before he was killed, 'We must see now that the evils of racism, economic exploitation and militarism are all tied together. And you can't get rid of one without getting rid of the other.'

King's anti-capitalist rhetoric throughout his campaigning is often air-brushed from history, particularly on the vapid and performative 'MLK Day' in January each year when capitalists, imperialists, Republican and Democratic politicians alike all clamour to join the celebrations of him as an icon of liberty, conveniently dismissing his vehement disapproval of capitalist injustice and white supremacist imperialism. Indeed, in the speech that the quote above comes from, he advocates for a form of universal basic income (UBI) to combat both racial and economic disadvantages (a policy tool only now being tested in various parts of the world (Torry, 2023)).

It also worth noting that the racism that pervaded the US (and the attempted eradication of it by King that led to him losing his life) was evident across the Global North at the time. Europe was in no way innocent. Because only two weeks after King was murdered, Enoch Powell stood up at the Midland Hotel in Birmingham in the UK to give his now (in)famous 'rivers of blood' speech in which he orated openly racist, xenophobic and hateful rhetoric. The speech directly resulted in an immediate uptick in race-related hate crimes around the country, and also laid the foundations for subsequent racist policies around immigration, housing and social services; some have argued (with justification) that the speech even foregrounded more contemporary UK policy decisions such as Brexit and the 'hostile environment' (Atkins, 2018; Solomos, 2019). But just as every action has an equal and opposite reaction, the speech also enraged, and emboldened, anti-racist campaigners in the UK in the subsequent years. Powell himself was kicked out of the ruling Conservative Party, effectively ending his political career, but his speech also rallied politically leftist student groups, socialists and communists against the rising nationalist and fascistic ideology of the racist National Front group, resulting in events such as Rock Against Racism in 1976, and the altogether more violent Battle of Lewisham in 1977. Suffice to say, in the UK at least, 1968 was an important year in European race relations, and while the urbanised resistance came later, activists built upon the anti-racist movements (if not the tactics) of the US.

It is clear, then, that in Washington DC, Resurrection City can be analysed as an *urbanised* outcome of a suite of anti-capitalist movements spawned from the civil rights movement, both tactically and politically. That it happened in May 1968 is undoubtedly more than a mere coincidence, and represents a concomitant US event of the more (in)famous events in Paris of the same month. The French uprisings, which started in Paris but spread throughout the country, have subsequently become a major event within postcapitalist discourse more broadly. They have been pored over by scholars, politicians, students and capitalist critics alike for decades, with every new study or commentary adding further fuel to the fire of their 'evental' qualities.

Taking a purely theoretical view of the term 'event' (see Badiou, 2007 [1988]), the term 'evental' refers to the persistence of a historical moment in time to cement itself as a fulcrum of ideological thought. Without wanting to rehash the entire philosophies of the event (I have explained these elsewhere: see Mould (2021)), the fact that May 1968 in Paris is still being studied as a seismic rupture of the capitalist order, despite the fact that it failed in its political goals to bring about change in the French government in its immediate aftermath, is evidence that is effects were felt deeply at the time and have reverberated throughout history to the present day (Harvey, 2012; Rojek, 2017).

What started as disgruntled students at the Nanterre campus of the University of Paris in March, the 'event' conflagrated into a nationwide general strike involving firefighters, the police, factory workers, government administrators and many others who shared a working-class and/or socialist sensibility. Alongside the strikes, there were riots, and, akin to Resurrection City, occupations. Indeed, the Sorbonne was taken over by students on 13 May to create the short-lived but nonetheless influential Sorbonne Occupation Committee (SOC). Attended by the members and advocates of the Situationist International (the 'SI': more on these important protagonists in the next chapter), the SOC were provocative in their actions, agitating the uprisings with ideologies of postcapitalism. Part of their agitation was the creation and proliferation of slogans. The famous slogan of the uprisings, '*Sous les pavés, la plage*' (beneath the pavement, the beach), is still uttered by revolutionaries today as a critique of the suffocating striation of contemporary urban environments. This metaphor was taken to the logical extreme at times, when the cobbled stones of the Latin Quarter in Paris were ripped up and thrown at the police, a tactic that was used in the Paris Commune (indeed the tactic was so notorious that the streets were latterly covered in asphalt to prevent further use as weapons (Kurlansky, 2005)). But beyond that, the SOC were keen for other (perhaps not quite as pervasive, but no less critical) slogans to diffuse through the protesting parties at the time. One of the communiqués from the SOC on 16 May read (and given the implicit and acerbic radicalism, is worth quoting in full):

Slogans to Be Spread Now, by Every Means

(leaflets, announcements over microphones, comic strips, songs, graffiti, balloons on paintings in the Sorbonne, announcements in theaters during films or while disrupting them, balloons on subway billboards, before making love, after making love, in elevators, each time you raise your glass in a bar):

Occupy the factories
Power to the workers councils
Abolish class society
Down with spectacle-commodity society
Abolish alienation
Terminate the university
Humanity won't be happy till the last bureaucrat is hung with the
    guts of the last capitalist
Death to the cops
Free also the 4 guys convicted for looting during the May 6th riot[1]

These slogans – perhaps more accurately, demands – are consonant with many contemporary demands today. For example, 'Death to the cops' clearly resonates with the anti-police sentiments noted in the previous chapter and the ACAB slogan, and there are many anti-university, factory-occupation and anti-consumerist movements (that are not discussed in this book but are no less prominent in the postcapitalist-city discourse) that echo these general sloganised cries of equality.

So it has been argued the 'evental' qualities of the Parisian uprisings are because of their theoretical and ideological foundations (Braidotti, 2008; Badiou, 2012; Harvey, 2012). Indeed, May 1968 was catalysed by a political climate in which socialist and communists had come together to form an electoral alliance with the 'February Declaration'. As such, the riots, strikes, sit-ins and marches were more than simply an attempt to gain better working conditions or specific changes to university policies. They coalesced around a tangible belief that a coalition of socialists and communists could realistically take control of the French government, leading to what some would argue were fatalistic decisions to stop the escalation of protests into full-scale revolution through instead engaging in the existing parliamentary democratic processes (see Bourg (2017) for a comprehensive and theoretical overview). Despite their immediate 'failure', though, the fact that the postcapitalist ideas and very *urban* practices of the uprisings are still relevant to the critiques of capitalism today speaks to the importance of May 1968 in Paris as a fulcrum of ideological thought (something I have argued elsewhere in more detail, about the ethic of 'failure' against capitalism (Mould, 2021)).

Moreover, such 'evental' qualities don't just mean an extension of their revolutionary potential through time, but also through space. That is because there was (and to maintain the 'eventalness', still is) an inherent internationalism to the Parisian uprisings that evidences the planetary movements of 1968 more broadly (and its own connections with the uprisings of 1848). The student 'leaders' of the Parisian uprisings have put on record that they were inspired by (and perhaps themselves inspired) other student revolts on US campuses such as Berkley (Kurlansky, 2005). But more than that, the planetary nature of the uprisings manifests in identifiable links to a former French colony, Tunisia. Having gained independence only a decade previously, Tunisia's post-colonial links with France were still strong economically, militarily, politically and intellectually (Hendrickson, 2017). Youth from Tunisia were students in Paris and vice versa. Indeed, one particularly famous French intellectual, Michel Foucault, had been teaching at the University of Tunis since 1966. In March of 1968, students at the university revolted. They were protesting against the arrest, beating and torture of a prominent activist and member of 'Perspectives' (a radical group of Tunisian intellectuals who met in Paris a year previously), Mohamed Ben Jennet.

Perspectives were active in local political dissent in Tunisia but also advocated for global justice, stemming from Tunisia's endorsement of Western neo-imperialistic policies in Palestine (still reeling from the Arab–Israeli War of 1967) and Vietnam. The university demonstrations of March 1968 were primarily fuelled by domestic concerns about the university's authoritarianism, but they garnered much debate and action focused on the internationalism of the post-colonial times they found themselves in (Hendrickson, 2017). Indeed, as Foucault himself admitted in an interview, 'it wasn't May of '68 in France that changed me; it was March of '68, in a third-world country.' (Medien, 2020: 493). The movement of people, students and university teachers under the migratory patterns of the post-colonial world undoubtedly led to information, tactics, ideas and revolutionary discourse being spread from Tunis to Paris and back again (and then to diffuse through the regional networks beyond).

As such, Tunis wasn't the only African city to be touched by the planetary spectre of urban revolution in 1968. In many African cities, there were similar protests in the form of university students revolting against a variety of interconnected practices of perceived imperial activities. The US was in the process of trying to establish military bases across the continent in a move to counter emergent communist movements. This was vehemently resisted by people, notably students, across Africa, whose ire was already high given the rampant anti-Vietnam War fervour in many African countries (Becker and Seddon, 2018). In January in Kinshasa, students protested against the visiting US vice-president, decrying the imperialism evident in the lavish state visit. The agitating student group were subsequently targeted throughout the year, with the leader eventually arrested. In Ethiopia, students had been mobilising throughout the 1960s in response to the government's strict control of higher education, as well as the presence of the US military. This came to a head in March 1968, when students were protesting outside an American fashion show in Addis Ababa, resulting in violent clashes, shootings and lootings. Other anti-US militarism student protests took place in Dar es Salaam, Nairobi and notably in Cairo. On 21 February, which was Egyptian Students Day, a hundred thousand students joined protesting workers to call for political reform of the militarised government, resulting in riots and the death of two workers (Becker and Seddon, 2018). Likewise in Dakar, students at the university were protesting against what they saw as the 'Americanisation' of the syllabus and called for its 're-Africanisation'. The students occupied the campus only to be violently repressed, with one student killed. This led to riots across the country and a general strike by the unions, and eventually to governmental concessions (Guèye, 2018).

That these protests (and many others across the continent) were in response mainly to the perceived interference of the US militarily and educationally is another example of the planetary nature of the uprisings of 1968 (and suggests too disquiet at the US attempt to quell the revolutionary forces ignited by Che Guvera's stay in the Congo in previous years). The urbanity of these protests comes from the fact that it was mainly students who catalysed these resistances; they met on city university campuses, no doubt fuelled by the images on their television screens and the reports on the radio of students taking over central Paris, or American Black students agitating against segregated university campuses. In the US, for example, by the spring of 1968 student demonstrations (mostly against the horrors of the Vietnam War, but also protests in support of other *perhaps* more trivial issues such as better food and more school dances) were numbering thirty or so a month (Kurlansky, 2005). But campus occupations, marches and sloganising were becoming so commonplace that further tactics were innovated. Indeed, as Kurlansky goes on to argue:

> Protestors understood that with constant protest they had to do more than just carry a sign in order to make the newspapers. A building had to be seized, something had to be shut down. To protest Columbia University's plan to build a new school gymnasium displacing poor black residents of Harlem, a student hopped into the steel scoop of an earthmover to obstruct construction. (Kurlansky, 2005: 81)

It seemed, then, that the student generation of 1968 were becoming radicalised by not only their teachers, but by the real-time events of US hegemony across the world that they were witnessing.

But it wasn't just American imperialism that catalysed urban revolts. In Czechoslovakia, the politician Alexander Dubček was attempting to loosen Soviet control by introducing democratic reforms and so-called 'socialism with a human face'. The USSR, though, vehemently disagreed, and along with the other nations of the Warsaw Pact, swiftly invaded Prague in August of 1968. Afterwards, many of the political reforms were reversed, but the uprising's 'evental' qualities rest in the tactics of the urbanites to resist Soviet oppression, notably that they were largely non-violent (Navrátil and Benčík, 1998). As the Soviet tanks rolled into Prague, the citizens barricaded the streets, took down road signs, daubed the walls in anti-Soviet graffiti, and even spread disinformation to the soldiers about the safety of the water supply, causing confusion and fear. Other tactics included self-immolation, famously by the student Jan Malach. The obdurateness of Dubček's popularity among the Czechoslovakian population meant that what the Soviet's thought would take four days took over eight months to accomplish (Lyu, 2023). Like in Paris, this so-called 'Prague Spring' didn't result in the ultimate goals of political reform or the removal of the oppressive power (the De Gaulle presidency and the USSR respectively). But its legacy in the annals of urban theory is testament to not only the protestors' innovative tactics, but their ideological imprinting into a planetary anti-capitalist and anti-imperialist spectre more broadly. Moreover, their use of the city as a protest 'tool' (via occupations, sloganising, barricading, rioting, graffitiing and so on) was vital in imprinting this ideological legacy. In other words, the urbanity of the resistive *practice* is linked to its ideological *praxis*.

As well as in Europe, North America and Africa, the dissent of 1968 was evident in Latin America as well. In Mexico City, a student uprising spilled over into bloody and fatal violence during the Tlatelolco massacre on the 2 October 1968, when over three hundred students were murdered by Mexican armed forces. The protests were against the Institutional Revolutionary Party (PRI), who were backed by US power in their attempts at capitalist reform in the country. Specifically, protestors were criticising the government's repressive tactics and its prioritisation of international prestige over domestic welfare, notably in the context of the upcoming Olympics (see Poniatowska's (1975) emotive first-hand account for details). The decision to host the Olympic Games in Mexico City was viewed as a cynical attempt by the PRI to showcase Mexico as a modern and capitalist nation on the global stage. However, the government's heavy investment in the Olympics came at a time when many Mexicans were living in poverty and political repression was rampant

(Bruhn, 1997). The juxtaposition of lavish spending on an international event with the daily struggles faced by ordinary citizens only served to exacerbate tensions, and students could be heard chanting *¡No queremos olimpiadas, queremos revolución!* (We don't want Olympics, we want revolution!: Estefania, 2018). The brutal and bloody repression of the students came only a week before the Olympics started, and cast a long shadow over them, with frequent protests by Mexican citizens and indeed Olympians. But they were perhaps surpassed – at least in terms of the lasting imagery of the games – by Tommie Smith and John Carlos, two Black American sprinters who famously gave the Black power salute when collecting their gold and bronze medals respectively.

1968: a year in which two Black Americans performed a symbolic protest against rampant racial capitalism in US society, in a Global South megacity stadium that had been built because the urban government were determined to gentrify their city at the expense of the urban poor and the blood of hundreds of students: a gesture that was beamed visually across the world by the then novel technological innovation of television. This is perhaps the reason why it can be thought of as the year of a planetary awakening of urban and ideological revolutionary potential; potentials that still live on today (Kurlansky, 2005). 1968 is just one year in a history of anti-capitalist resistance, but it contains many pivotal moments in anti-capitalist ideology for many reasons, and the impact of the events of that year resonate more than ever, some six decades later: the Arab Spring and Occupy movements of 2011; Black Lives Matter fighting against racial capitalism and facing multiple urban injustices in 2017 onwards; anti-immigrant sentiment is arguably at its most dangerously high levels across Europe since end of World War II, and is creating tensions and protests in cities across the continent. And today, there is also the existential threat of climate change bringing people, young and old, onto the streets in their millions. Resistance in the modern city is clearly very different (not least the integration of digital forms of protest and the use of the infrastructure of the smart city against itself (see Dekeyser, 2021)). There are also multiple theoretical interjections such as how changing the 'grammar' of injustices can affect protest (MacLeod and McFarlane, 2014), how paying attention to the emergent properties of resistance can embolden it (Hughes, 2020), and how the architecture and masterplan of a city itself can facilitate or deaden protest (Thorpe, 2014). Suffice to say, theorising and historicising resistance is an important part of understanding how postcapitalist cities can manifest in the twenty-first century, and 1968 provides us with the ingredients to do just that.

1968 was also an important time for one of the most significant processes of urban thought, namely housing. Today, the multiple housing crises experienced in many cities all over the world is a functional symptom of capitalism's innate desire to commodify everything, including the very places we call home. Madden and Marcuse (2016: 10) have argued that a 'housing crisis is not a result of the system breaking down but of the system working exactly as intended', and as such, these so-called 'crises' are simply how ordinary urbanites experience the result of the 'assetification' of housing under a capitalist urban regime. And like the revolutionary urban fervour that had an evental quality in 1968, so too can we look to that year for a number of events that saw the beginnings of the commodification of housing. First is that the Balfron Tower, one of the most iconic brutalist housing blocks of London, designed by Erno Goldfinger, opened its doors for the first time. The building was a testament to the grandeur of social housing in the UK, although nearly sixty-odd years later it has become the posterchild of the nefarious gentrifying process of artwashing (which I have discussed elsewhere (Mould, 2018)). But perhaps the most notable (and indeed shocking, particularly given its eerie echo of the Grenfell disaster) is when there was a fire in the Ronan Point tower block in Canning Town, East London. On 16 May, a gas explosion on the eighteenth floor led to the collapse of a corner of the building, resulting in, remarkably given the extent of the structural damage, only four deaths. This event became a watershed moment in the history of social housing in the UK, a 'blow from which high-rise public housing in the UK never recovered' (Gold, 1984: 374). It sparked a wholesale re-evaluation of building practices, regulations and the future direction of public housing policies in the UK (Smith, 2023), and emboldened the anti-public, capitalistic nature of city development that governed many of the processes and ideologies affecting housing supply right across the world.

In the immediate aftermath of the Ronan Point disaster, however, there was a public outcry over the general safety of tower blocks, which had been a politically popular solution to postwar housing shortages. Investigations into the disaster identified critical flaws in the building's design and construction, notably the panel system of construction where large pre-cast concrete sections were bolted together on-site, which failed to ensure structural integrity under stress (Gold, 1984). This led to big impacts on building regulations and standards including law changes at the national level, but also shifts in the construction and planning process itself. More broadly, though, it was often used as an example of the follies of large-scale, centrally planned, social housing programmes, leading to the advocacy of privatised housing instead. Coleman's (1985) famous book *Utopia on Trial*, which essentially became Thatcher's handbook for urban renewal, bemoaned high-rise living as dangerous, anti-social and generally unfit for modern urbanism. This signalled the genesis of neoliberal policy in the UK housing sector, which, of course, saw it grow and spread around the world (Slater, 2021).

On the other side of the Atlantic, in the US, a similarly modernist social housing estate was in the process of becoming the go-to symbol of inner-city urban blight. The Pruitt–Igoe housing estate in St Louis was famously iconified by the architect Charles Jencks (1977: 9) when he proclaimed that 'Modern architecture died in St Louis Missouri on July 15, 1972 at 3.32 p.m. (or thereabouts) when the infamous Pruitt–Igoe scheme, or rather several of its slab blocks, were given the final coup de grace by dynamite.'

While Jencks's claim was overblown (and as it turned out, wrong), it cemented the destruction of Pruitt–Igoe as a fundamental 'evental' moment in urban housing history (it was given further notoriety by Godfey Reggio's 1982 cult film *Koyaanisqatsi*, which put the images of the housing block's destruction to a Philip Glass soundtrack, creating a haunting spectacle of how the death of social housing is so entwined with the progression of capitalism in the twentieth century). But while the actual controlled demolition took place in 1972, the order for residents to leave was given in 1968 by the Department of Housing (Ramroth, 2007). An order of this magnitude had not been given before; it was a direct consequence of the 'Fair Housing Act' that had been brought into law only a few months prior in April 1968. The order signalled perhaps the first instance of what has now become known as 'decanting': a nefarious process of the violent dispossession of urban residents dressed up with neutral (and

rather patronising) language (Ferreri, 2021). Hence, we can look to
the initial governmental order in 1968 as a foreshadowing event
of what is now the standard practice – accumulation by dispossession – of contemporary neoliberal housing policy (Harvey, 1989).
But 1968 didn't just signal a shift to neoliberal housing processes,
it also sowed the seeds of some radical housing initiatives too. In
Uruguay, a law was passed which allowed funding for housing to
be given directly to families and communities, paving the way for
one of the most successful cooperative housing movements in the
last few decades (more of this in Chapter 7). And in another quirk
of timing, in August 1968, ground was broken on the site of the
World Trade Center in New York City: a development which became
not only an icon of phallocentric urban capitalism that symbolised
the globalised motifs of 1980s and 1990s American neoliberalism,
but also the site in which those very motifs were attacked by the
forces of Islamic terrorism, itself fuelled by the American militarism that underpinned the global spread of American neoliberal
hegemony.

Summary

Lenin famously said that 'there are decades where nothing happens;
and there are weeks where decades happen', and the fifty-two weeks
of 1968 certainly contained a myriad of seismic events with a
planetary reach that arguably contained far more 'happenings' than
many of the previous and subsequent years combined. Yet there are,
of course, a multitude of events that occurred which were completely
ordinary (and, indeed, other notable moments which have perhaps
gone unrecorded). But that so many media – books, films, documentaries, blog posts, anniversary articles, and the rest – focus on
1968 is evidence that there was something special about the year's
relationship with the development of urban capitalism and its associated discontents. The internationalism that it both came from (via
the televised events that inspired distant revolutionaries) and helped
to create (via a connected tissue of anti-capitalist action) is a key
ingredient in 1968's uniqueness. By stringing some of the more
relevant events together though in this specific analysis, I have
attempted to highlight how the year can be thought of as 'evental';

as a moment of significant rupture precisely because of the constant analysis (to which of course, this chapter can now be added).

The city, as a dense and (as the introduction explained) *intense* network of social, economic and political interaction, remains a potent arena for contestation and transformation; indeed, as I have quoted before (but it is worth reiterating) the city is the place where 'the powerless can make history' (Sassen, 2011: 574). The urban landscape, with its inherent complexities and contradictions, offers unique opportunities for solidarity, innovation and the reclamation of space and rights by those people and ideas that have been historically marginalised, brutally oppressed and/or silenced. Hence, in the rest of this book I want to evidence those threads of urbanism that have attempted to build spaces were these people, voices and ideas flourish. There are many spaces – from hyper-local and often fleeting pockets of de-commodified life to entire cities built with a communist dream – that strive for a fundamentally *post*capitalist city, and that have been 'won' from below because of the very actions detailed in this chapter. To build an urban world from the evental truths of these places, we just need to know where to look. Part III of this book can be thought of as an analysis of a collection of those places and what they're doing to enact not only a liveable but flourishing postcapitalism, and a vision of how they can be combined to usher in a more just, sustainable and equitable urban world.

But in order to get there, in order to exemplify the postcapitalist praxis that can aid in 'identifying' the city we want to initiate, we can look to contemporary practices of resistance that are both an exposition of the injustices that cities currently propagate, and a vivid exploration of the cities that need to be built. There are of course many tactics, processes, subversions, cultures and groupings that resist the capitalist cities of today, and all of them could form the basis of an entire book by themselves, let alone a single chapter (see Beissinger (2022) for a comprehensive overview). Instead, I want to lay the framework of an alternative viewpoint of contemporary postcapitalism resistive practices that I think has yet to garner much attention: practices with a distinctly *psychedelic* hue.

Chapter 4

Situationism redux and the psychedelia of postcapitalism

In April 2017, the then UK Conservative prime minister, Theresa May, announced a snap general election. Jeremy Corbyn, who had not long become the leader of the opposition Labour Party, embodied radical socialist values (which had been absent from mainstream UK politics since the 1980s), and began to mobilise large swaths of energised leftist grassroots groups to help coordinate what turned out to be a very effective political campaign. Despite narrowly losing the election in June that year, this campaign was credited with galvanising the rather fractious Left in the country, and providing a glimmer of hope for the disaffected and politically marginalised youth. One of the more surprising groups that emerged during the campaign was Grime4Corbyn – a collection of predominantly London-based grime artists including Stormzy, Skepta, Jme, Nadia Rose and others – who publicly supported the Labour leader and encouraged their fans to vote for him in the general election. Grime is a subcultural phenomenon which has musical roots in hip-hop with the lyrics often gravitating around social issues such as inner-city poverty, gang violence, police brutality and so on (Bramwell, 2015). One of Grime's more famous protagonists, Stormzy, iconically performed at the Brit Awards in 2018 with lyrics that directly referenced the perceived failure of the prime minister and her government to deal with the aftermath of the Grenfell disaster:

> Theresa May, where's the money for Grenfell?
> Just forgot about Grenfell, you criminals
> And you got the cheek to call us savages
> You should do some jail time
> You should pay some damages
> We should burn your house down
> And see if you can manage this

Hence grime, like many countercultural musical forms that preceded it (notably punk in the 1970s) is political (with a small 'p'). But given that it emerged at a time in British politics when neoliberalism had annihilated any viable ideological opposition within parliament, to engage with politicians and be Political (with a big 'P') would never have been thought of. So, the alliance with Corbyn – an above-middle-aged, allotment-tendering, corduroy-wearing white male career politician – was at the time, highly surprising to say the least.

But looking deeper into the activist tendencies of both, it is a clear match. Both grime artists and Corbyn (and the socialist-leaning governmental ideas that he represented) are vehemently opposed to the stifling and brutalising violence of contemporary capitalist cities. White (2020), when articulating the hyperlocal demarcation of racial urban capitalism (explained in Chapter 1), argues that this process catalysed grime's genesis in the council estates and street corners of East London in the 2000s and 2010s. And the subsequent success of the genre is because it spoke of the visceral harm and destitution that came about because of the intense urban institutional violence experienced at the time. White focused on Forest Gate in Newham, and the planning processes, gentrification, intense policing but also national policies such as austerity that went towards creating the conditions in which the genre of grime proliferated. Because young, largely racialised people are hemmed into a particular postcode through hegemonic and institutionally violent urban austerity practices (very similar to those outlined in Part I of this book), they create reactions that are at once social, cultural and (as will be explained as this chapter progresses) *psychedelic*. Corbyn, with his broad socialist appeal was an advocate for working-class solidarity, anti-austerity politics and anti-racist rhetoric, and so became an obvious ally to grime artists. The formalisation of the Grime4Corbyn group was therefore an example of a grassroots cultural and artistic movement that had its origins in a direct reaction to unjust urban policies 'crossing-over' to the more institutional political movement of parliamentary practices and general-election campaigning. From the perspective of postcapitalist city discourse and the arguments of this book, it is a prime example of how *reactions* to a capitalist city are borne out of movements that have a cultural and more-often-than-not artistic dimension. Without wanting to veer off into the complex debates about the inherent political actions of art (mostly because it would entail a whole separate book, but also because I have covered this elsewhere (Mould, 2018)), reacting to the capitalist city is as much an artistic action as it is a political one. That is because it is through artistic and creative practices that the alternatives to injustice are dreamed, envisioned and represented. Building these visions as viable alternatives is of course a political (with a big 'P') act given the requirements of institutions to change (which will be discussed in Part III of this book). But as part of the initial, visceral and community responses to injustice, artistic practices are the life blood of resistance.

In fleshing out the 'reaction' dimension to postcapitalist cities, this chapter aims to theorise, analyse and advocate artistic endeavours that not only highlight the clear and obvious injustices of the capitalist city, but also begin to paint a vivid picture of the joys of an alternative. What is more, there is a clear link between the artistic responses and the themes of the previous chapter, namely the evental qualities of 1968. Because it was in the fires of the Parisian riots of May that year that the most pervasive (and fetishised) resistance art movement reached its zenith: that of situationism.

Situationism redux

The late, great American science-fiction and anti-capitalist novelist, Ursula K. Le Guin, in 2014 when accepting a prestigious award, said these now oft-quoted words: 'The profit motive is often in conflict with the aims of art. We live in capitalism, its power seems inescapable, but then, so did the divine right of kings. Any human power can be resisted and changed by human beings. Resistance and change often begin in art.'

In these trying times of planetary climate catastrophe, geopolitical strife, ongoing genocides and the seemingly increasing ubiquity of capitalist realism, clinging to Le Guin's optimism may seem naive. And, given how skilled our capitalist overlords have become at co-opting the very essence of artistic critique, a decade or so since those words were uttered they seem, perhaps, laughably utopian. But this quite natural reaction is only so because the profiteers of capitalism have colonised the speculative future before it can even be imagined by the masses. There is a sense that such pessimism is too defeatist, as capitalism's co-optive juggernaut is fuelled by such counter-revolutionary mindsets; indeed, the very act of colonising our future requires violently disaggregating the ethical and political from any artistic endeavour (as I outlined in my previous works (Mould, 2015, 2018)). Such a violent division makes even the most subversive of art sellable (you only have to look at the works of Banksy to realise this). As Le Guin continued her speech, she bemoaned PR and sales departments that rule over artists (such as herself) like a dictatorship, flogging them 'like deodorant'. She pled that authors of political fiction – literary artists – craved freedom above all else.

To realise and actualise a postcapitalist city, one that resurrects the political imaginaries of 1968 (and those it spawned), I argue that the task of disaggregating artistic practices from the clutches of capitalism is paramount. In today's hyper-marketised art 'world' and media industries (meaning the amorphous, loose but mostly identifiable conglomeration of artistic practices, galleries, museums, media platforms, cultural critique and academic research) that manifest the bleeding edge of capitalism's territorialising process, this is a chronically difficult practice, but it is possible. Indeed, as Mark Fisher (2017) wrote in his unfinished work, *Acid Communism*, it is vital if we are to escape capitalist realism.

But where have we heard all this before? When did the story of urban subcultural, subversive and revolutionary practices that were forged in the fires of radical political thought get snuffed out? The Situationist International (SI) collective of Paris in the 1960s are often analysed and valorised as a visionary collective who pushed back against the stifling striation of capitalist life at the time, and laid the ideological groundwork for the coming revolution (Plant, 1992). The SI's artistic and political actions 'involved the continuous, conscious and collective recreation of the environment' and were the 'fruit of a new type of creativity' (Pinder, 2005: 165). The main protagonist of the SI, Guy Debord argued that creating situations – purposefully constructed events that seek to liberate individuals from the repetitive, dull and commodified experiences of daily life – are ephemeral, unique and vivid, standing in stark contrast to the homogeneity of modern capitalist existence (Debord, 1967). In an age where experiences were too often mediated by images and representations (and how much more are they now, sixty years later?), 'situations' aimed to facilitate direct, unmediated human interactions between each other and the materiality of the city around us. Over a number of years, the SI created and performed many different art works or enacted situations in the city, but it is perhaps their act of simply walking the city – *dérive* – that has become their lasting legacy (Marshall, 2023). *Dérive*, the *flâneur* and psychogeography are all concepts that have endured to today, germinating an entire universe of cultural forms that adhere, critique and augment these ideas (Routhier, 2023). Documentary films, online digitised pastiches, performance art pieces, academic conferences and everything else in between have been attributed to this most revolutionary of practices, *dérive*. Yet, the persistence of the SI, notably their very ableist, gendered and raced practice of walking-as-protest, evidences the very co-optive power of the capitalist city they were attempting to protest against (Elkin, 2016; Rose, 2021). As Swyngedouw (2002: 154) so acerbically noted, 'it is as if their [the SI] sting has been removed, as if they have been sapped of the life that once inspired a generation', with the confinement of the SI's political agenda limited to 't-shirts, mugs and serialised postcards', neutering their critique entirely. Such an extreme account does perhaps do a disservice to some of those SI-inspired practices that can genuinely provide spaces of protest and resistance to capitalist urbanism. For instance, the radical crip activist and geographer Morag Rose utilised her psychogeographical walks along the public footpaths of the river Irwell in Manchester and Salford in the UK to highlight how planned closures and privatisation of the paths by hotel developments infringed upon the public's right to the city. Via performative walks, alongside more traditional political activity such as gaining the support of local politicians, she was successful in getting the developers to drop the plans (Pidd, 2023; Rose, 2025). But there is no getting away from the fact that Swyngedouw's words holds weight more broadly; situationism as an artistic practice of critique has lost much of its 'sting'.

But refracting situationism through the more optimistic lenses of Le Guin and Fisher *can* bring a revivification to the ideological kernels of situationism, but the work of disentangling it from the capitalist agenda of mugs, T-shirts and postcards must be done. This is not easy work because largely it requires looking backwards towards the forgotten emancipatory imaginaries of the past, and sideways at the hidden and oppressed prefigurative politics of the present, rather than to the utopian postcapitalist horizon of the future. Fisher (2014) argued that during the first few years of the twenty-first century, the ubiquity of capitalist realism means that we are experiencing what he called (riffing on Bifo Beradi) the 'slow cancellation of the future'. By this he was referring not to a linear future of timelines, but to the very *idea* of the future as a radically different social arena to the present so often dreamed up and envisaged by artists (as Le Guin did so beautifully). Because of the appropriative and co-optive reaches of capitalism, any 'new' artistic form too often merely replicates a capitalist present to fend off any radical forms of social resistance that bubble up within artistic and/or cultural production practices (see also Bolstanki and Chiapello, 2005). Fisher gave numerous examples from music, cinema and art, and his prophetic stance has proved even more accurate as we have barrelled into the post-COVID 2020s, with the continual churn of Hollywood remakes and 'cinematic universes', bands who do constant reunions tours well into their octogenarian years, and the ubiquitous revival of past cultural forms as pastiche and 'nostalgia industry' (Cross, 2015).

For those of us critiquing capitalist practices in an attempt to build a more just postcapitalist future, this 'slow cancellation of the future' is evidently a highly pessimistic and gloomy mood to embody. Luckily, Fisher left us with a morsel of hope before he department this world with his text *Acid Communism*. Within it, he argues for a resurrection of the utopian energies of the countercultural revolutionary potentials of the past, and re-imagining them for the present. In particular, he advocated drawing on the radical potential of the countercultural revolution of the 1960s (and, I would add, 1968 in particular, as the last chapter highlighted) and applying it to current socio-political contexts. Importantly though, it required another ingredient, *psychedelia*.

Psychedelic ingredients

To use the term psychedelia in contemporary culture is fraught with baggage, notably that of illicit drugs. Magic mushrooms (possibly the psychedelic substance most widely available to humans) have, in their prepared form, been illegal for many years until 2019, when

Denver in the US became the first major metropolitan areas to legalise them. But psychedelic drugs have very ancient roots, with evidence of their use dating back thousands of years in various indigenous cultures (George *et al.*, 2022). The earliest recorded use of psychedelics can be traced to Mesoamerican civilisations, as apparently the Aztecs used *teonanácatl* (meaning 'divine mushroom') during religious ceremonies (Jay, 2019). These mushrooms contain the active ingredient psilocybin, which induces radically altered states of consciousness (Carod-Artal, 2015). Beyond that, though, the modern history of psychedelic drugs began with the synthesis of lysergic acid diethylamide (LSD) by Swiss chemist Albert Hofmann on 16 November 1938. Hofmann was working at Sandoz Laboratories in Basel, Switzerland, when he first synthesized LSD-25 while searching for a respiratory and circulatory stimulant. However, its psychoactive effects were not discovered until 19 April 1943, when Hofmann accidentally ingested a small amount and experienced the first LSD trip, a day now celebrated as 'Bicycle Day' as he was on a bike ride through Basel when the effects of the drug came on (Hofmann, 1980). The 1960s saw a significant shift as psychedelics moved from more clinical settings to the countercultural movement (and was used extensively in many of the student uprisings noted in the previous chapter). But more than its use in social movements and protests, music, art and literature from this era were heavily influenced by psychedelic experiences. Perhaps most famously we have The Beatles' *Sgt. Pepper's Lonely Hearts Club Band* album in 1967, but a favourite of Mark Fisher's was *Psychedelic Shack* by the Temptations, released in, yes, 1968. Fisher (2017) argued that the album 'describes a space that is very definitely collective, that bustles with all the energy of a bazaar. For all its carnivalesque departures from everyday reality, however, this is no remote utopia. It feels like an actual social space, one you can imagine really existing.'

The more-than-present atmospheres of an induced psychedelic trip were part of the appeal to the musicians, artists and student activists at the time, and they helped to foster a tangible revolutionary fervour (Gilbert, 2017). Hence, rather predictably, in 1966 LSD was made illegal in the US, and this marked the beginning of a broader crackdown on psychedelics worldwide.

The resurgence of psychedelia today is in part due to the clinical research conducted on psychedelics as to their efficacy in treating common widespread conditions such as depression, chronic anxiety and post-traumatic stress disorder (conditions that have become rampant under a suffocating neoliberal capitalism (Davies, 2021)). More worryingly, a number of Silicon Valley's neoliberal potentates such as Elon Musk and the late Steve Jobs have spoken about the influence of psychedelics on their creativity and problem-solving abilities (Kim, 2024).

Despite its co-option by greedy CEOs who have often looked to countercultural motifs and practices to get the edge over their competitors, psychedelia is not limited to the ingestion of drugs or natural compounds, illicit or otherwise. Instead, infusing a psychedelic sensibility into the subcultures of the present helps to challenge the sterile and oppressive modern capitalist-realist landscape, and envision new forms of communal and economic existence (Fisher, 2017). So the reference that Fisher and myself make to psychedelia is not limited to mind-altering drugs (although that can be included if that is your fancy); it is much broader than that. The etymology of the word is Greek, *psyche* ('mind') and *deloun* ('make visible' or 'reveal'). In relating to the Marxist trope of 'lifting the veil', psychedelia allows for people to fully experience the intense *abundance* of a life held in common: a life not predicated upon privatised, stifling and suffocating capitalist social relations, but instead upon the intimate connectivity between the self and the (human and non-human) matter of the world around them. Psychedelia is the affective presence of the more-than-human, experienced in the present. Characterised visually by intense and colourful motifs of fractal moving patterns that rarely conform to any obvious and recognisable icon or sign, psychedelia is the stage of experience *beyond* the immediate everyday life of the capitalist present: in the same way that it is more-than-human, but also more-than-present and includes tangible realities of past and future experienced in the situation of the now.

It is easy to see how this echoes the situationism of the SI, and how they looked to create 'unmediated human experiences' via artistic interventions in the city (via psychogeography and the like). I would like to argue, then, that infusing this situationism with a vial of psychedelia revivifies the situationist ethic and pulls it away from the appropriative clutches of capitalism. Such psychedelic experiences – or situations – may come from different cultures, traditions and social activities that we as individuals aren't used to or indeed comfortable with, but they nonetheless have a very material existence. Celebrating an important goal when your football team scores; the runner's high (if running is your thing); achieving Nirvana via meditation, worshipping at church or in a mosque; attending a concert: these are moments of affective and often collective experiences of a tangible excess that I would proffer we have *all* experienced at one time or another. And it is that intangible, atmospheric, affective and situational excess – however it is experienced – that is to be harnessed for a postcapitalist and common future.

City futures

I appreciate that this can all sound a little abstract and theoretical (not to mention, not very *urban*). But the artistic and cultural productions that such a theoretical (and psychedelic) mindset can produce are, as Le Guin so eloquently argued, the building blocks of resistance, and provide the embryos of a postcapitalist future beyond the one that capitalism realism dictates for us. In a Fisherian worldview (most readily readable in the collection of his K-Punk blog writings, which can be found easily online), there was indeed a psychedelic potential to contemporary subculture (less so the pervasive marketisation of the art world) if it can only navigate the alluring, yet dangerous, tentacles of capitalist appropriation. He found the same emancipation that Le Guin did with extraterrestrial and cosmological speculative fiction, in subcultural creativity (namely the very *urban* movements of rave, punk, hip-hop and art-house cinema), and even within individual artists (his essay on the Salford-based rock band Joy Division stands out in this respect). For Fisher, the beating heart of any subculture was its potential to serve as a catalyst for emancipatory social transformation, albeit on a 'small' (personal, local or urban) scale at first, but with the power to reverberate throughout the city (as a cultural 'movement'). The gatherings and expressions of like-minded revolutionaries and/or subversives, whether through underground politically charged music scenes, radical artistic communities, hackers or cyberpunk collectives, were not isolated phenomena. They were dynamic microcosms where new forms of resistance and resilience took shape. Subcultural city spaces, mostly in the western urban environment (notably around South East London where he taught in Goldsmiths), incubated innovative paradigms of anti-capitalist thinking, collective identities, and modes of critique. These, Fisher fervently believed, as did the SI back in the 1960s, were the building blocks of a new urban form and social order.

As Part I of this book outlined, gentrification and racial capitalism practices are producing cities that are designed to *continually* adhere to the accumulation of profit via the dispossession of raced and classed people and neighbourhoods. Cities are constantly changing, but they are not producing any new urban forms or social orders at all; there is a distinct capitalist realism to the city at play. To develop this concept further, we can refer to the work of Schwartz (2022: 1651) when he writes about 'nekronology', which is 'how excess wealth pollutes public spaces with a toxicity radiating from the future'. Schwartz uses the example of Thomas Heatherwick's much maligned piece of art/architecture/sculpture/capitalist monstrosity in New York, *Vessel*, and while he does not mention Mark Fisher specifically, there is a strong element of Fisher's 'hauntology' to Schwartz's concept of nekronology, in that capitalism's constant desire to accumulate for its future survival has meant a dispossession of the imaginaries of the present. So Schwartz (channelling Fisher, Le Guin, and others) argues that a revival of a kind of situationism (with a psychedelic and agonistic twist) to resist capitalist nekronology 'means NOT building the future; not transforming the present into the future. Let the future rot. No one has nor ever will live in "the future"; it's a hypothetical zone that justifies perpetual exploitation' (Schwartz, 2022: 1666).

In response to the 'wealth pollution' of a capitalist future, a revival of a situationist ethic resists futurist thinking that is so at risk of being sullied by that very pollution. It dwells in the very real and embodied experiences and practices of the present day, the here and now, the minutiae of the city all around us.

An ideal of example of this is the so-called 'Battle of Waterloo Bridge' that took place in April 2019. Not really a battle at all, it was an encampment of climate protestors, organised by Extinction Rebellion, who took over one of London's main thoroughfares, Waterloo Bridge. Initially by sitting in the road to block traffic, over the course of a week or so, the protestors defied police instructions to move (and subsequent arrests) and created a carnival of cultural activities including a skate ramp, an arboretum, Buddhist meditations, church services, sing-a-longs, and even a makeshift cinema popped up (Berglund and Schmidt, 2020; Molyneux, 2019). In so doing, the protestors were able to create a reality of climate action, one in which the forces of fossil-fuel capitalism were very distant indeed. As a moment of protest, the site was made into a vivid postcapitalist urban reality by the collective actions of activists, participatory onlookers, and even the police who were supervising it when they occasionally joined in (but who, then, a few days later, reverted to the role of enforcer of the status quo and hastily dismantled the site and arrested as many protestors as they could). What this *prefigurative*[1] encampment did (and many others like it around the world, including Resurrection City in Washington DC of 1968) was to enliven the forgotten or 'cancelled' futures of postcapitalism and, however briefly, give them a tangible reality in the present. Being involved in the site myself, it was difficult not to get captured by its vivacity; there was an atmosphere of intense joy, compassion and ultimately hope. This was borne out in many of the commentaries and interviews that protestors gave in the media after the event that spoke of a 'moment' of change in the entire climate discourse (Taylor and Gayle, 2019). Such hyperbolic optimism is easy to critique, and as the years have rolled on and climate catastrophe has only tightened its grip on the planet's delicate ecosystems, has sadly proven wildly misplaced. But it does speak to the euphoria clearly evident at the specific time and place; a euphoria that is 'unrealistic' given the surrounding realities of ubiquitous extractive fossil-fuel capitalism, but one that is nevertheless obdurately present, and tangibly *real*. In a sense, this was a psychedelic situation because it 'lifted the veil' of capitalist realism and the dead, climate-catastrophe riddled future it demands via an aesthetic and political atmosphere of excess, elation and overt optimism, and proffered, however fleetingly, a tangible reality of a radically different future, but one experienced in the present.

So, in order to admonish the pollution of a capitalist future, the work that needs to be done is to enliven the present moment as much as possible, to engage in politically charged situations that are psychedelic (in that they are more-than-present) and revolutionary (in that they are held-in-common). There are a myriad of ways in which this can be actualised, but I wish to focus on three that I have experienced personally and collectively, and have been the focus on my research journeys of late: agonism, proletarianisation and a form of neo-Luddism.

The first is Mouffe's (2005) concept of agonism, which argues that critical artistic practices (including production, circulation and audiencing) can incite a form of political dissensus; they can, and she argues should, disrupt the comfortable 'common sense' narratives sanctioned by dominant capitalist ideologies and bring to light the obscured and often obliterated realities; they should lift the veil of capitalist life. By challenging the dominant forms of consensus, art becomes a radical form of expression that does not merely critique and disrupt, but also offers alternatives and gives rise to social movements via a radical disassembling of the tacitly but often dominating consensual force, towards a dissenting form of agonistic socialising. In other words, critical art foments a necessary disruption in the smooth – and often invisible – practices of capitalist realism, making visible the invisible and giving voice to those silenced within the prevailing hegemonic frameworks. It is a form of 'staying with the trouble' (as I suggested I would do with this book) in the strict Harawayian (2016) sense which advocates for a deeper engagement with the problems at hand rather than a retreat to idealised solutions that are pre-offered. Art and culture, in this context, does not simplify, but complicates social narratives. It invites dialogue, questioning and confrontations with uncomfortable and often hidden truths. This form of artistic engagement challenges the spectator, no longer passive, to engage, debate and ultimately partake in the co-creation of alternative futures. Put bluntly, under capitalism, our resistance is so often performed for us by artistic practices that we consume passively and without agitation (at least not beyond that which capitalism cannot appropriate); to wrest ourselves from this performative apathy and enact a formative postcapitalism requires an active engagement with art that psychedelically unveils the injustices of capitalist life.

The second is to 'proletarianise' these situationist experiences and the artistic practices of postcapitalism more broadly. Class consciousness, and the raising thereof, is often at risk of being overlooked within protest and resistance more broadly. For example, one of the main (and largely valid) critiques of the current activist action against climate change is that it is overly white and middle class. There has been a great deal of work in attempting to 'undo' the whiteness of

environmental action (see Hickcox (2018) for examples in the US
and Hughey (2023) for the UK), and there is a strong advocacy for
how working-class sensibilities (and the rejection of 'professionalism'
that is entailed) are needed in the broader movement in order to
maintain and energise the climate movement (Eisenman, 2023). More
broadly, though, *any* radicality that is advocating for a postcapitalist
world that doesn't make a claim for working-class and intersectional
solidarity ultimately ends up as part of the neoliberalisation machine.
History tells us as much. We can look back to the Paris Commune
of 1871. Ross (2016) argues that the commoning practices that the
commune enacted back then blurred the boundaries between hitherto
immutable institutions such as education, art and politics. As she
argues,

> More important than any laws the Communards were able to enact
> was simply the way in which their daily workings inverted entrenched
> hierarchies and divisions – first and foremost among these the division
> between manual or artistic and intellectual labour ... What matters
> more than any images conveyed, laws passed, or institutions founded
> are the capacities set in motion. (Ross, 2016: 50)

Dwelling on the commune's *Manifesto of the Federation of
Artists*, Ross states that the Communards were using the social
experimentation of the commune to completely 'deprivatise' art and
beauty, and were integrating them into everyday and educational
life. The manifesto was an attempt by the artists of the commune
to therefore proletarianise artistic production, to take museums and
monuments back into public and working-class ownership, and have
the art and architecture on display subject to democratic control.
This reconnection between art, the public and the common sphere
was an important moment of the commune, and one that is vital
to the realisation of postcapitalist cities more broadly.

This revitalisation of the public sphere and commoning of art is
a direct challenge to the privatisation that clouds the present. Public
art as it's currently conceptualised is nothing of the sort; public
space as it's currently conceptualised is nothing of the sort. The
publicness of public space is a mere superficiality; it is more a language
of policy that is rubber stamped by planning officials, often signified
by the appearance of some insipid generic 'public art'. The same
with museums, galleries, biennales, festivals; if they exclude the poor

and the working class then what claim to radicality can they ever make?

And the third way in which it becomes possible to admonish the present 'wealth pollution' of a capitalist future is to engage in a form of neo-Luddism. The Luddite movement (named after the apocryphal legendary weaver Ned Ludd) of the early nineteenth century consisted of a group of English textile workers who arguably became some of the first organised opponents of industrialised and technological capitalism. They objected strongly to the introduction of mechanised looms and stocking frames, which allowed for the mass production of textiles and replaced skilled artisans, and significantly lowered the wages of many of the factory workers (Mueller, 2021). While in modern times, their name has become synonymous with an aversion to technology, the Luddites were not against technological progress nor the actual machines weaving themselves. Rather, they opposed the unregulated, exploitative practices of the burgeoning industrial economy that threatened their livelihoods. Again, contrary to popular narratives, their protests were highly organised and strategically targeted. They would assemble in secret at night to plan their attacks, often issuing warnings to factory owners before destroying the machines (Jones, 2013). But they also engaged in more official and peaceful ways of protest, in that they would attempt negotiations with the capitalists, and organised petitions for better working conditions and fair wages. However, their peaceful efforts were frequently ignored, and in 1812 the British government, clearly in the service of the industrial capitalists, formed the 'Frame Breaking Act', making the Luddites' actions illegal. The military were brought in, and often violent clashes would occur; protesters were regularly executed or sent to penal colonies in the 'new world'.[2]

The prefix 'neo' therefore has been added by more recent movements (see Lamont, 2024) to highlight how the Luddites' anti-capitalism (not anti-technology) is still relevant today. Neo-Luddism is more than simply recovering manual crafts, analogue technologies and a revivification of revolutionary practices of situationism, surrealism and their ilk (although that is an important part (Eiden-Offe, 2023)). Because refusing technology will only go so far. It is more about recovering the *materiality* of artistic and related activist practices, technological or otherwise. As Fisher (2014), channelling Marx, argued, there is an inherent materiality in the consciousness of revolutionary thought. A revival of the psychedelic culture that (as discussed above) he advocated for as revolutionary praxis necessitates a 'return' to this anti-technological materiality precisely because it is 'uncapturable' by the neoliberal machinery. He argued that 'despite all the mysticism and pseudo-spiritualism which has always hung over psychedelic culture, there was actually a demystificatory and *materialist* dimension' (Fisher, 2014). In other words, it is the essence of materiality – the intermingling of human and non-human matter that has characterised the development of our species ever since we first started using tools – that is being leached away by the neoliberal uses of technology.

And so, to return to the opening of this chapter and the subculture of grime and its allegiance with Corbyn's socialist political campaign in 2017, we can see how it has elements of all three of these psychedelic characteristics melded into one resistant subculture. It is agonistic, proletarian and material. Indeed, as James (2020: 2377, my emphasis) notes when discussing grime videos and their place in the broader landscape of the institutionally racist music industry: 'At a time of racist assertion, neoliberal marginalization, and decontextualized trans-local media flows, the human-voice-as-instrument then powerfully conveys the *agonism* and joy of the twenty-first-century multi-ethnic city through black diasporic form.'

Hence, grime is agonistic in that it deliberately disrupts the 'common sense' of the (racist) music industry, media and often urban forms of capitalist life. It is highly disruptive in the Mouffian (2005) sense, and 'lifts the veil' on the injustices of majority Black inner-city life. Because of this, it is also highly proletarianised. Grime is resolutely political in this sense as it arose from the working-class Black youth culture that has had to endure the last fifteen or so years of austerity politics in the UK (Perera, 2018). And much like the Communards in Paris one and half centuries prior, it blurs the boundaries between education, art and politics. And finally, grime is material. The artists have created a politically charged subgenre of music that often directly references local specificities (roads, estates, postcodes, etc.), and as James (2020) noted has an intense focus on the human voice as the main instrument, and ultimately stems from a deep connection with the very material factors of *place* (White, 2020).

Grime is therefore part of the universe of subcultures that have ebbed and flowed throughout the capitalist landscape of contemporary urbanised culture: rising from 'below', creating political and tacitly anti-capitalist atmospheres, perhaps spawning social movements and even political influence, before being targeted for commercialisation by capitalist registers (see Woods (2022) for an intricate discussion of how specific grime artists use their subversive and sometimes criminal pasts to rapidly commercialise their future). In that sense, grime echoes (not perfectly of course, but no less coherently) hippy culture, punk, rave, hip-hop, art-house cinema and the like. What links these together is a psychedelic sensibility; one that is agonistic, proletarianised, material and, above all, collective. In so doing, these artistic forms have the ingredients to resist the appropriation of the intense experiences of the present moment by the future wealth of capitalism. In all these urban subcultures (and the many more than I am personally unaware of), there is an intense situationism; an experience of the abundance of the present locality and temporality that is unrecognisable to capitalist mechanisms of resource extraction and commodification. Of course, these experiences are fleeting, temporal and bounded by all sorts of socialised parameters such as age, language, race, sexuality, neurotypicality and so on. And of course, as is the case with many, if not all, of these subcultural forms, their psychedelic tendencies cannot last against the relentless extractive pressures of capitalism; after all, twenty-first century 'creative' capitalism has perfected the *art* of co-opting critique (Mould, 2018). But in the psychedelic tradition outlined above, these sub-cultural forms *can* aid in the experience of the more-than-human, the more-than-present. They explode the situation of the 'now' beyond the repression of capitalist timing, and blend the past, present, future, near, far, subconscious, consciousness and the collective together into a situationism to which capitalism is blind, at least temporarily. The task we have (as a collective of activist and radical publics concerned in proliferating these postcapitalist tendencies rather than admonishing them) is to celebrate the psychedelic affect of these agonistic, proletarian, material and often very urban subcultural forms, and at the same time, hold back the opposing forces of homogeneity, professionalisation and codification of urban racial capitalism as much as possible.

Chapter 5

The city as canvas

In October 2019, a group of secondary school students in Santiago, Chile, began protesting against a 30 pesos rise in the cost of metro tickets (around 4 per cent). They coordinated a mass fare evasion, turnstile hopping and the shutting down of some stations with sit-ins and occupations. Only a month later, the Chilean government had agreed unanimously to hold a referendum to rewrite the decades-old, Pinochet-era constitution. From fare-dodging students to country-level political dissent, the protests known as 'Estallido Social' ruptured the political status quo in a very short space of time. Chile was 'at the barricades' (Alcarón, 2020), fuelled by a desire for change that saw a rapid cost-of-living crisis, unemployment and rampant inequality throughout the country.

It is of little surprise that Santiago was a tinderbox given it was the epicentre of one of the world's first national-level experiments in neoliberal policy making (see Edwards, 2023 for a comprehensive account). Since the 1970s, a cadre of economists known as the Chicago Boys, schooled under the tutelage of Milton Friedman and other eminent economists at the University of Chicago, were profoundly influenced by free-market principles, and a new post-dictatorship Chile – and the policy vacuum that was created by the military coup in 1973 – was the ideal test ground for state-level neoliberalism. Hence, Chile became a laboratory for punitive neoliberal policies such as reduced state intervention, deregulated markets, and privatised state-owned enterprises. Key industries, including telecommunications, electricity and even social services like health and education, were sold off to private investors. The 'success' of this model prompted the devotees of these economists, politicians such as Margeret Thatcher and Ronald Reagan, to roll out the same economic policies in core imperial countries (Klein, 2007).

And part of those destructive neoliberal policies was informed by what Vegara-Perucich and Boano (2011) called the 'big bang of neoliberal urbanism' in Santiago, which included (but was in no way not limited to) tax reductions on real-estate development, the dismantling of the central-planning bureau, and the transformation of land into a financialised asset. It is easy to see how Santiago was the 'frontrunner' of the symptoms of the neoliberal capitalist city, experiencing all the pinch points of gentrification, rising costs of living, rampant inequality and social disorder before many other cities following the same playbook.

Once the students lit the spark of protest with fare evasion, Santiago's streets filled with protestors, with over a million people taking to the streets on 25 October 2019, with the usual sights of marching, placards and the inevitable violent response from the militarised police filling the global news media. These will be the enduring images of the protests, and given that thirty-six people died and approximately 2,500 were injured at the hands of a brutal state, rightly so. But the protests have been noted also for the prolific use of art and creativity, notably on the streets themselves, to catalyse protestors and their revolutionary message (Salgado, 2019; Mattar, 2020; Gordon-Zolov and Zolov, 2022). This form of visual activism – that has a rich history of use around the world (McAuliffe, 2012) – transformed the urban landscape of Santiago (and beyond) into a vibrant terrain of dissent and postcapitalist hope, encapsulating the protesters' demands and visions for a more equitable and just society. As with many other protests, street art played a crucial role in the 2019 Chilean protests, as it can act as a powerful tool for communication, solidarity and resistance 'from below' (Mould, 2015). The walls of Santiago became canvases for a diverse range of artistic political expressions, from graffiti and murals to posters and stencils. These artworks, articulated the collective aspirations of the protesters, providing a visual narrative of the movement's ethos (Cobos, 2021).

In detailing and analysing the myriad messages and politics of this process of aestheticising the street, Cobos (2021: 545) indicates that there were five 'aesthetic-political milestones' to the protest that while having their roots in many resistance movements from the past were unique to the Chilean moment. Those five are: felling statues that represented the 'old' regime of Chilean capitalist hegemony; the prominence of feminist politics; dignity in dwelling; highlighting oppression; and the demand 'to be called people again' (Cobos, 2021: 550). These universal themes are a long way from protesting against a rise in the price of a metro ticket, but such is the nature of protest action as a part of postcapitalist resistance; it was the artistic actions of the movement that 'unveiled' the demands for justice lying beneath the suffocating striation of the capitalist city, and all that was needed was a spark. Slogans such as 'It's not thirty pesos, it's thirty years' encapsulated the protesters' grievances against decades of economic neoliberal policies that favoured the elite while marginalising the majority (Ojeda, 2023). The art also prominently featured indigenous images, particularly those of the Mapuche people – who had hitherto been depicted as terrorists by those looking to quash revolutionary potential – highlighting the intersectionality of class and indigenous struggles in Chile, but also a realisation of how such indigeneity can be a powerful force of change to the capitalist status quo. Many murals depicted Mapuche warriors, with their faces painted with traditional symbols, standing defiantly against a backdrop of flames. These powerful images not only celebrated the indigenous resistance but also linked it to the broader struggle against economic injustice (Gordon-Zolov, 2023). The artwork was also rich with historical symbolism. Many of the pieces drew on Chile's tumultuous history (not least its fractious relationship with the paragons of neoliberalism, the Chicago Boys in the 1970s), invoking figures like Salvador Allende and Victor Jara as representatives of past revolutionary hope against a tyrannical form of capitalism.

One of the more compelling and political aspects of the street art was its inclusivity. It was (as often is the case with mass social movements, as Chapter 4 outlined) started by students, but the production of the art was not confined to professional artists; it also included contributions from everyday citizens and amateurs (Mattar, 2020). This democratisation of art was part of the much-emphasised horizontality of the protests, reflecting a collective struggle that stretches back decades rather than an isolated moment of resistance. Indeed, the collective action of creative practices has been identified as a key component of the movement's success:

> The process of making itself had a unifying effect. Artists and activists consistently attested to the collective nature of cultural production.

Whether it be a graphic silkscreen workshop or a flash mob dance which gathered momentum through WhatsApp groups and was rehearsed *en masse*, creative endeavours often brought activists together physically and spiritually. (Gordon-Zolov, 2023: 52)

All in all, the creativity of the city and its inhabitants (artistic or not) came rushing to the surface, both literally and metaphorically. The surfaces of the city were adorned with political images, and the demands of the protestors were thrust to the top of the political agenda. Ordinarily, the contemporary capitalist city utilises itself as a canvas of consumption, with advertising, corporate and media messages, and branding motifs littering the city's multiple surfaces, competing for our eyeballs' attentions (Cronin, 2008; Coleman, 2015). But there are constant moves and countermoves to subvert this, with people sometimes taking corporate advertising down, covering it up with DIY or underground media, or the more coordinated 'subvertisers' who subvert the message with a political or activist theme (Dekeyser, 2021). These are then sometimes recovered by the official advertising company, and the cat-and-mouse game goes on. The process of contestation over the surfaces of the city is part of the political activism that went on in Santiago during the Estallido Social. As such, the surface of the city itself is a contested space, as Andron (2023: 3) has outlined, 'Surfaces are a stage on which urban stories unfold or become hidden; they are spectacle and surveillance devices, objects of desire and of maintenance. They are skins, borders, edges and contested territories of inscription and regulation.'

Through resistance and protest, Santiagans were utilising the contested surfaces of the city democratically, taking back some of the publicness from the increasing privatisation of urban space. In a sense, they were acting psychedelically upon the surfaces of the city, peeling back the layers of privatised capital to evidence an emancipatory aesthetic of resistance, indigeneity and proletarianised politics that would otherwise have been hidden.

Moreover, the citizens who daubed the surfaces of the city, danced through the streets, and filled the atmosphere with music exemplified an insistent reclamation of urban public space that transcended mere physical occupation. They infused the urban environment with a political vibrancy that challenged the privatisation of public infrastructure and spaces (and the increasing cost of using them), turning Santiago into a political canvas to reflect their collective aspirations, struggles and demands of a different, postcapitalist city. This dynamic interplay between the protesters and urban fabric of Santiago not only highlighted the psychedelic power of creative resistance (in that, as the previous chapter detailed, it had elements that were at once agonistic, material and proletarian), but also underscored the transformative potential of public art in enacting socio-political change. The aestheticisation of protest in Chile became a symbol of resistance that transcended national borders, demonstrating the universal language of art in expressing dissent and demanding justice.

The inclusive nature of the artistic production during the Estallido Social highlighted the potential for art to democratise political participation. By encouraging contributions from all citizens, regardless of their artistic skill, the movement emphasised that everyone had a role to play in the fight for a better future. This horizontality and inclusivity were crucial in sustaining the momentum of the protests and ensuring that the movement remained rooted in the experiences and aspirations of the broader population as a whole, including indigenous, working-class and marginalised people (Gordon-Zolov, 2023).

As 2019 turned into 2020, the COVID-19 virus made its way around the world via our hyperconnected networks of mobility, and Santiago was not immune. Curfews were put in place, and, generally, people stopped congregating to protest in order to protect the vulnerable. Rallies and marches still took place, but these were far smaller and had to work around the laws regarding partial lockdowns in Chile. The police and the government took this opportunity to remove a lot of the graffiti and street art, indicating just how important *they* saw it as part of the resistance movement (Gordon-Zolov, 2023). But despite this crackdown and the effects of the virus, the transformative change of the artistically inspired revolt had been realised; the referendum for the new constitution was held on 25 October 2020, with the overwhelming majority voting in favour. To date, various versions of the constitution have been drawn up, and although none, at the time of writing, have been voted in, this evidences just how vital the protests were in ushering in change at the very highest level nationally: in 2021, Santiago elected a communist and feminist mayor in Iracĺ Hassler (although she lost the mayorship in 2024). The political landscape of the city and Chile more broadly is still polarised like many other countries around the world, and the future of the city – as it continues to attempt to undo the very real effects of the history of Chile as a neoliberal laboratory from the 1970s onwards – is still very much in the balance.

However, the protests of Estallido Social in Santiago (and other cities in Chile) not only brought about significant political change at the national level, but also heavily re-animated the surfaces of the city as spaces for creative resistance and collective empowerment, with that re-animation diffusing into the social world of the city more broadly via empowering citizens, and even changing the political hues of the mayor. The transformation of urban surfaces into canvases of dissent and its potential to lever a city away from capitalist hegemonic powers to something altogether more *post*capitalist (or at least a city in political flux) highlights the enduring power of art to inspire collective action, lift the veil of capitalist realism, and enact social justice on a city-wide scale. As Santiago continues to grapple with its neoliberal past and envision a more just future, the lessons of the Estallido Social remind us of the psychedelic role that creativity, inclusivity and solidarity play in the ongoing struggle for a postcapitalist city.

Part III

Solutions

Chapter 6

From the care economy to the caring commons

Caring for each other (and increasingly ourselves) is now, sadly, some of the most radical and anti-capitalist acts we can undertake. In a world dominated by neoliberal capitalism's dogma of 'the enterprising self' and its design of socio-political institutions to promote competition, then rebuking that to care for one another goes very much against the grain. But spend any time in activist circles, social movements and postcapitalist urban environments, and you will experience that caring for each other is a far more 'natural' and human instinct than it is to compete with each other (Firth, 2022). Realising this, and shaking off the shackles of individual competitiveness, is a fundamental part of allowing postcapitalism to flourish as an urban society: the notion of care is essential for this.

But the word 'care' itself has capitalist overtones. In November 2024, a headline broke that was not only depressingly familiar but encapsulated the systemic failings of an industry tasked with the most basic of human all human needs, that of care. Centers Health Care, a sprawling conglomerate of nursing homes operating across New York state, agreed to an eye-watering (although, unlikely to be terminal for a company of their size) $45 million settlement following damning allegations of abuse and neglect of vulnerable residents in its facilities. Investigations revealed a grim reality of unsanitary conditions, untreated infections, and chronic understaffing that left vulnerable residents without dignity or medical attention for sometimes days. Finances meant to ensure the wellbeing of patients had instead been funnelled into bloating executive bonuses and further expansion projects, exposing once again the prioritisation of profit over care. For residents, the consequences were devastating. Reports surfaced of patients left in soiled bedding for hours, infections spreading unchecked, and minimal supervision leading to preventable injuries. Families who had entrusted their loved ones to these facilities were betrayed, witnessing first-hand how the commodification of care turns compassion into a bottom-line calculation.

I picked this story because it was 'live' at the time of writing, but I recall many more of this ilk, from the US, the UK and elsewhere across Europe. This scandal is not an anomaly at all; it's a symptom of a wider process, a care *industry* fundamentally structured to devalue its most essential labour while extracting maximum profit. It is a classic tale of the process of capitalism more broadly. But when applied to that most basic of human needs – care – the ugliness is far more pronounced. The obvious schism between profit and people is never starker than when it comes to care.

It is worth pausing briefly to define the nebulous notion of care, because it can hold a very different meaning depending on all sorts of intersecting conceptual, demographic, geographical and political inflections (see Tronto, 2020). Ultimately, from the perspective of postcapitalist cites, I share the view from the Care Collective (2020: 5, my emphasis) that 'care is ... a *social* capacity and activity involving the nurturing of all that is necessary for the welfare and flourishing of life'. In essence, this involves moving beyond a conceptualisation of care that embeds it in a purely deterministic framework around individualised physical health or mental wellbeing (as important as those things are), and towards a collective act of social reproduction away from capitalist registers. So while, for example, healthcare is vital, seeing it as an instrumental practice that simply nurtures people back to health so they can be productive capitalist workers renders it part of the neoliberal machinery and a catalyst for the privatised, insurance-based systems that, as the vignette above details, are so derided in the USA and other countries. This is the wrong way to view care. Instead, care includes everyday actions of solidarity, activism and community cohesion, as well as the more 'traditional' forms of care around nurturing children and looking after vulnerable, elderly and disabled people. It is essentially a political act of shifting the modes of social reproduction away from the market and profit motive, towards one that emphasises dismantling those very models in the first place.

And when viewed in this way, various forms of this postcapitalist care can be seen to be taking place in cities all around us: a very *care*ful revolution is taking root within the fissures, germinating in the soil of community gardens; it is there on the tables of mutual aid kitchens, and in the calloused hands of caregivers knitting together the frayed social urban fabric. Care, often relegated to the shadows of policy debates or dismissed as 'soft' feminised infrastructure, is a fundamental part of postcapitalist urbanism; without it, the fabric of everyday life would be torn apart by the extraction of capital. If, as Lefebvre (1968) posited, the right to the city is about claiming space for collective flourishing, then systems of a more radical postcapitalist care are the mechanisms through which this right is realised. To imagine a postcapitalist city is to build upon the very real parts of the city where care is not a commodity but a common, shared, reciprocal and regenerative practice.

To think such a way is indeed radical because under capitalism care has not only been commodified but chronically undervalued because of its intersection with feminist praxis. The logic of capitalism, in its prioritisation of bodies as labourers rather than human beings who have lives of leisure, pleasure and love, has systematically underfunded public care programmes (such as the National Health Service in the UK) in order to let the market take over. Of course, privatising health and social care only serves to speed up the race to the bottom, with large scale 'healthcare' conglomerates operating low-cost, high-yield services. Indeed, the media is often highlighting the inadequate care in private hospices, children's homes or disability services (Schwiter *et al.*, 2018). Low wages, insecure employment practices, and the exploitation of migrant workers are exposed, with the results often being abuse of vulnerable people in the care system. And for those people who are cared for at home by family members or friends, the financial systems of support have been slashed by austerity and its broader suite of policies that have destroyed any semblance of a safety net for long-term carers (such as the 'Bedroom Tax' in the UK where housing benefit was reduced for those with 'spare rooms' in their social housing, penalising those who required a room for caring facilities such as a special bed or mobility equipment (Nowicki, 2023)).

Ultimately, capitalist care has become a commodified service and/ or a burden borne by the family at severe financial cost. At the heart of this undermining is neoliberalism, of course, which Fraser (2016) articulates as creating a 'crisis of care', in which the systemic erosion of the social infrastructures that sustain life (so as to privatise it) is the ultimate goal. In this framework, care is divorced from its relational, communal and socialised roots and subsumed under market logics, becoming a site of exploitation, alienation and inequality (Care Collective, 2020). Fraser also evidenced how care is devalued within capitalism because it is so labour intensive: ultimately the 'surplus value' of the care labourer in caring for someone who will very rarely be able to go back to work as a productive body is very low indeed. Under capitalist logic, what is the point of caring for someone who will never be productive themselves? Hence, the wages are low to the point of criminality, or the work is outsourced to corporatised charities (as is so often the case with palliative care in particular).

Within the urban realm, this crisis of care is starkly visible. As Part I demonstrated, gentrification disrupts long-standing support networks (be they personal, neighbourhood or institutional) by displacing communities, while privatisation depletes the public goods that underpin collective wellbeing (such as green spaces, public parks, community centres and third spaces). Social services are stripped to their skeletal forms, and care work is outsourced to a labour force of low-paid, precarious workers, who are often women, and also migrants and people of colour, emphasising yet again the racial capitalism inherent in gentrification. Yet it is these workers who perform the intricate, emotionally heavy but 'invisible' work that sustains the life of urbanites (Gilmore, 2020).

The neoliberalisation of care under the usual rhetoric of 'efficiency' and 'cost-cutting' masks a deeper logic of capitalist extraction: the shifting of caregiving responsibilities from collective systems to individuals. Federici (2012) has used Marx's language to argue that this shift represents a form of 'primitive accumulation' where the unpaid labour of care is expropriated to sustain the broader capitalist economy, which, as Part I identified, has racism as an element of its functioning logic. Hence, the effects of this shift in care from the public to the private sector are profoundly gendered and racialised. Bhattacharyya (2018) has expressed vividly how care labour, particularly when outsourced to migrants and women of colour, becomes a form of neo-colonial exploitation; indeed, she argues that 'racialised divisions play a role in positioning women differently and enabling a kind of naturalised order of status and entitlement that hardens the devaluing of care and domestic work' (Bhattacharyya, 2018: 48). These workers occupy the 'bottom rungs' of global care chains and are often supplied via agencies where they are poorly paid, denied in-work protections (such as sick and maternity pay), and socially stigmatised. In this context, care work (not just of people but of the city itself through tasks such as cleaning offices, refuse collection and so on) becomes a site where the intersecting oppressions of race, gender and class are heavily reproduced.

In gentrifying neighbourhoods, rising rents and living costs push out low-income residents, often dismantling the intergenerational and communal care networks that have long sustained working-class and immigrant families. The privatisation of urban space exacerbates these losses, as parks, libraries and other communal resources are transformed into for-profit ventures. The result is what Wacquant (2008) calls the 'penalization of poverty', where the urban poor are excluded from both the spaces and the systems of care, further entrenching their marginalisation in the urban realm.

Care in common

Against this rather bleak backdrop, care emerges as a profoundly radical and postcapitalist act. Unlike neoliberal versions of the capitalist modes of production, which thrive on competition and individualism, care is inherently relational, cooperative, and oriented towards the collective, social wellbeing of everyone. To centre care in urban postcapitalist life is to reject the commodification of people as simply labouring automatons who must be chained to the factory floor, office cubicle or service desk, and to reimagine the city as a space of expressive humanity, love, joy and solidarity. In a society that devalues lives, the act of caring for one another – nurturing, educating, healing – becomes a way to affirm our collective humanity and challenge systemic oppression. The radical Black feminist bell hooks (2000) describes this as 'radical love', a form of care that is not only interpersonal but also deeply political.

In order to flesh out the notion of care and the role it plays in any envisioning of a postcapitalist city, it is worth spending some time considering the related, perhaps broader practice of commoning. Of course, commoning as a process is as old as human civilisation itself. It is not in the remit of this book to delve into this rich planetary history (I have done this elsewhere: see Mould (2021)), but ultimately it can be thought of as simply that which we create by being together. Taking an approach that builds upon the work of Gudeman (2001) and Gibson-Graham (2006), the commons can be thought of as the symbiotic relationship between a physical and/or natural resource and the community that develops around it. So, more than a forest, a river basin or a field of arable land, the commons develop as people begin to use, live and maintain that resource sustainably and responsibly, without privatising, depleting and extracting surplus value from the land for transformation into profit. Following many other scholars of the commons (see Linebaugh, 2008; De Angelis 2014; Federici, 2018, among others), I view the commons as less a discussion of resource allocation, and more a form of 'living resistance' to the hegemony of capitalist extraction; a resistance that has always existed in the darker corners, the hiding places, or the 'cracks' of capitalist life (Holloway, 2010).

This is no more evident than in the example of mutual aid, which is a lived practice of commoning (and, as we shall see, care). As political praxis, mutual aid involves providing reciprocal support, while, importantly, fostering an understanding of the structural inequalities that create conditions of vulnerability and need (Firth, 2022). It is first and foremost about raising class consciousness via the practical everyday provision of support (in that way it is 'prefigurative' – something which is discussed in the following chapters). The concept of mutual aid originates from the works of Kropotkin (2022 [1902]), a prominent anarchist and radical Russian philosopher. Kropotkin's thesis emphasises the innate human tendency towards cooperation and solidarity, challenging the social Darwinian doctrine of 'survival of the fittest' that dominated evolutionary and socio-economic paradigms of his time (and that, sadly, continues to do so today, with extremely deleterious social results). Instead of relying solely on hierarchical institutions, competitiveness or market mechanisms, Kropotkin (1902) argued that individuals are more inclined to engage in voluntary acts of aid and solidarity to address shared needs and collective challenges. It is only within the hegemonic nature of capitalism – something which has been 'naturalised' into education, social relations, and economic practices – that such cooperation seems 'unnatural' (Springer, 2014). Kropotkin's work is foundational within anarchist ideology as it radically critiques contemporary capitalist social relations based on class hierarchy, extraction, oppression and the enrichment of the few. Mutual aid, as part of anarchist praxis, focuses on how people can create radical new modes of sociality and solidarity that provide for the vulnerable many (Spade, 2020).

Mutual aid's radical nature today stems from how 'buried' it has become within prevailing modern capitalist societies (Mould *et al.*, 2022), but it has a prominent history, in the development of those societies, particularly around US cities. One of the most notable examples is the Black Panther Party's breakfast programme for Black schoolchildren that was formulated in 1968 (with its first actual free meal handed out in January 1969). These breakfast clubs provided healthy meals to many hungry, poor young Black children, directly addressing food insecurity in inner-city communities. Starting in Oakland in California but spreading throughout the US, the programme not only fed children but also made a very powerful critique of the state's lack of provision and the structural racism that underpinned these inadequacies (Heynen, 2010; Potorti, 2017). The Panthers' practices directly highlighted the government's failure to support marginalised communities and exposed the systemic inequalities of racial capitalism. What's more, it worked, and it worked well. So well, in fact, that J. Edgar Hoover of the FBI said, in 1968, that the Panthers were 'one of the greatest threats to the nation's internal security' and declared them a communist group, and therefore suspectable to state violence (Meister, 2017). So it was of little surprise that in the following month, prominent Panthers were murdered by the FBI, including treasurer Bobby Hutton and their main 'leader' Fred Hampton, who was shot dead in Chicago while he slept in December 1969.

More recently, the activist group Food Not Bombs (FNB) has continued this tradition of radical mutual aid in urban areas. FNB members cook vegan and vegetarian food in public squares and parks across US cities, often operating illegally and facing ongoing attempts by urban officials to shut them down. Their mission is to feed the homeless and urban poor, providing sustenance to those most affected by the failings of capitalist society (Parsons, 2018). The defiance of legal restrictions is a deliberate part of their strategy, underscoring their commitment to direct action and civil disobedience in the face of injustice. Also of note was the emergence of 'Occupy Sandy' during the superstorm of Hurricane Sandy in New York in 2012, when the public transportation network was flooded, and many people lost power, heating and food supplies. Shelter-in-place advice from the US government Federal Emergency Management Agency recommended staying home and calling emergency services, but this failed to account for those without sufficient food or safety for prolonged periods, notably those in the low-income neighbourhoods of Queens. In response, Occupy Wall Street activists and other networks organised medical aid, emergency power, and transportation hubs, providing 'mutual aid mobility' to marginalised groups excluded from state emergency responses (Conroy, 2019).

Unlike traditional charity, which often operates within the bounds of existing power structures, mutual aid efforts aim to challenge and transform those structures with a far more radical approach to that which charities supposedly foreground, namely care. As Heynen (2010: 1233) argues, based on an in-depth activist ethnography with FNB, 'unlike much charity, FNB works hard not to be complicit in the perpetuation of the capitalist states' biopolitics, but seeks to radically transform it'. And in relation to the mutual aid practice that proliferated during the COVID-19 pandemic, many groups provided food, emotional support, and shelter in spite of, not because of, institutional support (Mould *et al.*, 2022). These efforts demonstrate the power of community solidarity and mutual care support networks, and, moreover, tangibly show how class consciousness and solidary practices can sow the seeds for radical social transformation. Mutual aid, in this way, is more than simply *caring* for each other in times of need; it unveils the injustices of capitalism and directly evidences why it is needed in the first place. Ultimately, it can be summed up neatly by the words of Lila Watson, an aboriginal scholar who said back in 1984, 'If you have come here to help me you are wasting your time, but if you have come here because your liberation is bound up with mine, then let us work together.'

Mutual aid, as practised all over the world, is part of an urbanisation praxis in that it foregrounds collective actions of care and associated provisions (food, shelter, support, etc.). However, a crucial ingredient that can often limit the resistive power of mutual aid is that it often must fight for *space* to operate. Whether it's a building to operate from (which has to be rented often at market rates) or private land that they illegally occupy (such as FNB), there are often very spatialised restrictions that emanate from the privatised characteristics of the capitalist city. Securing urban land in the heart of the capitalist city for commoning practices is very difficult indeed, particularly when attempting to obtain land for that most fundamental of human right, housing (hence why mutual aid practices are rarely able to provide housing and shelter, and will mostly focus on more 'immediate' services that require little actual space, such as food provision, loneliness alleviation, and health care (Thornton, 2020)). As a corrective to this lack of space, Greenfield (2024) has called for the imposition of what he calls 'lifehouses' in cities around the world. These are imagined as spaces that occur very frequently in the city (every three or four blocks) where people can gain emergency shelter, water, power and food at a time of crisis, but also sites where in 'normal' times people can grow food, socialise and be educated. In anticipating the onset of more frequent and more damaging extreme weather events, Greenfield (2024: 170) sees a network of lifehouses as 'a space in which [residents] might realise a vision of social ecology, tending to themselves and the planet by practising and experiencing solidarity, mutual care and self-determination'. Mirroring old-school community centres but with more productive and useful services for emergencies, lifehouses, as a concept, contain the spatial element that's needed to realise mutual aid more pervasively, and would certainly be part of the inventory of any postcapitalist city.

A postcapitalist healthcare

To nurture the postcapitalist city and the commons it creates, care is clearly vital, but a population of willing, active and most importantly healthy people is paramount if this postcapitalist city is to flourish. Hence, when thinking about care in the city, the specificities of healthcare – and the structures and spaces thereof – need some extrapolating. And to do this, we can look to indigenous care practices, as they offer a model of social relationality that challenges capitalist logics. Rooted in principles of reciprocity and stewardship, these practices view care as a communal responsibility that extends to non-human entities and the land itself (Arteaga-Cruz and Cuvi, 2021). In countries predicated on a settler-colonialist logic (such as Canada

(Ray *et al.*, 2022) and Australia (Wicks *et al.*, 2024)), these alternative and postcapitalist frameworks disrupt the logic that separates care from politics, proposing instead a holistic vision of wellbeing that integrates social, ecological and even spiritual dimensions.

A good example of this more holistic form of socialised healthcare is from the Autonomous Administration of North and East Syria (AANES), known as 'Rojava'. It is a region of Kurdish culture that, since a revolution against the Syrian state during the civil war in 2013, has (as the word 'Autonomous' suggests) been a self-governing region. The area is not recognised politically as a country, region or city by any state or international agency, such is the intensity of their radical democratic governance (indeed, the only recognition they have received at all on the international stage is from the Catalan parliament). The area's governance is made up of several communes and hyper-local levels in which all residents discuss, debate and agree on how the locale is to be managed and run. A male and female representative of each collaborate as the 'next level' of a collective to share information and resources, but decisions are only made at the local level. As such, it is a form of *subsidiarity*: a system of government that makes sure all actions are decided, managed at performed at the 'lowest' level possible. The EU, to some degree, operates within a subsidiarity model, in that member states have sovereignty over much of their political decision-making, with the EU stepping in only when needed under the rubric of 'Europe where necessary, nations where possible'. In Rojava, then, all facets of governance are managed within the communes, including healthcare. As such, it is not a commodity to be purchased but a collective responsibility embedded within the broader framework of democratic confederalism (Hoffman and Matin, 2021). Decentralised, egalitarian and community-driven, Rojava's healthcare system directly challenges and systemically opposes the hierarchical, profit-driven models that dominate capitalist societies in the US and other private-healthcare countries. By prioritising gender equity, prevention and community education, this model provides vital insights into how health and social care might be reimagined in a postcapitalist urban future.

Rojava views medical knowledge as vital for everyone to know. The generational knowledge of healthcare, which was traditionally passed down by women, had been essentially stolen by the men of the evolving hegemonic state over the decades, guarded and then sold back to them for a profit. To counter this, each commune selects two heads of the health committee – one man and one woman. These people are trained by professionals in first aid, mental-health and basic medicinal care, and then disperse this knowledge throughout the commune. Medical supplies, drugs and equipment are bought collectively and stored for all to use, and there is a dual emphasis on 'natural' remedies as well as pharmaceuticals, given that much of the knowledge around herbal medicinal techniques was extracted over the generations from communities by the patriarchal systems of state governance (Manzinger and Wagner, 2020). Other examples include the education about child-rearing and its effects on the woman's body – giving those in Rojava the knowledge to decide how many children they want, and access to birth control. Overall though, the focus is on prevention rather than cure, making sure that the commune society itself is healthy and vibrant to begin with, reducing the chances that illness and disease can take hold (Hoffman and Matin, 2021).

Of course, it is not all a utopian healthcare vision. Financial resources for life-saving treatment, advanced equipment and hospitals are scarce, and given Rojava's autonomy and radical way of post-capitalist life, the threat of violence from Syrian and Turkish forces of the hegemonic state are never far away. But as a framework of democratic healthcare that focuses less on individual health as a precursor to capitalist productivity, and more on social, community and place-based flourishing, it is certainly radical.

It is also reminiscent of a model called 'The Hologram' by the US-based artist-activist Cassie Thornton. This is an ambitious and profoundly transformative model of grassroots community healthcare, as it offers a tantalising glimpse into how postcapitalist urban health systems might operate. The Hologram emerged from Thornton's work as an artist and activist deeply influenced by feminist economics, the social-practice art movement, and radical healthcare models like those practiced in Rojava. Thornton sought to address the pervasive crises of loneliness, exploitation and burnout in capitalist societies, particularly as these crises manifested in overburdened healthcare systems. The project began as an art experiment but quickly evolved into a robust framework for rethinking how care is provided, received and understood. Inspired by the Social Solidarity Clinics in Greece – networks of medical, pharmaceutical and therapeutic mutual aid-style care in austerity-hit Athens after the financial crash of 2008 – The Hologram foregrounds the centrality of care in sustaining life under capitalism.

At its core, The Hologram is a system of collective care in which an individual is supported by a triangle of three other people who attend to their physical, emotional and social wellbeing. Each of these three supporters (who may or may not be medical professionals, but between whom medical knowledge is shared) focuses on one dimension of care but works collaboratively to ensure the hologram – the fourth person – receives comprehensive and continuous support. In turn, the hologram becomes part of a triangle for someone else, creating a network of care that is both horizontal and reciprocal. In this way, the system decentralises care networks, reduces a reliance on professionals, creates a form of radical reciprocity, allows communities to take ownership of their own health systems (like in Rojava), breaks down the silos of professionalism, and creates resilience to economic shocks (such as Greece experienced after 2008).

Such a democratic model of care provision is, of course, a difficult model to scale to the multitude; it suffers from what Harvey (2012: 102) has referred to as the 'scale problem', in that what works at one 'level' of geographical scale, such as the local, won't work at another, such as the global. In attempting to do so it butts up against the profit motive that comes with 'economies of scale', the problem of apathy that comes from caring for people who aren't immediately present, and, of course, the constraints of time along with everything else that capitalism leaches from society. And perhaps even more problematically for a 'scaling' process is these radical systems of care require a sympathetic governing context; trying to implement a commune-style healthcare system in a highly privatised city alongside a privatised healthcare system would be very tricky indeed, and would likely fall foul of predatory processes. But the issue with this (and with many ideologies that bemoan the lack of 'scaling' of systems and resources held in common) is that perhaps 'scale' is the wrong word here; there is a sense that the kinds of horizontalized democratic healthcare system evidenced by Rojava and the experimental artistic forms like The Hologram can be *extended*. Like the planetary forms of resistance networks that aided in the blossoming of a 'global' revolutionary event in 1968, practices of radical care can be shared, distributed and connected to places that are receptive to them.

A careful urbanism

It is good news, then, that those 'receptive' urban locales do exist. There are many examples of how the urban form – architecturally, infrastructurally and governmentally – has been adapted from prevailing capitalist schemas to revolve more around community and social wellbeing. For all the privatised and capitalist care systems that exist (with clearly catastrophic results, as the opening to this chapter shows), there are systems that go against that ethos and prioritise the health of people over profit (or at least try to).

And we don't even have to look that hard if we broaden the way we conceptualise care in urban contexts because it exists in official programmes such as mobility and wellbeing policies. In Barcelona, for instance, the city's 'superblock' initiative reclaims streets for pedestrians and creates communal spaces for recreation, socialising and green spaces (Mueller *et al.*, 2020).[1] Cities like Bogotá, Taipei, Ljubljana and the more obvious choices of Copenhagen, Berlin and Amsterdam have extensive biking networks and pedestrian-friendly designs, with advocates claiming they improve physical and mental health as well as provide the obvious environmental benefits of reduced vehicle pollution (Schwartz *et al.*, 2022). Moreover, mobility infrastructures and architectures that are sensitive to disabilities often elevate accessibility for all. Blind architect Chris Downey (2013) has long advocated for designing 'cities with the blind in mind' as it also benefits the urban experience for sighted people via simple details such as wider pavements, and allowing more sunlight onto the street (which is often used by blind people to orientate themselves if they feel the warmth of the sun on one side of their face).

Beyond mobility, the obvious inclusion of blue–green spaces in cities has been evidenced to improve mental health. Indeed, in the US it has been reported that for every 10 per cent increase in access to green and blue spaces, there is a 7 per cent reduction in risk of anxiety and depression (NIHR, 2024). The therapeutic qualities of green and blue spaces in the city are obvious (Bell *et al.*, 2018) and are now very much part of the neoliberal urban agenda, given their clear ability to gentrify neighbourhoods; and so any emphasis on the 'greening' of the city for health purposes should also not be disaggregated from the need to hold, manage and maintain these spaces in common with residents. Community gardens often fulfil these criteria, such as those found in and around Tompkins Square Park in New York City, notably La Plaza Cultural. It was created in 1976 by local residents who essentially 'seed bombed' a vacant, derelict lot. Today, of course, many of these gardens have been commandeered by parks and recreation authorities, and while this aids in their finance and helps to 'spread' the resources and networks of gardens as spaces of community care around the city as a whole, they are run as part of a programme of urban renewal and tacit gentrification. Hence, while these gardens operate on a day-to-day level as an open space of community cohesion and mental wellbeing, they are still part of the neoliberal urban hegemony of the city. For a postcapitalist city to emerge (or perhaps *re*-emerge) in and of these spaces, the state needs to be defenestrated completely, and they should be put back in the hands of the communities that created them from scratch in the first place. The common resource of a community garden built by residents in a vacant lot during a city in crisis doesn't require the New York Department of Parks and Recreation to connect it with other gardens around the city or, indeed, the world. This can be very easily done with the already existing lines of communications we have as a planetary population. As such, there is no scale problem here; the issue is connectivity, and while the state has a monopoly on this, it is a monopoly that can be, and often is, broken (McGuire *et al.*, 2022).

A more radical and resistance-led example of this kind of connectivity is the anti-raids network in the UK. The expansion of immigration-enforcement power due to years of the Conservative government's 'hostile environment' (Bahita and Burnett, 2022) reflected a broader capitalist logic of 'bordering' that reproduces labour precarity while securing capital's access to exploitable migrant labour (Mezzadra and Neilson, 2013). Immigration raids, often marked by violence and psychological intimidation by the police, therefor serve as a dual-purpose mechanism for the capitalist city: deterring undocumented migration and disciplining racialised communities to enforce societal hierarchies.

The anti-raids movement directly confronts this logic by attacking the state's monopoly on coercion and surveillance. By disrupting raids, the movement challenges not just the spectacle of state violence but also the structures of exclusion and exploitation it upholds. It operates through localised 'cells' of activity, which are small, autonomous groups connected by loose yet resilient communication systems (often Telegram, Signal or other encrypted messaging services). Central to the anti-raids movement is the principle of active and very public solidarity, which acts as a form of visible counter-power against the state's narrative of individualism and fear. A classic case of this was seen on Kenmure Street in Glasgow in 2021, when a raid by the police was quickly alerted to the anti-raids cells in the city, and within only minutes of the raid beginning, hundreds, if not thousands, of activists flooded the street to halt it, with some of them positioning themselves under the wheels of the immigration van for over eight hours. After a protracted stand-off, the police finally gave up (see Brooks (2021) for details). It was testament to the networked nature of anti-raids resistance, and evidenced just how effective this can be if mobilised quickly and efficiently. And like the community gardens, it is a 'model' of activism and resistance that does not need to 'scale' as such, because the same tactics of horizontality are used right across the UK. The anti-raids movement is an exemplar of how radical, bottom–up movements do not require a centralised vanguard or a 'state' to organise across space (as the traditional Marxist ideologies espoused by Harvey (2012) above would have you believe). All that is needed is a will, and the means to communicate.

In this, the anti-raids movement is reminiscent of the Hong Kong protests of 2019, the motto of which was 'be water', allegorising the fluid and networked nature of activism during the pro-democracy protests (Ting, 2020). These protests and their networked, water-like nature were enabled by the use of encrypted messaging apps like Telegram to facilitate connections. These apps played a big part in Hong Kong (as they did in Glasgow in 2021). However, the use of physical zines was also prominent, notably in the proffering of care. Indeed, it has been suggested that these zines aided in a number of ways to help create practices of self-care that 'expand the emotional habitus among protesters and movement supporters to accommodate debilitating bad feelings … and contribute to voluntary kinship among protesters beyond the state-sanctioned nuclear family model' (Yam and Ma, 2023: 668). As such, while these networks of resistance create a weapon of activism against the violence of the state, they also couple this with networks of community care that that activism requires. It is within these kinds of networked actions, as Butler (2015) argues, solidarity emerges, not only through a shared vulnerability and susceptibility to the racist violence of the state, but also through the deliberate act of standing together against it. In anti-raids actions and the networked protests of Hong Kong, solidarity assists in the action *and* the care. After all, in the postcapitalist city, care and activism are mutually co-constitutive, and one cannot happen without the other. Indeed, as Kelly Hayes and Mariame Kaba (2023: 51) have noted in their book *Let This Radicalize You: Organizing and the Revolution of Reciprocal Care*, 'we are living in era where refusing to abandon people can be a revolutionary act'.

Summary

As we confront a future shaped by climate crisis, economic precarity, and social fragmentation, the case for care grows ever more urgent. The postcapitalist city, grounded in systems of care, offers not just a vision of survival but a shared connection of thriving. It is a city where everyone has access to the support they need to live with dignity and free from state violence. It is a city where the networked, fluid notion of an active community is not a resistive afterthought but a foundation. Of course, these careful actions would fizzle out very quickly if people had nowhere to live, and sadly, in the rapidly gentrifying global city, stable, functional and dignified housing has become a dream that many simply cannot afford. That is why a postcapitalist city requires a radical rethink in the provision of housing: to move away from the profit-driven, corporatised and privatised housing supply that is the cause of so much immiseration of urbanites, towards a housing system that is cooperative, communal and, above all, postcapitalist. And so it is to housing that the next chapter turns.

Chapter 7

Urban commoning

Trawden, a small village in the Lancashire countryside about an hour's drive from the city of Manchester in the north-west of England, is not the first place that springs to mind when thinking of how the behemoth of the capitalist city can be subverted. In the 2010s, the local community centre faced closure because of the lack of funding from the local council. The national policy of austerity was in full force, and like many other local councils, Lancashire's central funding had been drastically cut, and they were forced to reallocate their already scarce resources to those services they had a legal obligation to fulfil (such as social care, provision for special educational needs and so on). First on the chopping board were relatively valuable local real-estate assets, like community centres in the heart of the village. Selling them off to a private-housing developer or a retail giant could provide valuable additions to their income stream. This story was repeated across the country; the neoliberal weapon of austerity was brought in under the guise of reducing national debt, but really it served as an ideological battering ram to privatise the urban environment, and 'let the market rip' (for a recent analysis, see Dagdeviren (2024)).

The close-knit community of Trawden weren't about to let this happen, though. Their community centre was a hub of the village and provided a safe and warm space for vulnerable people and those who had been plunged into poverty because of the prevailing economic headwinds (felt particularly strongly in northern rural areas of the UK, suffering as they were from disproportionate investment in the south and major metropolitan areas). After a co-ordinated campaign and a successful fundraising drive, the village collected enough money to buy the community centre and save it from being sold off. Not stopping there, they also purchased the neighbouring library, also under threat from closure. Fast forward to 2021, and the local pub across the road – again a valuable place of community cohesion (as many watering holes are in villages like Trawden) – was in danger from closure. Not from austerity, but because of the pandemic's economic shocks to the hospitality sector, and a rising cost of living. Again, the village mobilised its community capital to fundraise over half a million pounds to buy the pub and keep it in the hands of the community. Furthermore, in order to delay the sale, they successfully campaigned to list the pub as an 'asset of community value', which put restrictions on who could purchase it and allowed them valuable time to raise the funds to purchase the pub themselves.[1] The community centre, the library and the pub are run by locals and thriving. Indeed, as The Alternative (2022) state:

> The library is now heat-pumped and solar powered, with a highly successful locavore shop attached – featuring all kinds of local produce, and refill canisters for full sustainability. The post office is in a corner of the library, and very busy – a communal talking shop as much as anything. The newly acquired pub is also building social capital with folk nights, craft workshops and employment of the local youth. The levels of local volunteer labour – and increasingly paid posts – is high.

Trawden has inspired many other similar initiatives across the country, with village and indeed urban neighbourhood communities attempting to purchase assets themselves, maintaining local ownership, and keeping financial and social capital circulating within their communities. It is also more democratic, given that local people are engaged in the decision-making that effects day-to-day activities. It is not without its issues, of course; Trawden is a relatively affluent area, and one wonders if something similar could happen in areas that don't have as much spare capital to invest in their local communities, and a portion of the funds raised was from charitable donations as well (Rubin, 2021). But even with, and perhaps because of, those caveats in place, this small unassuming Lancashire village is a microcosm of how urban commoning can survive, and perhaps even thrive, in the suffocating milieu of globalised capitalism that sees small villages as it does traditional urban land: an asset to exploit.

What happened in Trawden is an example of a type of urban commoning, which, as this chapter will detail, is a broad movement of urban processes – from buying small village pubs to the construction of massive urban housing programmes in megacities – that are contributing to the emergence of the postcapitalist city. Commoning is not a new process (as discussed in Chapter 6) and has existed as a panacea to the intersectional violence of urban gentrification for as long as the capitalist city has. Any postcapitalist city that has emerged from urban commoning has done so because of the collective will and power of local residents, and to some extent the relative 'blindness' of the capitalist class to the value of the urbanism that has been created. In other words, those pockets of urban life that have succeeded in resisting the suffocating gentrification of the capitalist city have done so through constant (and often difficult, exhausting and, yes, privileged) action from below, and not because of any 'help' from the overtly capitalistic and neoliberal urban officialdom, at least not at the beginning.

For a postcapitalist city to develop beyond these prejudicial structures, the process of commoning needs further investigation, analysis and advocacy as a viable means of urban life that works *collectively* across bounded space (be that the de-mapped but very real (red)lines of racial demarcation within cities or national geopolitical borders). The violence of the capitalist city (as Chapter 1 outlined) has always viewed these processes as a direct threat to capitalist accumulation, and therefore has repressed them at every turn, yet as this chapter will detail, places of urban commoning still find spaces to flourish and provide real urban alternatives to all types of citizens. This chapter will therefore work to identify the threads of commonality among these disparate forms of commoning, and weave together the image of a postcapitalist city that has the potential to be taken forward as a vision of urbanism that defies the logic of capitalist accumulation in providing a more just, sustainable and equitable way of life.

Common housing

When theorising the urban commons, Huron (2015; 2018) suggests that one of its fundamental properties – and how it relates to the capitalist city more broadly – is that of acquiescing to a sense of 'strangeness'. Specifically, the city is a place of a high concentration of people and resources (often far more so than in a rural or suburban environment), and, as such, there is a higher propensity to need to work with strangers to achieve success in commoning. She argues that 'strangers coming together to work on a common project is a distinctly urban phenomenon. The experience of working together with strangers – people who do not come from the same place geographically, culturally, or perhaps even politically – is [a] defining trait of the urban commons' (Huron, 2015: 7).

This stems from her examination of how low-income residents of Washington DC came together to collectively manage and own their housing in the 1970s and 1980s. These cooperatives were formed in response to broad process of racial capitalism outlined in Chapter 1, but were specifically related to the widespread sale and conversion of rental apartments into condominiums, a trend that threatened to displace long-standing, predominantly Black communities in the nation's capital. Within these housing struggles, she describes commoning as an active, participatory process involving the creation and maintenance of common resources through collective action. Similarly, with research in Dublin, Bresnihan and Byrne (2015) show how the commons comes from not simply the production of collective housing (i.e. through purchasing or building homes) but through the (often very difficult, and 'messy') maintenance and management of those homes, often with strangers (something which under traditional capitalist regimes would be done by for-profit management companies or the local authorities). As such, it is important, of course, not to fetishise commoning – particularly given the emotionally fraught process of having to engage with strangers – as internal conflicts, financial sustainability, and the pressures of surrounding market forces are a threat to the commoning process, just as much as the threats from capital are (Huron, 2018; Vidal, 2019).

It is clear from the urban commoning literature that housing is a key provision and rightly so. As such, there are many other studies from around the world that focus on the variations of housing forms that urban commoning can produce. Hence, it is possible to identify various 'established' forms of housing commoning with their own set of discourses, literatures, ideologies, cultures and global idiosyncrasies. The rest of this chapter, then, will detail a few of these, namely squatting, community land trusts, and co-living (and working) spaces. Threading these together analytically is a deliberate ploy to highlight the emancipatory potential of such processes, but it is not to ignore that these various processes may butt up against each other, not least because of some conflicting political ideologies, varying degrees of charitable donations, and land-ownership models (as will be discussed). The aim, though, is to highlight potential sites of collaboration, consensus or constructive critique so as to take the positive, emancipatory postcapitalist elements forward into a viable future that is different – hopefully, radically so – from the suffocating capitalist present.

Squatting

In April 2024, the globally renowned multimillionaire media darling and real-estate tycoon (and occasional chef) Gordon Ramsey was in a legal battle with a group of people who squatted his empty London pub. The group set up a community café, and provided food for the residents of Camden in defiance of the authorities. Given the fame of the owner, it is unsurprising that this made the news, but the fact that squatters had commandeered a multimillion-pound property, one that is surrounded by even more expensive private dwellings, was itself quite remarkable. Their stay was inevitably brief (two weeks in total), as this is London after all, a global city *par excellence* that rarely tolerates such brazen defiance of the strict rule of real-estate capital. However, the squatters had all the legal recourse available to them to make sure that they were able to eke out as much space as possible to practise the fundamentals of a postcapitalist city – briefly, but spectacularly.

Vasudevan (2015) has articulated how squatting is a fundamental part of any form of anti-capitalist urbanism, in that it is direct action from those people who are claiming their right to the city (à la Lefebvre (1968)). And despite recent domicidal practices by the UK government via Section 144 of the Legal Aid, Sentencing and Punishment of Offenders Act 2012 – which was essentially the criminalisation of squatting (Nowicki, 2023) – this particular group threaded the needle of UK law to defy the police's attempt to evict them. In the process, they carved out a viable space in which no rent was paid, but people were fed, shelter was provided, and, generally, urban lives were being led.

At the same time, on the other side of the planet in Melbourne, there was an individual calling himself 'Purple Pingers' who garnered a massive online following by not only exposing the often cruel practices of landlords (via letting properties deteriorating massively in living standards), but also pointing people in the direction of empty homes in the major cities around the country. In Australia, breaking and entering is of course illegal, but squatting is not. Purple Pingers simply made – and continues to make – an inventory of empty homes that were accessible without criminal damage. In so doing, he provided housing for hundreds, if not thousands, of people, all the while drawing immense ire from the landlord class (and their media champions).

These two examples, while perhaps fleeting given their unabashed resistance to capitalist urban power, point to the *prefigurative* nature of squatting practices. Prefigurative politics, a term first coined by Boggs (1977) that has since become an important part of anarchist and anti-capitalist lexicon, is fundamentally the rejection of traditional forms of political engagement that attempt to defer social change to future legislative victories or the capture of state power (i.e. the traditional Marxist view of resistance). Instead, the practices of prefigurative politics focus on *collectively* constructing new (or at least new to the specific time and place) social relations and forms of organisation in the here and now, embodying future societal goals *through* current practices. It is an approach which actively (i.e. via its very 'doing') criticises the strategic and often hierarchical methods of conventional resistance politics, advocating for a celebration of everyday community life that operates outside of formal political spheres, and is rooted in a collective endeavour (and this is why it is clear the climate encampment on Waterloo Bridge detailed in Chapter 4 can be thought of as prefigurative). Many squats operate collectively, with decisions about future practices decided democratically via consensus rather than voting (Vasudevan, 2015), and in so doing eschew the privatised nature of urban living which is so often the default. Prefiguration is the very political practice of living as the world *should* be. Indeed, 'to prefigure is to anticipate or enact some feature of an "alternative world" in the present, as though it has already been achieved' (Yates, 2015: 4). Hence, squatting is inherently prefigurative as it enacts the postcapitalist urban worlds that it seeks to see more of. Put (very) bluntly, prefigurative politics is doing it rather than talking about it.

Squatting therefore manifests in the here and now (i.e. prefiguratively) as a critical response to the capitalist urban order, challenging the hegemonic narratives that put property ownership and market mechanisms over basic human rights. Historically, the phenomenon of squatting has been intricately linked to broader socio-economic and political crises of various depths. Post-World War II Europe, for example, saw squatting emerge out of necessity in cities laden with bomb-damaged homes and a dearth of housing (Vasudevan, 2015). However, by the 1970s, squatting had evolved into a form of radical prefigurative praxis, critiquing private property laws and articulating alternative urban futures (Pruijt, 2013). It became an urban form of experimenting with autonomous living, communal practices, and direct action against the neoliberal commodification of urban space. Through the direct occupation of abandoned or under-utilised buildings, squatters challenge the notion that the city's value is best determined by real-estate markets and financialised urbanism (Fields, 2017a). Instead, as those in London and Melbourne have shown, they propose a radical reimagining of urban spaces as inclusive and importantly, *collective* habitats.

The legal recognition of squatting varies widely, reflecting broader societal attitudes and political climates. And even within squats themselves, the prefigurative nature of them means that they are not always as 'pure' an example of postcapitalism the neat theorisations would suggest. After all, they are lived spaces with all the nuances, complexities and messiness of the city writ large. While some European contexts have seen periods of relative tolerance or legal accommodation for squatters (the areas of Christiania in Copenhagen and Metelkova in Ljubljana are two examples of large, long-term autonomous squats that have existed relatively peacefully among capitalist city landscapes), others, notably in the Global South, exhibit more contentious dynamics. One of the more famous examples is that of Torre de David in Caracas, which became a stark embodiment of this struggle (McGuirk, 2014; Irazábel-Zurita *et al.*, 2020). Originally intended as a commercial skyscraper, the tower became derelict and half-finished during Venezuela's banking crisis of 1994. Subsequently, nearby favela residents who had fallen victim to slum landlords occupied this building, and it became one of the world's tallest informal settlements through the collective action of thousands of squatters. Images of people making a gym out of elevator equipment, siphoning electricity from the city grid, and stringing washed clothes across half-built atriums were splashed all over the glossy media of the West, championing (and in effect, fetishising) the grassroots urbanism of 'entrepreneurial' Global South citizens. Despite its rather crass mediatisation (it was even used as the background to major Hollywood TV shows), it represented a form of urban reclaiming, not just of unutilised space but of the right to the city itself, amid Venezuela's broader housing crisis. Despite its portrayal in some media as a lawless enclave, the tower developed its own internal systems of governance, with clear rules and communal responsibilities that ensured safety and order. The prefigurative nature of the squat, and the fact that it was home to over five thousand people, meant that it evidenced the 'messiness' of such prefigurative urban politics. As the in-depth study by Irazábel-Zurita *et al.* (2020: 26) highlights, the building had 'charged tensions in-between the formal and informal, modern and traditional, modernity and postmodernity, reality and imagination, and capitalism and socialism'. Despite various attempts to evict the squatters as Caracas' mayoral administrations came and went (and not to mention an earthquake which left the top twenty-five floors severely damaged and highly perilous) there are still squatters there to this day, living a precarious, but prefigurative postcapitalist city.

Clearly, squatting in the cracks of the official capitalist city that is so violently defended by state power it is not for everyone, and the constant precarity and fear of brutal revanchism by the dominant hegemony of the city renders squatting a fleeting form of postcapitalist living. But its inherent prefiguration is not so fleeting – instead it can be thought as a fundamental building block of postcapitalist urbanism that can be realised within state structures rather than against them. It is more difficult, of course, and it takes longer to realise. But there are indeed examples in the here and now that have taken this prefiguration and attempted to mould it around, within and through the often obdurate but sometimes malleable urban state structures. The next chapter will give some more empirical examples from my various site visits to postcapitalist cities around the world, but it is important to first outline some of the more specific and articulated urban housing systems that are viable and long-term alternatives to capitalist urbanism, and analyse them individually, before going on to show how they meld together (sometimes conflictingly, but always prefiguratively) in actual urban places from around the world: those specific models being Community Land Trusts and cooperative housing.

Community Land Trusts

Originating in the US as early as the 1960s, the idea of the Community Land Trust (CLT) has mutated and transmogrified over space to create different forms of urban life as it 'touches' down in cities with vastly different cultures, social contexts and demographics (indeed, the very success of CLTs requires flexibility and responsiveness to local specificities). At their core, CLTs are non-profit, community-based organisations designed to ensure the collective stewardship of land. Central to the CLT model is the separation of land ownership from the ownership of the buildings (like homes or commercial spaces) that sit on the land. The model aims to provide authentically affordable housing and other community benefits (e.g. commercial spaces, community gardens, social services, etc.) by removing land and housing from the speculations of the volatile housing market, thus ensuring that these resources remain affordable for long-term, sustainable community use. In the US, CLTs are governed by a tripartite board comprising CLT residents, community members, and public representatives, which ensures that decisions are made in a manner that balances individual interests with the broader community's welfare and the CLT's mission (Gray, 2008). An early example is Dudley Neighbors Inc. in Boston from the 1990s, a 'company' set up to collectively purchase a large parcel of land (known as the Dudley Triangle) to own in perpetuity. Houses were built on the land by members of the 'company' with financial help if needed, but as those houses were subsequently bought and sold, the land itself remained in the ownership of the collective (Medoff and Sklar, 1994). Since its inception, it has been widely praised as successful in revitalising a distressed neighbourhood through community empowerment and sustainable development practices (Engelsman *et al.*, 2018).

CLTs, particularly in the capitalist cauldrons of Global North cities, are of course not without their issues. Decision-making can be a labour-intensive process, and often the purchase of the land initially requires the input from larger institutions such as charities, local government and sometimes philanthropy from the elite, which means that sometimes the 'transfer' of ownership is legally complicated, and the provider can often maintain some element of control. In addition, it has been noted by Martin *et al.* (2024) that CLTs have problems in scaling beyond the local community because of the 'stickiness' of the land portfolio available to be used in this way. Furthermore, CLTs are ultimately a legal vehicle, and their postcapitalist success (or not) depends upon the activism of those committed to it. As Engelsman *et al.* (2018: 120) note when discussing the Dudley Triangle CLT, 'The stewardship role that the CLT adopts is not only a technical requirement but dependent on the intangible quality that comes with organising that in turn, may lead to political agitation.'

Ultimately, though, the separation of land and housing, and collective ownership of the former means that CLTs can play a critical role in resisting more 'traditional' forms of gentrification and speculative real-estate practices that often lead to displacement of low-income and marginalised communities (Davis *et al.*, 2008). Fundamentally, the CLT model has demonstrated its versatility in addressing diverse housing needs within a specific location, ranging from single-family homes to multi-family apartment buildings. This adaptability not only enhances the model's applicability across different urban settings but also enables it to cater to the varying needs of the community in the longer term.

Such versatility is important internationally, particularly when attempting to implement a 'model' such as CLTs in Global South urban environments. Indeed, as this book has emphasised throughout, the very term 'model' is wrong because it assumes a certain immutability that can render it problematic as it crosses borders. The urban geographical literature is awash with examples of how 'models' are simply agents of neoliberalism that are orchestrated by corporate actors to gentrify more of the urbanised world (sometimes labelled 'fast urban policy' (Peck and Theodore, 2015)). Furthermore, the informal settlements of Global South megacities (i.e. the favelas, ghettos, barrios, shanty town, *champerío*, slums and other locally specific and/or stigmatising terms) have for many decades been sites of the collision between informality and formality. Heralded as a unique form of urbanism that is grass roots, DIY, bottom–up, they are also subject to the brutal edge of neoliberal urban policy that includes pacification, gentrification and experimental financialisation (Lees *et al.*, 2016). Sites of violence as well as genuine emancipation, they possess an aura of experimentalism, laboratories of urbanism that have been pored over by academics, architects and activists alike. As such, they contain kernels of post-capitalist urbanism that provide genuinely new forms of city life that are more sustainable, just and equitable than current prevailing capitalist urban systems, but in doing so they are often snuffed out by the violence of those overarching systems.

As such, the CLT model has been implemented in these urban laboratories precisely because of their malleable urban form, architecturally and socio-politically. For example, there has been a very successful implementation of a CLT in San Juan, Puerto Rico. Based on an initial threat of gentrification via compulsory purchase by the municipality, residents gathered together democratically (and over countless meetings over many years) to collectively purchase the land that was under threat. Like CLTs in the US, they separated out the land and the housing, but created a third strand, namely the infrastructure. Divided into three different institutions, but with overlapping personnel managing them, residents were able to fend off real-estate developers and create a thriving CLT in the Canõ (canal) region of the city. Such was the success, that campaigners and activists have attempted to spread this version of CLTs to other Global South megacities. Through online meetings, festivals and site visits, the residents of San Juan's CLT met with like-minded activists from Rio de Janeiro in an attempt to implement a similar housing provision. This process of implementation is analysed in detail by Basile and Fidalgo (2022); ultimately, a successful implementation requires stripping out any institutional desires (such as financial motives or international recognition) to focus on the needs of the residents and the local legal and political contexts. They argue that

CLT implementation requires a collaborative process in which communities possess and maintain agency and are empowered to make decisions, leveraging existing governance structures and organized leadership. Thus, CLTs are not simply a model of supplying houses or formalizing land/real estate. Rather, CLTs have the potential to facilitate an emancipatory process with profound and lasting effects for its members. (Basile and Fidalgo, 2022: 57–8).

This democratic realisation in different spaces, rather than its potential 'copy-and-paste' implementation, is what makes CLTs a viable part of a postcapitalist city. They *require* international collaboration between incumbent residents, learning off each other and exchanging stories of success, failure and everything in between. As such, their implementation requires an active form of 'stretching' rather than 'scaling', which is the foundation of postcapitalist urbanism.

Cooperative housing

The cooperative 'system' of alternative socio-economic life has been in place and existed alongside burgeoning neoliberalism for decades. Indeed, the official story of the cooperative movement dates to the Rochdale Pioneers in 1844, when twenty-eight workers in the cotton mills pooled their scarce resources to access the raw materials they needed to work at a lower cost. Today, the cooperative movement has large, national industrial institutions such as the Mondragon Cooperative Corporation that originated in the Basque region (which includes a university, a bank, factories and retail outlets), the Co-operative supermarket in the UK, the Zen-Noh agricultural cooperative in Japan, and the banking cooperative Crédit Agricole in France. Many of these institutions, through being owned cooperatively (i.e. not via traditional shareholders or single individuals), spread the wealth generated by their economic activities more broadly, and their size indicates how they operative very comfortably within a competitive market system, employing capitalistic motifs of efficiency, advertising, organisational hierarchies, and so on. Their operation within nationalistic frameworks of regulation – tax, law, etc. – means that any internationalism inherent to their business practices is far from the resource sharing and mutual learning that has come to characterise postcapitalist urban imaginaries, and is shaped more in purely capitalistic contours of economic and 'global production networks' (Coe and Yeung, 2015). While there are some industrial and manufacturing cooperatives that have leaned towards more radical and anti-capitalist forms of production (famously the Empresas Recuperadas in Argentina after the country's deep recession in 2001 (Thorpe *et al.*, 2019)), many of the cooperative movements operate very much as traditional capitalist units. As Marx (1998 [1894]: 438) noted in *Capital, Volume III*, 'co-operative factories of the labourers themselves represent within the old form the first sprouts of the new, although they naturally reproduce, and must reproduce, everywhere in their actual organisation all the shortcomings of the prevailing system.'

Hence, within the factory setting at least, the role of cooperatives needs to 'reproduce' the capitalist organisational form in order to progress. In the centuries since Marx penned those words, it would be only the most fiercely optimistic of us that could claim the many cooperatives around the world have sprouted new forms of radical postcapitalist economic alternatives that threaten the global capitalist hegemony.

Within the realm of housing, though, the cooperative movement is more embryonic, and while it has perhaps not fully sprouted into a radically new form of housing on the broad urban scale, it has certainly germinated. That said, one of most successful cooperatives started in, yes, 1968 in Montevideo, Uruguay. Known as Federación Uruguaya de Cooperativas de Vivienda por Ayuda Mutua – FUCVAM (which translates as the Uruguayan Federation of Mutual Aid Housing Cooperatives), it was made possible by significant pressure on the national government to change the public financing law so that funds could be given directly to families and communities, rather than housing developers and government 'intermediaries'. The 'Housing Law' (as it became known) passed in late 1968. In response to a rampant national housing crisis, the government created a land bank that essentially set aside parcels of land for communities who had received funding to purchase them (at very reduced rates). Like the CLT movement, this separated out land and housing in order to dilute the dominance that market forces could enforce upon urban spaces (Nahoum and Valles, 2014). The initial impetus for FUCVAM came from a group of working-class residents of Montevideo who were desperate for affordable housing. By purchasing a block of land through the Housing Act, they formed the first cooperative, which soon led to the creation of a federation that would support the establishment and management of similar initiatives across the country. The model was simple yet, at that time and place, revolutionary: members would contribute their labour to the construction of their homes via 'sweat equity', thereby significantly reducing the cost of housing in purely financial terms. One of the key features of FUCVAM's approach was its inherent mutual-aid system, where those residents who wished to join actively participated in the construction of their own homes alongside professional builders and existing residents. This lowered costs but also fostered a strong sense of community, skill-sharing and solidarity among members, but more importantly foregrounded collective ownership. This granted 'ownership to the group where families are entitled to use and enjoy the common property. This is a reassertion of the concept of housing as a right instead of as a tradable commodity, thus keeping speculation at bay' (Nauhom and Valles, 2014).

FUCVAM has of course not been without challenges. While the Housing Law meant that it was able to seed other cooperatives around the country, the 1980s and 1990s saw a big shift towards neoliberal national governance which curtailed its anti-corporate ethos. Because of its staunch rejection of the central role of capital in housing and ideological insistence upon mutual aid and collective ownership, FUCVAM have had to battle for their land from the forces of urban privatisation and gentrification (Santoyo-Orozco, 2023). But the first decades of the twenty-first century have seen these neoliberal policies largely overturned, and FUCVAM has become a model of cooperative housing that other Latin American countries have taken on. Like the CLT movement, international networks of cooperative housing have been established connecting nearly 17,000 families in 408 cooperatives in Brazil, Bolivia, Paraguay and others, as well as initial conversations with communities in sub-Saharan Africa (World Habitat, 2024). And it hasn't just seeded housing projects; there have been schools, health centres and social community centres built as well. FUCVAM have a strong reliance on education not only within their own communities, but globally as they spread the cooperative model around the world. It is part of their modus operandi to instil the radical ideologies of collective ownership and mutual aid. It has been noted by Santoyo-Orozco (2023) that 'popular education not only exists in the consciousness of the communities that embrace it, but also in the practices of maintaining and reproducing a collective space'. Indeed, the motto of FUCVAM from the outset has been 'Housing is only the beginning, not the end'.

One of the fundamental ingredients to the success of FUCVAM has been the involvement of the state as a key provider of land. Without the cheap access to the 'portfolio' of land parcels that are reserved for the cooperative movement, an expansion of its post-capitalist ideology would have been nowhere near as widespread as we've seen so far in Montevideo. In the Global North, where urban governance is decisively more neoliberal in its approach to the allocation of urban land, cooperative housing is far more difficult to create. That is not to say that there aren't instances that point to its radical possibility. In many European, US and other imperial core cities, housing cooperatives manifest in various forms, but they typically encompass single buildings occupied by an association, or cooperative, of members (and as such they more often than not operate as oases of collective ownership in a wider ocean of privatised cityscapes). Cooperative members, who contribute rent significantly lower than market rates, collectively finance the maintenance of the property (some will have charity or government funding as well). Operational tasks and management responsibilities are generally undertaken by the members on a voluntary basis via sweat equity, or if needed, professional tradesmen are used and paid for out of the central funds (and decided democratically). Members, though, typically do not hold any financial capital in their residences. Rather, the properties are held by the cooperative itself, which is a distinct legal entity in many countries, thereby decoupling individual members from direct ownership (Birchall, 1988; Andrusz, 1999). There are often strict rules to being a resident, too: some cooperatives will shun couples because of their perceived volatility in living arrangements (under the rather clunky assumption that childless, unmarried couples will be more likely to change their relationships and hence living arrangements more frequently). More generally, because these cooperative housing practices and their affordability benefits are so rare, they can inadvertently create their own forms of exclusivity. As Vidal (2019: 174) has noted, 'The cooperative's collective property might be closed off through insider nepotism and held as a commons only among members or may be dissolved as a commons altogether from within through its individualization and monetization.'

To mitigate this, perhaps, there are other examples which also extend the cooperative model to a notion of 'co-living', where the units have been deliberately designed to provide a more communal form of life and keep such individualisation at bay. A recent and relatively successful example is Marmalade Lane in Cambridge in the UK. It is a cooperative, and indeed co-living, housing development that was built on a plot of land that became suddenly vacant during the financial crisis in 2008 after the initial developer went bankrupt. The city council, after years of unsuccessfully trying to sell the land to other developers, took a more radical step in selling it (below market rates) to a cooperative of residents, an architectural firm, and a small urban developer (but yes, still a developer). The development has caught the eye of architectural and urbanist critics not only because of the focus on sustainability (cars are not allowed on site), but because it is where forty-two families live communally with a large kitchen for multiple families, joint laundry facilities, and large open common spaces (Wainwright, 2019). Extending the cooperative ownership model to a co-living arrangement too is of course not to everyone's living tastes, but it is a clear example of an urban council (in this case Cambridge) taking a risk to provide something radically different to the norm.

There is no escaping, though, that within the intense capitalist cities of the imperial core, the radicality of the cooperative model is stunted by distinctly neoliberal and privatising tendencies of urban management systems. In many Global North countries, cooperative housing is an exception to the rule. Despite a rampant housing crisis fuelled by a chronic dearth of social and truly affordable housing, city councils continue to develop housing using the traditional capitalist routes of private real-estate developers, who will provide housing as assets for the upper and middle classes, rather than as homes for the urban poor. Any alternative forms of housing provision – be they CLTs, cooperatives or anything else – are tolerated for as long as they occupy spaces in the 'downturn'. Once the rent gap is big enough, they will inevitably be enclosed, privatised and gentrified. In sum, without a state that can provide some sort of support, these postcapitalist models will only ever be exceptions. Initiatives such as FUCVAM turn this on its head, working in conjunction with the state to provide for the poor and marginalised communities. Indeed, through these models, 'marginality' is exposed for what it is, 'a myth constructed through capitalist exploitation to naturalize social relations of dominance' (Santoyo-Orozco, 2023). The relationship between cooperative initiatives from below and state policy from above is always a risky alliance, though (Vidal, 2019), and, as such, fetishizing them can led to privatised gentrification through the back door. But given the rampant dispossession felt by urbanites across the globe, the cooperative ideal represents a workable model that allows citizens to work *with* rather than *against* the state to provide a viable and lasting form of urban commoning.

The trials of house-building

All this sounds rather utopian, of course. The detail is too often where the devil lurks, and the everyday life of building, maintaining and perhaps even expanding these democratically controlled alternative housing models can be a hurdle in itself. But these radical housing models reshape not only physical spaces but also the subjectivities of those who inhabit them (Jaureguiberry-Mondion, 2023). The substantial amount of mutual-aid labour (or 'sweat equity') that is needed to carve out these spaces is deeply relational, involving persistent organising, navigating legal frameworks and obdurate state administrators, and mobilising financial resources. Such efforts demand not only technical expertise but also sustained commitment to community organising, advocacy and care. But it is often hugely beneficial, with Ehwi *et al.* (2022: 1) arguing that, with regards self-building, it 'is associated with giving people agency and control in the design and building of their homes ... and fostering a strong sense of community and the development of important social skills such as tolerance, compromise and mutual respect among group members.'

Living in a cooperative, self-built home, or CLT (as the research tell us), can foster a sense of collective identity and agency that contrasts sharply with the alienation often experienced in market-based housing systems. These alternative housing spaces become sites of postcapitalist learning, where residents can acquire skills in governance, construction and conflict resolution, as well as develop a deeper understanding of collective responsibility (de Jong *et al.*, 2015).

But the state also plays a role, as we saw in Uruguay. Often this can be as simple as getting out of the way, but it can also leverage its financial might to create broader progressive economic national contexts. The participatory budgeting method (often referred to as the Porto Alegre model) has been used for nearly four decades as a way of engaging local residents in financial decisions that affect their community, but there are even broader policies such as universal basic income, the four-day working week with no loss of pay, and policies of subsidiarity (such as those employed in Rojava detailed in the previous chapter). And broader still, these housing models also problematise the very notion of the nuclear family unit that is so pervasive in the western world. Margeret Thatcher proclaimed so famously that there was no such thing as society, only individuals and families, but the 'traditional' family unit so beloved by Thatcher and her neoliberal peers continues to wane (Sarkisian and Gerstel, 2012). As housing affordability (and the general cost of living) continues to soar out of reach for many younger people, some are shunning the traditional nuclear family in favour of co-living, childless partnerships and even neo-nomadic lifestyles (Trujillo, 2021).

But it is clear that from Trawden to Caracas, from Boston to Montevideo, urban commoning is a fundamental practice of human beings looking to live collectively and democratically. The capitalist city machine, as outlined in the first part of this book, constantly suffocates any attempts at resistance or alternatives, and while it is an effective process, like all machines it is not perfect and sometimes breaks. While it is being repaired and honed, fissures of possibility open up, and people have the opportunities to create alternative 'machines' that can begin to be sustainable. It is never easy, of course, as it requires radical shifts in fundamental structures of urbanism that have become so ubiquitous and commonplace that they are seen as 'natural' and therefore immutable. Private property, familial living, market forces, urban governments in the service of real-estate capital, profit over people; these are all seemingly eternal truths of the contemporary city. Yet as this chapter has highlighted (and since you have managed to get so far into this book without throwing it away in disgust, you will undoubtedly know of many, many more), they are not as concrete as the architects and technocrats of the capitalist city would have you believe. Through the prefigurative politics of squatting, the internationalist mutualism of Community

Land Trust models, the deliberate financialised separation of housing and the land it occupies as distinct taxable entities, and the anti-individualist urbanism of co-living, a postcapitalist city is not only possible but also very real. Instead of private property there are urban spaces of common ownership; the nuclear family is not always the unit of housing; the real-estate market has been defenestrated; governance is collective and democratic and not paid for by developers; postcapitalism truly puts people over profit. Collectivising these themes is what a postcapitalist city will do, and prefiguratively, does. It is a form of common urbanism that cannot be reduced to a single act but is continually performed and enacted; it is a postcapitalism that is lived.

Chapter 8

Prefigurative postcapitalist cities

What follows is a journey. Specifically, my journey to a few select urban (and I use that term in its widest possible 'planetary urbanisation' meaning (Brenner and Schmid, 2011)) areas that in one way or another evidence a postcapitalist sensibility. It is by no means meant as a narrative that somehow totalises the experience of postcapitalist cites, nor are there really any ways in which these areas can act as benchmarks for other urban areas (however commensurate or not) to follow. It is an empirical account of the very small selection of urban areas that attracted me via their attempts – at various scales – to enact a 'city wide' postcapitalist ethos. As can be seen, there are threads of exciting potentiality, but also spectres of capitalist capture; there are instances of utopian urbanism, others of violent dystopia. But by visiting three places across three continents focusing on three very different 'prefigurative' actions (in that they are living and attempting to enact urbanism that is distinctly post-capitalist but with different ideological hues – anarchism, Maoism and agonism), I hope to entice and excite you by demonstrating that alternative urban systems are not only possible, but very real indeed.

Slab City

The five-hour long drive through the Californian desert had been a struggle. Following the (thankfully) reliable satnav had been straightforward enough, but coming off the I-10 at exit 168 around Joshua Tree Park onto roads that had signs stating 'No cell signal for 10 miles' the anxiety really began to set it. The searing and

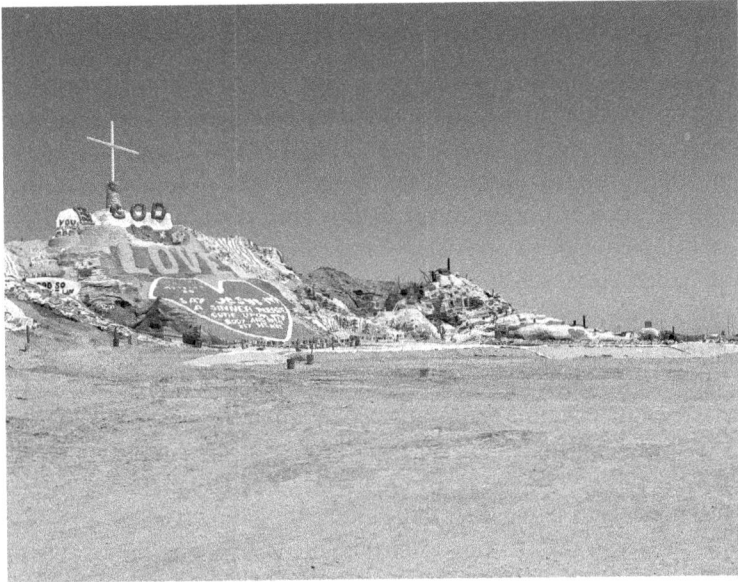

8.1 Salvation Mountain (Author's photograph, May 2023)

relentless heat was penetrating even the full-blast clanky air condition-ing, and the paper maps that I now relied on were beginning to make very little sense as I doubted my (now very antiquated) map-reading skills. I admitted to thinking at an increasingly frequently rate, was the trip going to be worth it?

But as I drove through the desert town of Niland, the last vestige of 'civilisation' before my destination (I use the term civilisation very loosely here, given the large array of burnt-out vehicles, Wild West-style saloons and the odd Confederate flag flying over porches), the sight of Salvation Mountain (Figure 8.1) greeted me as an oasis of boundless human creativity and spiritual devotion in the vast expanse of the surrounding arid and deserted landscape. The mountain itself was crafted by the hands of the American folk artist Leonard Knight; this vibrant mound of dirt, straw and countless gallons of paint stands as a beacon of hope and (very biblically inspired) love in a landscape otherwise marked by oppressive heat and starkness. Its vivid colours of swirling blues, radiant reds, and verdant greens blazed like a gargantuan Matisse painting under the desert sun, incandescently complemented by the surrounding monochrome bright blue sky.

The mountain greets all visitors to Slab City; it is the perfect gateway to the infamous settlement of travellers, outcasts, marginalised and those who would otherwise simply find 'normal' capitalist societies uncomfortable, oppressive and stifling. It is the exemplar of folk or outsider art, a testament to the slightly gaudy but incredibly homely aesthetics of amateur and fiercely anti-elitist creativity. A lone woman sat under a makeshift tarpaulin tent with a small dog greets me with a smile, and hands me a small card with a Bible verse, website and PayPal handle scrawled on it.

I sit beside her, exhausted by the drive and the (as I check my watch) only ten minutes of walking around in the stifling sun. Before even beginning my exploration of the rest of the city and meeting up with the people I've been emailing, I had to familiarise myself with the heat: a living, breathing entity, wrapping itself around you in a sweaty embrace. Yet, amid this intense climate, the people of Slab City extended a welcome as warm as the desert sun itself. They formed a rich tapestry – artists, fixers, wanderers, dreamers – all seemingly united by a shared desire for freedom from judgement by mainstream society. Their homes are a testament to a non-linear ingenuity and homesteading creativity, crafted from repurposed materials and adorned with murals and sculptures that tell stories of hope, rebellion, neurodiversity and folky aesthetics that speak to the vast constellation of human experiences. Every structure is in itself a unique manifesto, a declaration of independence from the constraints of capitalist society.

In this community, you are greeted not with suspicion, but with open arms and open hearts (despite the fact I was driving a modern, relatively clean and large Japanese-made SUV). Conversations flowed as freely as the desert breeze, ranging from philosophical musings to tales of personal transformation. I was given food free of charge, as much as I wanted to drink, and all the time I needed. I was told before I set out to bring some bottled water, so I had stopped at the CVS Pharmacy store en route to buy five large containers of water, but my gracious hosts insisted I save my drinking water for the return journey.

I met up with the librarian, a trans man who, despite the library being officially closed, welcomed me in to peruse the collection

8.2 Slab City library (Author's photograph, May 2023)

of books, toys and what I could only fathom were piles of metal frames, wooden crates and other casts-off from building projects, all joined together in a weird interplay of material masquerading as 'public' art (see Figure 8.2). I came armed with a few copies of my books to donate to the library, which they were more than happy to take, as long as I signed them. Not wanting to devalue them I declined, but they insisted as apparently it was a library tradition to get authors to sign their donations. And there was me thinking I was being unique.

I journeyed to East Jesus, the outdoor art gallery that is the apotheosis of subversive material art. It uses 'everyday objects' that have been disassembled, inverted, turned inside out, or just destroyed to create a very deliberate anti-capitalist message. The wall of stacked old-style TVs with slogans such as 'This machine kills braincells' and 'Democrats are evil' written across the screens, is one of the more evocative pieces in the gallery. There are 1970s Buicks covered in CDs and naked Barbie dolls, tyres and old bike parts reassembled into humanoid figures, and a geodesic dome

8.3 East Jesus gallery (Author's photograph, May 2023)

covered in netting. But the material oddities of the gallery are repeated right across Slab City; people's homes are just as symbolic. One of the more famous residents, Dot, lives next door to the gallery, but her home is an extension of it. It is a mixture of semi-permanent wooden sheds, stationary (and presumably undriveable) camper vans all draped together with nets and fabric. She even has a large lounging pool made from rubber and inflatables, which she jealously guards for obvious reasons, particularly in the hot season.

As the sun began its descent, painting the sky in hues of crimson and lavender, Slab City transformed into a realm of shadows and soft light. The heat began to ease its grip, replaced by a gentle cooling zephyr that breathed new life into the desert. Around communal fires and makeshift bars, the din of raucous, drug-fuelled laughter and music escaped into the cloudless night. Here, under a canopy of infinite stars, the true emancipatory beauty of Slab City reveals herself, not just in the physical manifestations of DIY culture, anti-capitalist aesthetics, and a fiercely communal affective atmosphere,

8.4 Bills Bike Shop (Author's photograph, May 2023)

but in the spirit of its people and the profound sense of freedom they exuded. I retreat to my SUV, rented specifically because I wanted to try and sleep in it, but even in the relative cool of the night, the heat is not conducive to slumber, and so I find myself wandering the desert, intermittently meeting Slab City residents, some of whom are suspicious (mostly of my accent), but most of whom are simply happy to see a new face.

Clearly, the anti-capitalist, communal and convivial city that I encountered is not ubiquitous. It is punctuated by officialdom and hierarchy, and it hasn't managed to escape the reach of the US dollar as a form of trade and barter. There are even some of the hostels and spare rooms listed on Airbnb. There was also clear evidence of violence upon my visit. I went to see one of the other famous residents, Charlie the bike-repair guy. His shop – called Bill's Bike Shop after his dad – had featured on a number of TV documentaries that I had watched prior to my visit, but when he took me there, it was a landscape of ashes, twisted metal and burnt tree trunks (see Figure 8.4).

He explained how a local resident of the city had set fire to his lot because Bill had stood up for someone recently at a bar. Despite clearly losing a great deal of his livelihood and stock of old bikes, he was very philosophical about it all. In fact, he said that it had given him something else to do and was an opportunity to rejig the layout of his bike yard. Another abode that I passed had numerous threatening signs outside such as 'You loot, we shoot!', confirming what many people had said to me that that kind of messaging evidences the self-policing mantra of the city. Because of its remoteness, Slab City is very rarely visited by the police, government officials or any other form of capitalist state representatives, and so the policing here is community driven. So, rather than the Gramscian view of a police force that en*force*s the will of capital (as discussed in Part I), the policing here is performed by the residents, albeit with firearms it seems (I was lucky enough not to encounter any in my short visit). For all the talk of abolishing the police in many activist circles in the US, Slab City has never had a police force and is clearly surviving (if not thriving) to tell the tale.

Other people spoke of their fear that the growth of the site over the last few years would attract the police more, and the inevitable violence and eviction that that would bring about. Numbers fluctuate depending on the season, but the permanent residents (called 'slabbers') number around 150; in the 'peak' season, that number can swell to 3,500, many of whom (it was suggested to me) come less because they have been rejected by mainstream society, and more because they see it as a space from which to learn from, extract inspiration from and essentially use as an experimental testing ground for ideas that may end up catalysing entrepreneurial activity (it was mooted by some, albeit rather intoxicated, residents that Silicon Valley venture capitalists have been seen in the city, which wouldn't surprise me in the least).

I was there for only a fleeting moment (and hence could easily be bracketed into this process of extractivism for external kudos, given you're reading about it in a book published by a corporation that no doubt will aid in my own career path) – a mere blink of an eye for the slabbers that have taken up residency there permanently and call it home. But even in my ephemeral stay, there were undoubtedly distinct postcapitalist, perhaps most readily anarchist, and very *psychedelic* urban sensibilities that were impossible to not be enamoured by. As the previous chapter outlined, squatting is a practice of prefiguration, itself a vital component of realising and concretising postcapitalist cities, and Slab City has been described in various media as a 'squatters paradise', 'America's most dangerous squat', and 'The Last free town in America'. All of these labels. while being largely uttered for clicks, are perhaps partly true as it is, after all, a squat. The site was an old US army base that disbanded in the 1960s and was subsequently used by RV-based nomads as somewhere to congregate, given the large concrete slabs that were the foundations for the barracks remained and were very useful in the desert (Hailey and Wylie, 2019). So yes, it's certainly a squat and it has the DIY (or, as one slabber corrected me, DIT – 'do it together') aesthetics and precarious infrastructures that are synonymous with squatting. And the collective democratic processes that maintain civility and a sense of 'order' are multifarious, fragile and based on a 'live and let live' philosophy rather than anything more codified. There is no rule book to living in Slab City; the only real 'code' that I heard talked about was that you mark out the area you want to live in with tyres, and thereby anything you do with that space is up to you. And yes, the slabbers will use money when needed, i.e. going into 'town' to purchase fuel for generators, food and/or water, and if they don't have enough money at any given time, there is always a workaround via mutual aid practices and sharing of existing resources. And some of the people I spoke to worked periodically in places outside the city (one man I drank with worked at an RV park over three hours' drive away). Any new 'road' that is forged will be given a name by those that use it most (and after a while, it ends up being written into reality, first, by a handwritten sign, and then by Google Maps using it).

So yes, it has all the *academic* characteristics of a squat, but viewed through the lens of postcapitalist cities it *feels* far less like a squat and more like a psychedelic city – one that, as Chapter 5 outlined, goes beyond the capitalist here and now. The postcapitalist futures that haunt the present are not ghosts here; they are alive and have been for years. It is as if the Fisherian psychedelic subcultures have spawned a city that has championed over capitalist attempts to either violently destroy it or co-opt it via appropriative capitalism. It is a permanent residence that isn't under constant threat from the capitalist city (as many squats often are). This permanence is of course most evident in its longevity; it's been around in some form or another since the 1980s. The distinct lack of any state activity is aided no doubt by its vast geographical marginality from land that could be considered even remotely the thin end of a rent gap. It's been used in some contemporary and capitalist media: it featured in the 2007 Hollywood film *Into the Wild* and has been subject to numerous travel documentaries and YouTube explorers. All this spectacularisation gives the place a distinct psychedelic quality befitting of an anti-capitalist pilgrimage (hands up, guilty, but to be fair, upon viewing Salvation Mountain for the first time, it is easy to see why). But ultimately it is the people who reside there, the slabbers, that provide the tangible psychedelic ethos in their concrete rebuttal of mainstream society. The various media portray them as *weird*, and taking a quick walk around Dot's house you can see why. But postcapitalist cities are nothing without a population determined to make it work, and the slabbers' refusal to align with 'normality' is the engine of the city's postcapitalism. They are trans, neurodiverse, conspiracy theorists, amputees, addicts, queer sex workers; the collective population is an embodiment of many of those groups so violently marginalised by mainstream capitalist society. Its size, geographical location and extreme living conditions make it some-where that quickly sifts out those who don't really abide by its ethos. But conversely, those conditions mean that as a 'model' of postcapitalism it is certainly not replicable nor scalable; indeed, to even think it could be goes against the postcapitalist, read psychedelic, sensibilities that it pervades. It is a city that is more-than-human (via its obvious re-use of everyday objects beyond their capitalist function), but also more-than-present in that there are actual realities of a postcapitalist future experienced in the situation of the now. And all that is required to experience it is a five-hour drive into the Californian desert (and a very high heat tolerance).

Chongqing

At the very extreme 'other' end of the postcapitalist cityscape is the Chinese city of Chongqing. If you search online for this most captivat-ing of cities, you will undoubtedly be met with spectacular images of skyscrapers emblazoned with lights curated to form a definite

8.5 Cyberpunk Chongqing (Author's photograph, February 2024)

cyberpunk aesthetic akin to Ridley Scott's 1984 classic film *Blade Runner*. And wandering through the dizzying downtown areas at night it is difficult to disagree (see Figure 8.5). As a huge fan of science fiction, walking the cavernous city streets fired all the emotive emblems of orientalist urban dystopias that have been the mainstay of a western rhetoric for many decades. But adding to the often vertiginous affective atmosphere of the city is its underlying topography: Chongqing is a very mountainous city that resists more traditional forms of urban planning that could be applied to flatter terrains (Roast, 2024). Within the broader geography of China itself, Chongqing is also fairly remote, relatively 'new', and away from the bustle of the coastal cities, and hence has found that shaking off the 'rurality' as a spatial, cultural and social logic fairly difficult (Cheng, 2015). Indeed, it has been suggested that the city embodies the ancient (and intricately complex and manifold) concept of *jianghu* (江湖). This literally translates to 'rivers and lakes' but also can be used to refer to a broader concept of 'wilderness'. Originating from ancient Chinese literature, it articulates a parallel society to the mainstream Chinese one (be that ancient or contemporary), inhabited by martial artists, outlaws, wanderers and those living on the fringes of conventional society. This quasi-mythical realm, distinct from the structured and hierarchical imperial society of Chinese dynasties and the Chinese Communist Party (CCP), is a space of freedom, adventure and often moral ambiguity. The concept of *jianghu*, with its connotations of mobility, fluidity and alternative social structures, has been associated with many forms of subcultural and criminal activity, including the Triads.

From the point of a view of urbanism, this relation is theorised by Li (2014: 113), who argues that 'like rivers and lakes, streets in Chinese cities can often induce careless behaviours; their possible status as spaces of *jianghu*'. This is expanded by Roast (2019b: 123), who argues that *jianghu* constitutes of form of 'deterritorialization of place: a space of transition and disorder that rejects the niceties of the city for a more horizontalized (yet less secure) ethic of social relations'. The freeing disorder of *jianghu* was particularly evident when attempting to find somewhere to eat in the city. Many of the eateries and dining rooms (I hesitate to use the term 'restaurant') in the less touristy parts of the city that I attempted to dine at were delighted to have a lone western tourist, but I found myself sat at a round table with six or seven other people, scooping hot pot out of a large metal bowl in the middle. My Mandarin is virtually non-existent, but with the help of someone who spoke relatively decent English (and a translation app on our phones) it became clear that this was how people ate in the city; it was only relatively recently (and only in the wealthier westernised parts of downtown) that more individualised dining experiences were to be found. But after some initial embarrassment on my part, I found the collective (and brow-sweatingly spicy) dining experience very much part of the *jianghu* that I had read about so much. One elderly diner told me (very clunkily, via an app) that this was how people ate before the city arrived. In the mountainous, often very cold climates in pre-urbanisation times (which, given the rapidity of Chinese urban expansion, wasn't that long ago) families and communities would huddle around large pots of hot spicy food and talk about their worries, their hopes and pass on generational knowledge of farming and industrial techniques. This cultural ritual, of the collective consumption of food and sharing of knowledge, is clearly a fundamental part of Chongqing's urban fabric, and perhaps one of the driving 'more-than-human' forces that catalysed the creation of what is now known as the 'Chongqing model'.

The model was the brainchild of Bo Xilai, who was the Communist Party Secretary of Chongqing between 2007 and 2012. Before this, he was a promising politician within the ruling CCP and seen as a then potential rival to Xi Jinping, which may explain his rather controversial story. His appointment was viewed as an effective demotion, given before 2007 he was the minister of commerce for the whole of China, so perhaps it was a move to marginalise his political prowess. He was from the Maoist school of politics, and he championed the proletariat as the true drivers of the Chinese project, as well as the rightful heirs of its bounty. Mao's horrifically violent cultural revolution of the 1960s and 1970s was something that the CCP leadership under Xi were quite rightly keen to dissociate themselves from. The then 'new' form of Chinese geopolitics was far more about attracting foreign investment, championing entre-preneurship, and expanding Chinese 'soft' power to match its clear global economic power. But Bo was old school; he looked to Mao's policies to develop Chongqing, and if success is measured in pure rapidity of growth, he was enormously successful. The city was only really formed in 1997 when it separated from the Sichuan province to become a province in its own right. Today it is the most populous city in China, at around 30 million people (Jaros, 2023). [1]

Hence the 'Chongqing model' refers to the very specific Maoist (and hence resolutely postcapitalist) policies that aided in creating the burgeoning megalopolis from 2007 to 2012. The model drew significant attention both within China and internationally, specifically around housing, anti-corruption and infrastructure, but also because Bo (re)initiated a form of Mao's 'Red Culture' that was either critiqued as communist indoctrination or praised as national pride (depending on your political hues). Chongqing, even before 1997, had a history as a strategic and economic hub, given that it sits at the confluence of the Yangtze and Jialing rivers. During the early part of the twentieth century, it served as the wartime capital of China, but post-1949 Chongqing became an industrial centre under Mao's industrialisation policies, particularly during the Third Front Movement of the 1960s and 1970s (a massive infrastructural investment programme of the interior of China seen as a defence against the expansion of the

8.6 Chongqing housing estate (Author's photograph, February 2024)

USSR). However, after it became a city in its own right in 1997, Chongqing experienced rapid urbanisation and economic growth, partly fuelled by the central government's 'Go West' strategy (which doesn't refer to looking to western nations for development, but was a set of infrastructural and socio-economic programmes aimed at developing China's western interior regions).

Bo Xilai's appointment as Party Secretary of Chongqing in 2007 marked a significant turning point for the city. His vision for Chongqing was ambitious, aiming to transform the city into a showcase of Maoist principles within what he saw as the growth of a westernised and capitalist market economy (Cheng, 2015). He put into place massive economic redistribution and social welfare programmes, focused on large-scale public housing projects aimed at providing affordable homes to low-income residents, which at the time was in stark contrast to the market-driven housing policies prevalent in other Chinese cities. Massive housing estates, full of skyscraping residential blocks, but also schools, public space, retail parks and health centres were built to house rural migrants on low incomes, in order to rapidly increase the housing provision for the workforce for the city (an example is shown in Figure 8.6). Educational programmes for children were put in place, as were courses for rural workers to train them in the city's massively expanding manufacturing industries. Indeed, David Harvey (2012: 64) argued that the Chongqing model therefore aimed to 'reduce the spiralling social inequalities that have arisen over the last two decades across China [due to it embracing capitalist policies]'. To aid with the growth of these industries (providing jobs for the millions of rural migrants flocking into the city), Bo oversaw significant investment in infrastructure, including the construction of new roads, bridges and railways. Given the mountainous nature of the city, some of these infrastructural programmes were highly innovative and utilised never-before-seen engineering feats. The metro system of the city stands out in this regard and has become world famous through the striking images of trains going into stations that have been built in skyscrapers, cable cars that thread themselves through tight gaps in residential tower blocks, and public squares that appear to be at 'ground level' on one side, but are actually twenty-two floors up on the other. As I sauntered my way around the city, these spectacular and innovatively engineered infrastructures added to the cyberpunk and futuristic aesthetic of the city, aiding in the general affective atmosphere of being in some sort of postcapitalist utopia (or perhaps dystopia, depending on your cultural lens).

The social and economic burgeoning of the city wrought by Bo's Maoist policies between 2007 and 2012 would in itself perhaps not make it too different to other cities in China which were experiencing similar kinds of population explosion. Yes, Chongqing focused on social housing for the rural poor as a primary, but that didn't exclude private developers from capitalising on the growing real-estate market; after all, postcapitalism rarely happens in a vacuum. But the Chongqing model was perhaps at its most controversial with Bo's use of Maoist cultural and socialist values through initiatives like the Red Culture movement. This included promoting old revolutionary songs, organising mass public singing events, and encouraging the study of Mao political texts and speeches (Cheng, 2015; Mei, 2017). These actions were intended to foster a sense of collective identity and loyalty to the Communist Party, but it ended up irking the CCP hierarchy who were looking to shed the Maoist image in favour of a more globalised, outwardly looking – dare I say, ideologically *capitalist* – version of their *communist* policies. This, of course, sounds oxymoronical; and while this is a debate rehearsed in far better detail elsewhere (see Coase and Wang, 2016), there is an ongoing ideological tension when referring to China as a geopolitical entity, a tension that has manifested in ugly political discourse, international policies, and widespread Sinophobia in Western narratives.

But perhaps the most controversial, at least for the CCP's immediate self-preservation, was Bo's crackdown on organised crime and corruption, dubbed 打黑 (*dǎhēi* – roughly translated to 'striking the black') campaign. This initiative was popular among the local residents but controversial further afield due to reports of abuses of power, illegal detentions, and the use of extra-legal interrogation methods to extract 'confessions'. The campaign led to many thousands of arrests, including several high-ranking CCP officials and police officers. It was these arrests that eventually led to Bo Xilai's downfall. In 2012, his police chief, Wang Lijun, fled to the US consulate in Chengdu, revealing details of corruption and the apparent murder of British businessman Neil Heywood, allegedly orchestrated by Bo's wife, Gu Kailai. This scandal led to Bo's removal from office, his expulsion from the Communist Party, and his eventual trial and imprisonment. To this day, his conviction remains highly controversial and there are ongoing appeals and counter-appeals. Bo's rivalry to Xi is often cited as a clear reason as to why it was a 'show trial' with very little transparency (Hill, 2013); suffice to say it signalled an end to the Chongqing model as a form of Maoist, socialist, proletarianised and ultimately postcapitalist project.

The Chongqing model has left a complex legacy since 2012. On one hand, Bo Xilai's policies significantly improved public services (notably transportation and housing infrastructure) and social welfare for many residents. The crackdown on crime made the city safer in the short term, and indeed as a foreign visitor to the city more recently (one who often likes to wander into areas of the city that tourist guides often tell people to avoid for fear of crime), I never felt unease (although as a western, white male there are clear reasons as to why this is). Since 2012, the city has fallen in line more with China's national urbanisation policy, and the city has seen a massive uptick in technology industries, notably hosting an important branch of Foxconn's factories to make Apple products. But as a result of these more entrepreneurial and capitalist modes of economic development, many of the large-scale housing projects that were built for rural migrants to offer a dignified life while they transitioned to urban society have become glorified dormitories for the factory workers who live in poor conditions on the outskirts of the city (Roast, 2019b). And while my visit to the city was unsatisfyingly brief, I walked as much of it as I could, and only once did I come across a homeless individual in a metro underpass soliciting for money. This could speak to the city's excellent social welfare programme and housing policies, but anecdotal evidence of those residents, students and retail workers I spoke to suggests that the homeless (and visibly disabled) are moved on very quick and rarely seen in public, a symptom of a city obsessed with image and with effacing anything that would detract from its clear development as a location that inhabits the social mediascape as the cyberpunk city *par excellence*. Despite this, the city's rural past remains resolute in the social actions of its inhabitants. The streets were filled with low-level commerce, conversations and a cacophony that represented a clear living *jianghu* of the past (that I experienced so vividly around the hot-pot bowl).

As this book has explored, postcapitalist cities exist in the cracks and blind spots of the capitalist machinery. Such machinery, in this instance, is the (re)writing of Chongqing's history and the redrawing of its surface as a slick, spectacular image-laden city that can flow through global media networks to draw in tourists, investment and other forms of free-moving capital. But peel back this layer, and the legacy of Bo's Maoist policies remain in the quality of the housing, the efficiency of the infrastructure and, more importantly, the affective presence of *jianghu* on the streets.

Mechelen

In the middle of Belgium, nestled roughly halfway between Brussels and Antwerp, is Mechelen, a non-descript small city of around 90,000 inhabitants that is arguably stereotypically Belgian in its architecture and canal-side culture. However, beyond its picturesque facades, obligatory striking cathedral, and the cobblestone streets synonymous

with Benelux urbanity, Mechelen drew me in because of one innovative, experimental art piece that has the potential to radically redraw
urban democracy. The art project is called 'The Ground of Things'
and is (at the time of writing) still ongoing. It is a multi-faceted
endeavour that incorporates artists, museums, the local council and,
crucially, local communities and residents. I was alerted to the project
by a group of academics who talked about it at a conference in
Antwerp I was invited to back in 2021 (indeed, it was the first
in-person event I attended post-COVID so the anxiety and trepidation
of many of the attendees including myself was palpable). At the
time, because of the COVID-19 restrictions, I was unable to go to
Mechelen, but the radical democracy of the project gnawed away
at me, and I had to go back, simply to know more about how it
worked in practice.

The Ground of Things, or De Grond der Dingen in Dutch, is at
its heart, an initiative that aims to radically reimagines public space
and civic engagement. Since 2019, the theatre company Arsenaal/
Lazarus and the museum Hof van Busleyden under this banner have
conceived of a number of different projects and art pieces, but their
essential purpose is to gather ideas from the people of Mechelen by
asking them a similar question to the one that opened this book:
'What is your idea of a perfect city?' After a few speculative conversations with the local authority, the people of Mechelen quickly became
part of the project themselves, and before long the city authorities
had offered 20,000 m² of various parts of the city to the project
(Otte and Gielen, 2020). This was in no doubt in part due to the
liberal tendencies of the Mechelen mayor, Bart Somers, who had
previously won international acclaim for his work on integrating
refugees and asylum seekers in the city (Dudman, 2017).

The collective of people and institutions quickly moved into action
and created 'The Never-ending Park', a sort of agora-type space
that overtook part of the basement of the Hof van Busleyden museum,
extending it further underground. In this space, over the course of
two years (culminating in an exhibition in September 2020), the
residents came together to discuss, debate and experiment with
various uses, and how many of the square metres would be needed.
Some of the projects that were proposed included a community
garden, eco-communes, a sculpture park, an 'eco-corridor', gaming
zones or simply some retail outlets.[2] Crucially, though, as part of
the democratic process, each resident had to agree to their square

being used in the designated way. In all, 206 projects have been proposed since 2020, and many have gone forward into 'production' in conjunction with the city government.

There are many similar kinds of participatory democracy projects that take place all over the world; participatory budgeting, pioneered by the Porto Alegre model (Sousa Santos, 1998), is one such example that has become a mainstay of urban, regional and some national economic policy agendas. What makes the Mechelen case more radical is that it is an ambitious initiative that aims to reconceptualise the very nature of public spaces in the first place through participatory design and community involvement. The Ground of Things challenges the conventional top–down approach to urban planning, advocating instead for a bottom–up active methodology where the community participates in shaping their environment. More acutely, the democratic process rarely involved voting; all the decisions about the use of the space were arrived at by discussion, and eventual consensus. In that sense, it is reminiscent of Mouffe's (2005) concept of agonism, which as discussed in Chapter 5, is a radically participatory form of democracy and artistic practice that *antagonises* the traditional forms of democracy as imposed from above. As part of the agonisitic tendencies of the project, from the outset the question was asked by the organisers: 'Who are the citizens that come to negotiate about proposals? Are they not again mainly the white, empowered, and skilled middle-class people who feel at home in a deliberative model?' (Otte and Gielen, 2020: 152).

The uncomfortable truth about supposedly radical democratic processes, particularly those that involve a great deal of discussion, is that, yes, they privilege those with access, articulation and the space in their lives to give over to those processes. Too often it is the underprivileged in society who are unheard, and so their voices remain outside the democratic process. The organisers recognised this and included in the project a 'touring chair' that visited lower-income and marginalised neighbourhoods in an attempt to canvass their opinions. The organisers have admitted that this is far from ideal, and while the 'voices of the unheard' are filtered through the privilege of the organisers and the residents who were more fully involved, they have been able to include projects that these communities deemed important. And of course, the entire project itself, like many other subversive and countercultural artistic endeavours around the world, is couched within, and was dreamed up by, capitalist cultural institutions, so its postcapitalist sensibility is perhaps somewhat limited to a mere 'window' into the practices of deliberative community-based formulations of public space.

Another tangible benefit of the project has been the impact on cohesion throughout the city, which itself is clearly an important part of the mayor's remit, given his background in refugee integration. As the main project itself came to an end and the government picked up their recommendations, it would have been easy to slip back into the old hegemonic patterns of top–down democracy, with the official urban hierarchy making the decisions about the use of public space. However, to date, a number of the projects have been realised, and the process of deliberative community-based democracy that the project has pioneered has been used in other parts of the city's development plan, including a 'garden of food' that has used the space in a public park to create a vegetable garden, a silent forest, and even a pizza oven (Architecture Workroom Brussels, 2024).

Despite its postcapitalist sensibilities around the use of radical democracy, the scale of this project renders it rather fleeting in the ongoing transition away from the suffocating injustices of the capitalist city. Being in the heartland of empire (notably a short train ride away from Brussels, a city built on the back of massive injustices of racial capitalism as Chapter 1 outlined) any threat to the established order of the capitalist city is minimal at best. But there are many other instances of cities further afield that have not only threatened, but completely overthrown the capitalist hegemony to establish a postcapitalist city that has *lasted*. These places have, so far at least, eluded my travel plans (much to their benefit, no doubt), and so the following is less an empirical account and more an overview of the places and their ideological positioning with the spectrum of postcapitalist urban praxis. Ultimately, they warrant some discussion, given how they have firmly established themselves as prefigurative utopias (as far as that is possible in these days of suffocating capitalist realism) of a *true* postcapitalist city, broadly defined.

Other variations

One of the more (in)famous examples is Auroville, in the South Indian state of Tamil Nadu. The commune city is often heralded as a beacon of alternative living, horizontal anarchist governance, and ecologically sustainable development (see Clarence-Smith, 2023). Founded in, yes you guessed it, 1968 by the spiritual guru (and yoga teacher) Mirra Alfassa (simply referred to as 'The Mother') Auroville (which translates as the 'city of dawn') was envisioned as a universal town where people from all over the world could live in peace and progressive harmony, transcending nationality, politics and religion. The city's 'economy' (such as it is) deviates significantly from traditional capitalist models in that it does not function on a profit-driven basis. Instead, residents contribute to the community according to their abilities and receive what they need in return as a form of mutual aid or perhaps 'gift economy' (à la Mauss (1954)). Like many other communes, squats and anarchist communities around the world (one of the most famous being Christiania in Copenhagen, a place I have written about in the past (Mould, 2015, 2018)), Auroville operates a model of collective ownership, sustainability and self-governance. Much like The Ground of Things in Mechelen, decisions are made through a participatory process, involving all members of the community. Auroville's legacy and durability has, of course, not been without its challenges and controversies: because of its inclusive philosophy it takes in tourists, and as such there are paid-for hostels and rooms, creating what has been described to me rather disparagingly as an 'anarchist theme park', and, like all prefigurative postcapitalist cities, it is not immune to violence, racism and other prejudices, and has been threatened with demolition many times in its history (Ellis-Peterson, 2022). But its longevity is testament to its ethos of spiritual anarchism, as well as its relative isolation deep within the forests of Tamil Nadu.

If Auroville can be thought of as an anarchist flavour of postcapitalism, then Marinaleda in Spain is very much of the communist variety. Born out of abject rural poverty, this Andalusian village was led vociferously by a communist mayor named Sánchez Gordillo and has become a self-described 'communist utopia' where the land is collectively owned by the community (producing olives, artichokes and other crops), workers earn equal pay (regardless of the job), and there is affordable housing to residents, with a nominal mortgage payment of just 15 euros per month (Hancox, 2013). The community holds regular assemblies where every resident has a voice in decision-making, with education and healthcare systems being free. Large murals of Che Guevara adorn the walls, and Gordillo gained national notoriety in 2012 for a series of raids on nearby supermarkets to steal food to give to his starving residents (earning him the title of the 'Robin Hood mayor'). The prefiguration of Marinaleda is highly evident in the many quotes by Gordillo, e.g.

> We have learned that it is not enough to define utopia, nor is it enough to fight against the reactionary forces. One must build it here and now, brick by brick, patiently but steadily, until we can make the old dreams a reality: that there will be bread for all, freedom among citizens, and culture; and to be able to read with respect the word 'peace'. We sincerely believe that there is no future that is not built in the present. (Hancox, 2013: 3)

Gordillo stepped down from the mayoral role in 2023 citing poor health, although critics (of which there are many inside the Spanish national government) will tell of his waning popularity in the village due to his harsh treatment of political opponents (Gomez, 2023). There is little doubt though that Marinaleda represents for many an achievable vision of how a postcapitalist urban environment can not just emerge but thrive in the midst of the capitalist onslaught of financialisation, gentrification and appropriation (Candón-Mena *et al.*, 2020).

Somewhere in between these two (ideologically rather than geographically) lies the city of Preston in the UK, which represents another version of the postcapitalist city from a more government-led municipal-socialism perspective. The so-called 'Preston model' is rooted in the concept of community wealth-building (Brown and Jones, 2021). Preston has developed a city governance structure (through assembling political will at the local council level) that maximises the economic potential of local assets and thereby leverages the spending power of local anchor institutions – e.g. hospitals, universities and the local council itself – to support businesses and community cooperatives. This approach is a departure from the traditional economic development models that often prioritise attracting external investment, which has led some local councils in the UK to bankruptcy (e.g. Birmingham and Woking). Some of the major factors inherent to the model include encouraging anchor institutions to procure goods and services from local businesses, promoting the establishment of worker cooperatives, advocating for fair wages and working conditions to reduce economic inequalities, community banking, and, crucially, bringing outsourced services back under public control to ensure better quality and accountability (Hanna *et al.*, 2018). Any postcapitalism within the Preston model is present in its economic practices: it prioritises localism, circular economy practices, and community wealth-building over pure economic growth and returns on investment. So, while still using the fundamentals of the market to generate income, the rationales for its generation remain distinctly different to more traditional neoliberal forms of urban government.

Summary

While the models explored in this chapter offer compelling glimpses into prefigurative postcapitalist urbanism, there are of course real-life limitations that remind us the road to transformative system change is fraught with contradictions and limitations. These urban spaces, as vibrant, different and aspirational as they may appear, are not immune to the spectres of capitalist capture, structural inequality, and internal fragility. In Slab City, the fierce independence and creativity of its inhabitants are tempered by the city's reliance on broader capitalist structures; whether through the use of money for essential goods or the presence of Airbnb rentals within an ostensibly anti-capitalist haven. The Chongqing model, despite its roots in Maoist ideals of equity and communal welfare, was mostly the vision of a charismatic and politically motivated individual, and has now succumbed to the inexorable forces of global capitalism and the weight of the Chinese state hegemony. In Mechelen, the radical participatory processes underpinning its artistic democratic performances, in the end, still relied on established cultural institutions and the uneven participation of marginalised voices, revealing the broader challenges of such experiments in truly subverting existing power dynamics.

Even in longer-standing examples like Auroville or Marinaleda, the spectre of exclusivity, external commodification, and internal conflict looms large. These utopias are neither immune to the pressures of a globalised capitalist city nor to the reproduction of alternative hierarchies within their radically democratic structures. But these critiques do not – and I would argue, must not – negate the postcapitalist value of these spaces; on the contrary, their very imperfections are instructive. They underscore the need for vigilance against the co-option of postcapitalist aspirations and a recognition that no single 'vision' of postcapitalism offers a panacea. Instead, they collectively suggest a mosaic of possibilities, a shifting, imperfect terrain where the seeds of a postcapitalist urbanism might grow in the cracks of the capitalist city.

These urban experiments, as far as Slab City is from Preston, are as varied in their approaches and contexts, but they home in on a common goal: to envision and enact a form of urban society (in the pure Lefebvrian (1968) sense) that breaks free from the constraints of capitalism. They psychedelically reveal both the exciting potentialities and the persistent challenges of creating postcapitalist cities at scale and for duration. Through these examples, it becomes evident that alternative urban systems are not only possible but already in existence, offering glimpses of futures, presents and pasts that prioritise communal values, social equity, and environmental sustainability. In envisioning pathways forward, we must embrace the paradox of prefiguration: the simultaneous necessity and insufficiency of creating spaces that embody postcapitalist principles within the present capitalist system. By learning from their flaws and tensions, we can refine our understanding of what it means to craft cities that not only resist but also transcend the logics of capitalism. The challenge, as always, lies not just in imagining new worlds but in building them, brick by agonistic brick, on the imperfect foundations of the present.

Chapter 9

Harvesting hope: Exploring solarpunk cities

What follows is text that was fairly uncomfortable for me to write, as I deliberately moved away from a traditional academic position of cynicism and critique to engage in that most scarce of resources: hope. That's because, in recent years, a novel urban phenomenon has been steadily gaining traction in various parts of the non-commercialised Internet and in underground media (such as independently published books, zines and DIY visual media), and, in so doing, has been stimulating the collective imagination of urban planners, architects and eco-conscious individuals to operate a planetary vernacular. Termed 'solarpunk' and born initially as a set of images and conversations, it has steadily grown into a literary subgenre, an artistic trope, a social movement, and now, with actual solarpunk cities having been built, a genuine urban form (Gillam, 2023). To unpack the concept, the following chapter will proffer data and analysis that have been gleaned from a variety of media, but mostly online forums, Mastodon hashtags, blogs, short films, and Pinterest boards, with site visits to some cities in the Netherlands that online are described as archetypically solarpunk (to ascertain with as much academic rigour as I could whether or not they deserve such a claim).

Etymologically, solarpunk has clearly riffed on cyber-, steam- and dieselpunk, with the 'punk' suffix referring to a cultural movement of subversion, anti-establishment and rebellion, and the solar prefix being both literal and figurative. Literal in that it is often solar power and images thereof that fuel the movement, but figurative in that it's a shining light of optimism in a world that, today, is gripped with a ubiquitous darkness and despair of climate catastrophe and the fascist horizons it has ushered in (Connolly, 2019). The abundance of solar power is obvious: indeed, according to NASA (2016), 173,000 terawatts of solar energy strike the Earth continuously. That's more than ten thousand times the world's total energy use. But it is an abundance of that most precious and most allusive of resources in this world so full of despair – that of hope – that solarpunk is trying to level up. Because spend any time with solarpunk aesthetics, literature or in a solarpunk city, and you cannot help but be infected, perhaps overwhelmed, by its sheer hopefulness.

But where does this hope come from? It's all well and good having a term for a movement which is a signifier of hope, but what about the practice, the politics, the movement that any 'word' or slogan tries to bring into being? What exactly *is* solarpunk? At its most basic, it is a sociocultural and urban development phenomenon, and finds its origins in grassroots social, and importantly, artistic responses to the rapidly mounting environmental challenges associated with urbanisation, climate catastrophe, imperial occupations, and social inequalities (Regenerative Design Collective, n.d.). Rooted in a tapestry of influential movements such as eco- and Afrofuturism, permaculture and a wellness aesthetic, solarpunk synthesises these diverse inspirations into a unique and visionary conception of future urban landscapes that differs radically from the status quo of the capitalist city and the ecological damage it causes. It is a deliberate symbiosis of nature and technology, transcending the often capitalist-inflected green design and green urbanism, to envision cities that actively *regenerate* ecologically, economically and socially (Gillam, 2023).

Embedded within it is a form of urban 'commoning' that was discussed in Chapter 7, a process that enlivens city workspaces with its incumbent and very *present* communities, rather than for the extractive and very *absent* private interests. So far from an institutional form of 'the commons' that is purported by the World Bank and other Bretton Woods institutions, it takes an approach more in line with a 'planetary commons' (Mould, 2021), in that it sees the material world and human communities from a symbiotic rather than extractive perspective.

But while solarpunk could be dismissed as a mere fad – an overly artistic movement that smacks of naive utopianism and/or something ripe for capitalist appropriation (and I have seen enough of these kind of movements sell or fizzle out over time) – it has all the ingredients to capture the yearning for emancipatory change that is latent within the global multitude (indeed, the first ever anthology of solarpunk literature came from Brazil, from the relative margins of the Global South (Lodi-Ribeiro and Orsi, 2013)). Put bluntly, solarpunk names a social, cultural and ecological movement that is not only befitting *theoretically* of current postcapitalist urban activities that this book is attempting to articulate, but *politically* as well. But before landing on these conceptual frameworks, it's important to outline its aesthetics and how it relates to some of the more psychedelic forms of postcapitalism that this book has detailed so far.

SOLARpunk: Aesthetics

While nascent, the 'look' of solarpunk is rooted in an amalgamation of science fiction, indigeneity, Afrofuturism, ecofuturism and, increasingly, anime (particularly that of Hayao Miyazaki). But its infancy also means it is very fluid, diffuse and difficult to pin down. As it was born online, it has a broad visual culture, which can be loosely categorised into three broad motifs.

The first, and most fundamental, is one of a seamless integration of renewable energy infrastructures into the urban fabric. There are obviously a lot of solar panels, but also wind turbines, hydro and other renewable energy sources that meld into the architecture of buildings and urban infrastructure. The solarpunk aesthetic ultimately celebrates the visibility of sustainable energy solutions, turning them into aesthetically pleasing and integral components of the urban landscape, rather than trying to hide them into existing infrastructure and/or architecture. Second, there is the DIY and upcycling trope familiar to the squatting movement, such as that seen in Slab City (in the previous chapter). They relate to a Jugaad-style design or 'squat tech', which is handcrafted with repurposed items, such as recycled materials used in building structures or sustainable furniture, and contributes to a sense of community engagement and a rejection of mass-produced capitalist consumerism (see Kaur, 2016).

These two motifs are largely present in many other aesthetic genres (and fairly familiar), but where solarpunk differs is in the third; namely, its use of futuristic but humanistic science-fiction technologies. It envisions advanced technology that coexists with a human-centred approach. So, there are advanced gadgets, smart infrastructure and humanoid robotics, but all are designed with a focus on accessibility, sustainability and human wellbeing (contrasting with the impersonal, vast, violent and dehumanising technological scales often depicted in cyberpunk genres that Chongqing exudes). But along with this technological element is often an artistic calmness and a serenity stemming from a softer colour palette, sounds of nature, and a preponderance of green–blue landscapes. Like so many postcapitalist practices (as discussed in relation to Santiago), solarpunk encourages the integration of art and creativity into technology to create functional designs that are artistically vibrant. This may include interactive public art installations, sculptures that also serve as renewable energy sources, or kinetic artworks that respond to environmental conditions.

Beyond these three broad themes, the aesthetics also include more processual idioms such as community-oriented design practices. Public spaces in solarpunk cities are designed for community gatherings, shared resources, and collaborative activities reflecting the post-capitalist commitment to communal living, and the tangible examples of this includes community gardens, co-housing projects, and decentralized power-sharing systems that promote social interactions and mutual-aid networks. Many of the imagined solarpunk cities that can be found online – and some in real life – have a very mixed-use urban-planning feel that emphasises the coexistence and often co-location of residential, commercial and recreational spaces, and crucially promotes walkability (and perhaps treads into that most controversial of topics, the fifteen-minute city (Willberg *et al.*, 2023)). Finally, solarpunk aesthetics seem to envision a gradual transition between urban and rural environments, with cities blending into surrounding natural landscapes. This involves contemporary planning technologies such as ecological corridors and green belts, but generally this is done to deliberately minimise the ecological footprint of urban expansion, and vociferously rejects sprawl and unchecked suburbanisation (Harlock, 2024). So, from an aesthetic and urban-planning perspective, solarpunk imaginaries represent a departure from the bleak and dystopian imagery commonly associated with speculative science fiction, instead offering a vibrant and hopeful vision of a sustainable, community-driven future.

SolarPUNK: Politics

But, of course, we've seen all this before. The Bauhaus movement, and before that Art Nouveau and modernism more broadly; artistic movements that incorporate urbanism have become overly aestheticised to the point of being anesthetised, or they have been drawn into the clutches of capitalist appropriation, losing all their political potency in the process (Pinder, 2002, 2015; Forlano *et al.*, 2019). And perhaps as a harbinger of solarpunk's impending co-option, a tech CEO used the term favourably at SXSW in March 2024, and the (albeit activist, but nevertheless embedded) Hollywood actress Emma Watson posted a solarpunk image and summary of a Ted talk about it on her Instagram account back in 2021. But this is all the more reason why solarpunk emphasises its political and very deliberate postcapitalist ethics: much of the online material is at pains to emphasise its community, degrowth, guerrilla, resistive, rebellious and overtly anti-consumerist tendencies. Steinkopf-Frank (2021) put it bluntly when she wrote 'solarpunk is not about pretty aesthetics. It's about the end of capitalism.' So while not explicitly based in hard-line political activism (I have yet to see solarpunks take to the streets as we saw people do in Part II of this book), it can be said to occupy an activist-political space that seeks to build new worlds with new tools. While not totally congruent, it echoes Lourde's (2018 [1984]: 1) refrain that 'the master's tools will never dismantle the master's house', hence solarpunk can be said to relate to the Black anarcho-feminist tradition which seeks to prefiguratively build new worlds without any semblance of the old.

Perhaps a more fitting theoretical frame would be Guattari's (1989) notion of 'ecosophy', which is a holistic framework that integrates three interconnected ecological registers: the environmental, the social and the mental. For Guattari, radical ecological thinking must go beyond addressing environmental crises in isolation, and instead engage with the broader socio-political structures and individual psychological processes that underpin them. This 'threefold ecology' recognises that the degradation of the planet is intertwined with the systemic social inequalities of capitalism, and the alienation or oppression of the human psyche that this engenders. Ecosophy calls for a fundamental reimagining of subjectivity and collective relationships, promoting a transdisciplinary and ultimately very creative approach to building sustainable futures. Creative in that, rather than prescribing fixed solutions, it emphasises the cultivation of new, experimental ways of living, thinking and organising that challenge hierarchical systems and foster interconnectedness, regenerative relationships with the land, and respect across all dimensions of existence, human and non-human (Guattari, 1989).

Via its focus on sustainability, community and art, solarpunk could be said to align neatly with this ideal. Furthermore, within Guattari's ecosophical ideas, the urban fabric requires reworking not just with officials and technocrats (architects, planners, lawmakers, etc.) but with inhabitants of the present and, in a psychedelic way, the future as well via a regenerative model where a sustainable future is dependent upon the practices of the present (and hence defenestrates the 'wealth pollution' of a capitalist future (Schwartz, 2022)). Indeed, Guattari (1992: 101) wrote 'only in a climate of freedom and emulation can new habitat approaches be experimented, and not through laws and technocratic bulletins'. As such, solarpunk cities characterise several political and ethical positionalities that feed into an ecosophy mantra, in that they envision cities that are *regenerative* rather than extractive. Like an embryonic forest, solarpunk cities ebb and flow with the seasons and climate, they don't exceed their resource limits, and they create an environment that encourages diversity (of flora and fauna), ecological richness, and the sharing of resources. Such a regenerative characteristic of solarpunk cities can be seen with its championing of sustainability, social equity, and radical democracy.

Furthermore, solarpunk's vision for the urban fabric of tomorrow transcends the reductionist confines of pure ecological preservation that is the purview of many capitalist and private urbanist visions of 'sustainability'. Instead, solarpunk embraces a multifaceted approach encompassing not only renewable energy sources but also innovative water-management systems, waste-reduction strategies, green roofs, vertical farms, and the promotion of public transportation and non-motorised modes of commuting (Agee, 2023). In addition, mirroring ecosophical commitments to collaboration, the solarpunk ethos is inextricably linked to a steadfast commitment to social equity. By prioritising, for example, affordable housing solutions and the establishment of vibrant communal spaces, solarpunk actively promotes inclusivity of the urban poor (Wagner, 2023).

Hence, class consciousness is vital. To paraphrase Chico Mendes' famous phrase: ecological politics without class consciousness is just gardening.

Any city that does not have a radical democratic form of engagement for all citizens, but specifically the urban poor and marginalised, is doomed to fail before it can even begin.

Democratically, then, the solarpunk paradigm presents an avant-garde stance on urban governance and infrastructure, advocating for decentralisation in all aspects (hence why conservative economists have been so dismissive of solarpunk, given it has 'socialist' tendencies (Pethokoukis, 2022)). It posits that by decentralising energy production, water management, and governance structures, urban centres become more robust and resilient.[1] The term 'sociocracy' is used in conjunction with solarpunk regularly, which denotes a far more discursive kind of democracy than representative democracies. It is a Mouffian (2005) form of politics by dissensus, one that, as Chapter 7 outlined via squatting (Vasudevan, 2015) and Chapter 8 via Mechelen's 'Never-ending Park' experiment, can be complex, time-consuming and perhaps inefficient; but it entails that *all* voices are heard and acted upon. These features – sustainability, social equity, and radical democracy – together create the vital ingredients for a city that doesn't just grow extractively, but renews regeneratively and hence has ecosophical features shot through.

Solarpunk in global praxis

Existing as an online 'movement' is one thing, but where is the solarpunk practice 'on the ground'? Do these cities actually exist and do they *work* as a postcapitalist visions of alternative urbanism? Arguably, we've tried them in the past. Ebenezer Howard, a visionary urban planner and social reformer, laid the foundation for the Garden City movement in the late nineteenth century in England. He envisioned a novel approach to urban planning, one that harmoniously blended the advantages of both city and countryside living. The Garden City model proposed the creation of self-contained communities surrounded by green belts, with a careful balance between urban and rural elements. These communities were designed to be economically self-sufficient, with a mix of residential, industrial and agricultural spaces. The aim was to provide citizens with access to nature, ample green spaces, and the benefits of modern amenities while avoiding the pitfalls of overcrowded, polluted urban centres. Welwyn Garden City and Letchworth in the UK became the testbeds of this utopia, and remain the only garden cities ever built. Also, the Transition Town movement, with Totnes in Devon being the pinnacle, could be thought of as embodying some aspects of the solarpunk dedication to sustainability (perhaps less so its democratic and class-consciousness ideals, given the town is overtly middle class with, until 2024, a Conservative MP).

Solarpunk is more than just a European phenomenon (although, in fairness, not much more). In the rural outskirts of Nairobi, where maintaining a reliable supply of electricity remains a challenge, local communities have adopted a proactive stance towards solar power. Through the installation of small-scale solar micro-grids, residents have not only achieved self-reliance in power, they've been able to bridge energy access gaps (Bahaj *et al.*, 2019). They've also helped to spur economic development while expanding access to electricity in areas that state-level power-grid infrastructures would have no hope of reaching (Vernet *et al.*, 2019). It is a stretch to call it a solarpunk community, but use of solar power and its successful adaptation provides a sense of tangibility to the Afrofuturist strands of the solarpunk movement online. In most progressive 'movements' attempting to enact environmental justice, too often marginalised and indigenous people and their practices are either left behind, ignored or, worse, deliberately marginalised (Hickcox, 2018; Kline, 2022). Solarpunk is not immune to this, which is why part of the movement is attempting to make sure that as it develops, this isn't the case. Indeed, some creatives and 'clifi' writers 'include indigenous community farming practices in solarpunk. Not just because these communities may have discovered years ago the answers to some of today's ecological problems, but also because solarpunk's narrative/ manifesto … is of a future woven from the experiences of non-dominant peoples' (Cameron, 2019).

Afrofuturist aesthetics therefore are a critical part of the solarpunk movement for similar reasons outlined throughout this book as to why the capitalist city is inherently racist. This is perhaps why the Marvel film *Black Panther* is often heralded as a 'solarpunk, afrofuturist superhero film that helps spark discussions about three aspects of climate literacy: access to natural resources … [and] the interconnectedness of racial justice and climate justice' (Gliddon, 2023). In the film, Wakanda, the hidden African country, is a technologically advanced civilisation that is depicted in complete harmony with the natural environment. The solarpunk aesthetics of the film are readily apparent, and the fact it is part of an Afrofuturist genre renders it an important addition to the solarpunk movement. Before we get carried away, though, it is important to note it is a film produced by the billion-dollar conglomerate Disney, and the film has been critiqued as promoting 'capitalism with a Black face', and a form of 'othering and orientalism' that is inherent to neoliberal discourses of contemporary capitalism (Saunders, 2019).

So, in terms of actually existing solarpunk cities that are not European, perhaps it is worth re-emphasising Auroville as outlined in the previous chapter as a solarpunk settlement, given that its anarchist politics and sustainable architecture certainly align well with the solarpunk imaginary. We can also look to the thirty-three 'Climate-Smart Villages' across five countries in South East Asia which are part of a regional drive to increase the climate resilience of agricultural practice. Their use of AI and smart technologies specifically as a means of scaling up the benefits of indigenous agricultural practices certainly aligns with solarpunk tropes of embracing technology (but again, AI is not without its eco-critics, given it consumes a huge amount of power (Dhar, 2020)).

In terms of my own research, though, despite the relative privilege of my academic position, I was only able to cast my solarpunk research net to northern Europe, and one city that is mentioned frequently in the online material (see Jens, 2023): Almere in the Netherlands, largely because it exhibits a pragmatic realisation of key solarpunk tenets (and it also helps that the city is very new and has a geographical tabula rasa, being as it sits on reclaimed land from Lake Ijsselmeer). Visiting Almere you are greeted with a fairly mundane, newly built, non-descript small urban centre. It is unspectacular in its design and typically Dutch in its plentiful cycle infrastructure. But on the outskirts is the suburb of Oosterwold, which is a site of radically innovative urban planning and community-driven, self-build development. It was conceived by the architectural firm MVRDV as a large-scale experiment in self-sufficiency and community governance, and was officially launched in 2013 as part of Almere's broader vision to

9.1 Oosterweld, Almere (Author's photograph, May 2024)

accommodate a growing population while promoting sustainable practices (see Figure 9.1).

Central to Oosterwold is the ethos of self-build, where residents are the primary agents of development. Unlike traditional residential developments where homes are constructed by (mostly) corporate developers, Oosterwold asks residents to design and build their own homes in conjunction with architects if needed. The self-build paradigm fosters a sense of ownership and personal investment in the community (Lloyd *et al.*, 2015), and each plot of land sold in Oosterwold (by the local government at very low prices) comes with the condition that the buyer must develop it in line with certain sustainability guidelines, which include providing for green space and water management, that at least 50 per cent of each plot must be dedicated to green-space agriculture, and promoting self-sufficiency and environmental stewardship (Knikker, 2021). And the area certainly has a strong DIY aesthetic as well as community cohesion. Residents I spoke to were at pains to emphasise that they collaborate on shared projects and infrastructure, such as communal gardens, renewable energy sources, and waste-management systems (using

9.2 Aardehuizen on the right, Olst on the left (Author's photograph, May 2024)

smart and AI technologies). This collective approach not only enhances the sense of community but also ensures that sustainability is a shared responsibility. While some spoke of the rising costs of living, and some of the newer inhabitants found that the cost of the land was nearing that of the nearby city centre, the self-build and up-front sustainability goals means that it, aesthetically at least, has a distinct solarpunk ethos.

But perhaps one of the *most* solarpunk places I was able to visit in the research for this book lies a few miles to the east of Almere. The small community of Aardehuizen is a bounded site of only seventy or so people but is explicitly solarpunk in the way the architecture is designed, the energy is produced, and the community in governed. Driving towards it you have to go through the usual Dutch-style low-rise housing, but as you approach, the ditches at the side of road separate the asphalt from various walls of wooden crates, hand-smoothed plaster, and what look like old car tyres filled with straw, all covered in an array of different creeping vines and greenery (Figure 9.2).

9.3 Aardehuizen (Author's photograph, May 2024)

I park up and walk around it, wondering where the 'gate' is and checking my phone for a reply from the contact who said they'd meet me. Nothing yet. I find the entrance, past a large wooden garage structure with what look like upcycled CDs repurposed as solar panels. I wander around the 'buildings' on small paths, past structures that look like something out of the Shire from *The Lord of the Rings*, some with geodesic domes on top (see Figure 9.3). I pass chickens, dogs, a goat and rows of vegetables and apple trees before I get to dwelling number 17, where the contact I'm due to meet lives. I knock on the door; still nothing. So, I amble around seeing some children playing on a trampoline, before I'm greeted by a smiling older woman who offers me a pear. Soon, a man on a bike arrives and, despite not knowing who I was (and my bumbling attempts to explain I did have an invite from a resident but they weren't around), he welcomes me into the house (the older woman was his mother-in-law) and offers me a coffee, going through the history of Aardehuizen in detail, his role in it, and the architecture of his 'house'.

The settlement was dreamt up as part of the 'Earthship movement' – a sustainable architecture genre formulated by the US architect Michael E. Reynolds (Harkness, 2011) – which has mushroomed to include technological innovations, but also politically to be a truly 'sociocratic' society. The man who took me into his home and the other residents who joined us later for a beer (although not my contact, who it transpired got her dates confused) were keen to emphasise sociocracy as the politics of Aardehuizen because it is a more radical form of democracy (indeed they didn't like the term 'democracy' because of its European etymology, emanating as it does from ancient Greece). In essence, a sociocracy is a horizontalised governance system that aims to create productive and harmonious organisations by ensuring that all members have a voice in decision-making processes; there is no voting, only discussions until a consensus is reached. A quick search online will show you that the solarpunk movement has sociocracy very much at its heart. Furthermore, the residents work hard to create a sustainable community: all new residents have to help build their home; they recycle all they can (including human waste), but, unlike other eco-squats, they don't actively shun technological advancements, such as heat pumps and AI software to optimise energy usage (indeed they embrace their ability to increase the sustainability of the community), and to date they have produced 90 per cent of the energy they use. The site is now 'full', and the surrounding empty fields have been or were being built on, although the residents pointed out that while the developments were officially part of the local government's housing provision for asylum seekers and low-income residents, they were so enamoured by Aardehuizen that the architecture of these developments is aiming to mirror the 'Earthship' style. I was there for only a few hours, so I was unable to really get a sense of how close to the sociocratic politics the community functioned, but I did get a sense of the comradery that permeated the group, and to my surprise, an overwhelming sense of hope amid the dread of a suffocating planet. And so aesthetically, politically and indeed emotionally, Aardehuizen is as solarpunk as it got for me.

All these examples I've given, they are obviously real world and so none of them live up to the utopian vision that the solarpunk movement – with all its aesthetic, artistic, political, economic, social, ecological and technological optimism – has in mind. Indeed, the more you seek out examples (both online and in the 'real' world), the more holes you find, the more sheen and spin you have to fight through, and the more these supposed solarpunk communities and cities are either just ecovillages that are doomed to fail and become subject to the same urban pressures as everywhere else, imaginaries of global corporations, or private investments looking to greenwash their capital. They are *places* after all, and so susceptible to the same political pressures, gentrification and lack of resources in the capitalist city that this book has detailed; solarpunk cities (as they exist in real life) are inherently anti-capitalist and so will butt up against capitalist realism eventually. And to one of my more critical colleagues, this is all very reminiscent of that most pernicious of anarcho-capitalistic, tech-bro populated, self-congratulatory hellscapes – the Burning Man Festival. And in all honesty, I can see *exactly* where he is coming from. Essentially, pessimism *can* win. But perhaps that is the point; maybe that's what at stake.

Mies van der Rohe (1924) famously argued that 'architecture is the will of an epoch, translated into space', and for all the brilliant visions of a postcapitalist future that the final part of this book has outlined, perhaps that is what is lacking – an architectural urban *vision*, a cohesive aesthetics that we can aspire to, a political will to latch on to and an ideology to aspire to. Solarpunk has a great deal of *potential* in this regard (so long as it continues to be critical of its Eurocentrism). For all the capitalist appropriation, for all the spin, it does seem that there are real kernels of urban radicality, perhaps of revolutionary thought.

Solarpunk's anti-capitalism and resistance is inherent in its architecture, infrastructure and politics, but it is also more than a patronising view of the world (i.e. not another kind of favela chic (Cummings, 2016)). It is characterised by what it wants to avoid as much as what it wants to be: after all, naming the enemy is an important step in avoiding them. But, in being relentlessly *hopeful* (which, as I mentioned in opening this chapter, is an uncomfortable position for most academics, as we all too often prefer cynicism and critique), it is in effect naming that opposite. In being unapologetically optimistic, solarpunk shows dystopian capitalist futures to be what they inherently are: a failure of the imagination. And that is the critical factor: to create cities fit for the future, a hopeful collective vision over pessimism is required.

I am tempted to end by quoting Gramsci (2017 [1927] 40), when he wrote, 'I'm a pessimist because of intelligence, but an optimist because of will.' But perhaps (because it comes from a form of speculative fiction that is better known than solarpunk but no less optimistic), a more fitting summation can be found in the words of Jyn Erso from the Star Wars film *Rogue One*, when she says, 'Rebellions are built on hope.'

Conclusion
Yeni Istanbul, 2075

Xiwang was nervous. In her two and half decades on the planet so far, she had never exhibited any leadership qualities. In fact, she actively looked to shy away from them. She took direction well but felt grossly uncomfortable in giving it out. She much preferred being a background kind of person. But sadly today, she no longer had that option. In just a few hours, she would be inaugurated as the chairperson of the Yeni Istanbul City Assembly (YICA), effectively making her the mayor of the city (in old speak). As much as she had studied the copious amounts of written material that came with the posting, which insisted the chairperson was only an administrative role (and was only able to use a power of veto if policy consensus couldn't be finalised), she still came out in a cold sweat thinking about having to *actually* do it. Despite her predecessor, Amir, having shown her exactly how mundane, officious, collective and downright boring the position was in the three months of shadowing, Xiwang was overly anxious about having to make any form of decision on the behalf of others. Of course, in the span of the nearly thirty-five years of Yeni Istanbul's transition to management by sortition, no chair of YICA had even come close to having to make an executive decision on any policy, but that didn't comfort her at all. 'Why her?' was always playing in the back of her mind. Why was she the unlucky one that had her name pulled out of a hat? Of the millions of qualified citizens that were available for (or 'at risk of', as she preferred to put it) being part of YICA, her name came up. It was of course blind luck. Sortition is a well-versed ancient practice, and the transparency of the process means that there is no way (that she could think of at least) there'd be an inherent bias, but she had always been superstitious. Her discomfort wasn't just down to the fact that her name was selected as chair, it was because she knew that this term was going to be a difficult one politically. Largely because of the months of anti-trans violence in the Tarlabaşı district that would need to be dealt with if it continued to spiral out of control.

Despite years of tireless community outreach work in both religious and queer groups, and the Anatolian Confederation's banning of Neuralink's Gender Affirming Implant device back in 2068, the trans community were still under attack by Muskian religious zealots who clung to the old ways. The murder of three transgender sex workers last year over consecutive nights saw weeks of protests and looting. While the perpetrators had been sent to the healing lodges on the foothills of Mount Ararat, having been sentenced (not uncontroversially, it has to be said) by the Citizens Congress of Justice, there was a latent atmosphere of unease, conflict and tension that any single mis-timed spark could turn into yet another conflagration of anti-trans sentiment.

Xiwang, though, was always planning (or as her legal guardian would say, plotting); that was just a feature of her neuronal-mapped autism-B3. She was luckily born in 2050, a couple of years after the Hologram healthcare network was rolled out right across Byzantia, and as such she received all the support for her neurodiversity she needed, given that previously her guardians would have no way been able to afford it. So, while she was not a leader, it didn't mean she didn't have a plan.

She was not from Tarlabaşı, but she knew the area well enough through her previous role as a mutual-aid facilitator for the queer youth of the city. During her time in that role, it became clear that the integration of queer children into their more traditional and religious communities was facilitated by a cooperative housing model, supported by the community-owned trusts of YICA's land registry. There is a simple truth that living together in proximity as a collective community aids massively in breaking down cultural differences and social barriers, and had worked time and time again as a successful tool in YICA's flagship social policy of community conflict resolution. It wasn't just the housing though, it was the auxiliary practices of community urban farming (both traditional and with the help of public robotics technology), sustainable energy implementation, and place management. It was fortunate that most of the land in Kadıköy where she was focused was still underdeveloped since the 'Great Quake' in 2041, and so housing was relatively straight-forward to secure.

Ah, the Great Quake. In retrospect, it was rather poetic that it was a natural disaster that would be the event to usher in a political revolution, but it really didn't feel very poetic at the time. Largely because in the immediate aftermath of the largest earthquake ever recorded (not just on the North Anatolian fault line, but anywhere in the world), the response by the ageing Emperor Erdoğan was violent, disastrous, disgusting and, as we know now, formed the legal foundation to dissolve his empire. Of course, the legal work came after the bloodshed on the streets. The radical group 'The Students of Dev-Yol' mobilised far quicker than the lumbering state to provide mutual aid and disaster response, but then of course they did have a great deal of expertise to draw on, given that half the world was responding to the regular extreme weather events (the classic text *The Occupy Sandy Handbook of Mutual Aid* was vital in this regard). Istanbul University's campus was one of the few places in the city not to be flattened by the gigantic earthquake, and the students set it up quickly as a meta-lifehouse, aided (eventually) by the resources of the trade union DİSK and leftist Sol political party. Other lifehouses had sprung up around the city, and it soon became clear to Erdoğan that he was being completely embarrassed by the effective mobilisation of these students, trade unions and community groups, and so the violent rebuttal was swift. But of course, you all know the history after that: the massacre of Vezneciler, and the story of Adilly Özdemird whose selfless act ensured the revolutionary forces were victorious, and that Yeni Istanbul could be born. Their name will be forever told in children's story books and cartoons, and will eternally adorn T-shirts, mugs and postcards.

But the redevelopment of Yeni Istanbul has been painfully slow, funereal, glacial. The political wrangling after the fall of Erdoğan took a long time to settle, largely because the old guard demanded a voice at the governmental table while their trials were taking place. The leaders of the student group, trade unions and Sol Parti were quick to identify themselves as a 'transition government' of (then) Türkiye, and of course were understandably unwilling to let anyone potentially responsible for the massacre of Vezneciler to be anywhere near government, even if they used the old excuse that they were 'just following orders'. But the predatory international developers, who saw the flattened city of Istanbul as a massive rent gap that could create billions of crypto, still had some sway at the old 'national' level. Hence, after many in the upper echelons of the Turkish Empire were charged with murder, conspiracy and other serious crimes, there was very little of the old guard left. So, the radical action was taken of politically dissolving Türkiye into its more culturally variegated regions – called the Federation of Byzantia – each with an administrative city (helped enormously by the ancient communes of Rojava to the south). This ensured that, each city had to look to its citizens to form a government, and many of them used a random process of sortition simply because they didn't know what else to do. Yeni Istanbul, as it became known, was the first to form such a government, and the first iteration of YICA was born.

Sorry for the detour. Back to Tarlabaşı and the anti-trans violence that Xiwang knew YICA would have to tackle. There wasn't really the availability of land for a cooperative housing model that had worked so effectively in Kadıköy, so she would need to either try to retrofit the existing housing provision towards a cooperative model or find another way of ensuring conflict resolution networks. The other ace up her sleeve was artistic performance in the form of 'festivals of forgiveness'. She remembers going to them as a child. They seemed very strange at the time, with members of the Muslim communities performing elaborate and creative dances as a form of (what I would later find out to be) contrition for their role in oppressing minority Christians when we were all part of Türkiye. For a couple of weeks in the spring, the streets would be closed off to bicycle traffic, and people were encouraged to use the space to express their emotions through art and dance (and often synth-psilocybin). There were artists at hand to help, with materials both analogue (such as paint brushes, spray cans and easels) and technological (drone projectors, lab-grown bodily appendages and immersive robo-architecture) available to use. Community kitchens were set up where food from different regions was served, and there were also some educational classes for the kids. Her guardians were keen musicians and very proficient in the mechalute, and used to compose what were, to Xiwang, beautiful noises that were calming, almost meditative. She remembers these festivals fondly now as they enabled people to open up and learn, and while some were weirded out at times, they helped in a communal understanding of the nuances and specificities of the lives of their neighbours. Despite the violence of the religious zealots of Tarlabaşı, Xiwang knew that it was a vocal minority who were being radicalised (and probably heavily funded) by the Muskian fascist ideology emanating all the way from the Republic of Gilead, which couldn't tolerate any form of social identity that aligned with difference over tradition, whatever hemisphere they lived in.

So, armed with little more than some good ideas, she set off for her first meeting of YICA. As she stepped out of her ecosquat, Xiwang's footsteps echoed on the cobblestone streets, now reclaimed by pedestrians and flanked by buildings where vertical gardens, interwoven with solar microcells like threads of handcrafted silver, cascaded down their facades like waterfalls. The development of New Istanbul post-41, as we've heard, was slow, but that was only because they wanted to get it right. The lack of the quick buck of international real-estate finance meant that they could build the new city with sustainability and commonality as their driving forces. Hence much of the old 'rubble' from the Great Quake was repurposed, and the rebuilding programme was split into neighbourhood divisions. Each division was free to build up as they wished, so long as sustainability goals set by the local Community Commissions were met. As such, green walls, DIY wind turbines and solar panels, windcatcher towers, and where needed reflective media doors littered the streetscapes of Yeni Istanbul. As Xiwang continued her walk to the metro station, the air was fresh, purified by the city's vast green lungs on the outskirts, and the sillage of the early morning bakeries' produce clung to the heat of the day.

After a short ride on the metro, she alighted at Adilly Özdemird Square, the location of the YICA meeting rooms: a fairly non-descript combination of 'Earthship Movement'-style buildings (basically, disused tyres stuffed with straw), a large flat disc made deliberately from the rubble of the old CBRT Tower from the financial district, and a geodesic dome at the centre that was covered in translucent solar cells and a thick blanket of Cappadocian navelwort. She entered the dome and was greeted by a smiling Amir who gave her a giant bearhug. He pulled down his mask to proclaim, 'Today is the day

Xiwang!' while grabbing her shoulders. 'Have you your inaugural speech ready?'

'I do,' she replied. 'I'm going to go with something a bit different if that's ok?'

'As long as you're not coming out as a Muskian capitalist, you can do what you please!' he chuckled as he ushered her towards the interior of the dome. The glass ceiling housed the lush gardens and open-air forums where the people were already gathered, no doubt deliberating under the morning sun's nurturing gaze.

As they settled into the humming atmosphere of the assembly, Xiwang's heart began to swell with a rather odd sensation. Perhaps it was pride? Responsibility? Either way she felt like she could get used to it. 'What did you say in your inauguration speech Amir?' she asked.

'Did you not see it on socials?' he quipped.

'Er, no, sorry.'

'Not much. I simply reaffirmed the ideals of YICA's slogan, "Collaborating in action, living in unity". Or something like that – I'm not a details person!' He stared off towards the ceiling and wafted his arms in a theatrical gesture. 'But I do recall emphasising that Yeni Istanbul's strength lies in our diversity and our willingness to give us all the space to listen to each other. To heal the wounds of the past, we have to weave a rich tapestry of conflicting voices into our decisions, ensuring every thread is valued, seen and noted.' He turned to her and gave a wry smile.

'I like that,' said Xiwang, flipping through her notes. 'But I found this old prose from the '20s, just before the ecological collapse, which I think works. It's an old anti-capitalist poem, I think.'

'The '20s? I remember them, I was young and carefree, but they were hard times.' Amir paused as if to recollect. 'In fact, they were bleak. People hoarded billions of cryp—, sorry, dollars, and government used to let them.'

Xiwang stopped in her tracks and looked confused. 'Really? That's crazy.'

'Yep. And they used that money to buy entire cities pretty much, and made them inaccessible to everyone other than their rich friends.'

Xiwang scoffed. 'Oh, I did hear about *that*. I remember my uncle talking about how much rent he had to pay in Old Istanbul.'

Amir continued. 'Get this, though. We also had to actually pay for food, and if I remember correctly, they used to ship it around the world on old dirty fuel ships only to put a third of it in landfill.'

'Land … fill?'

'Basically bury it in the ground.' Xiwang's eyes widened in amazement, her lips stretched outwards in disgust.

'I'd heard capitalism was stupid, but that's just insane,' she exclaimed.

'Yes it was. So I'm looking forward to this poem!' Amir smiled.

He led her to the main meeting hall, entering through double doors towards the side of a large wooden stage in front of an auditorium of near a thousand seats. Already some of them were filled with eager members of the press, and there were camera drones already in place. She took her place on the seat marked 'Chairperson' and sipped the glass of water that had been left for her, as there had been for all the other new members of YICA that would be joining her on stage.

After only a few more minutes there was standing room only. Five other people joined her on stage, each looking equally as nervous and sheepish as Xiwang. Amir was busy laughing with someone to the right of the stage, but after a man in a sharp suit whispered something in his ear, he hopped onto the stage and stood behind the glass lectern to a ripple of applause. He thanked the gathered press, YICA members, citizens and foreign auditors for making the time for attend Xiwang's inauguration, joking that while his own was only five years ago he felt he had aged a lot more. After a few more bad dad jokes that got little more than polite laughter, he introduced Xiwang. To rapturous applause, she stood up and shuffled to the lectern, gripping her notes.

She waited for the applause to die down, cleared her throat, and began her address:

'What is a city? Is it a collection of people? A form of bustling urban sociality and joviality? Or is it a site of economic practices that has miraculously sprung from the hard work of powerful capitalists? Or perhaps an arena of activists who struggle, a place of dissent, or a battle between those who have and those who haven't?

'Eridu, the first city in Mesopotamia, just south of here, in modern-day Iraq, and yes, now it's a ruin, a place of sand and dust, and a salty land which proved to be its undoing – but its cityness is still with us, enrichens us even today with its prestigious history of the first time that we came together to grow something much more beautiful than we could do alone.

'So New York, London, Tokyo and Katmandu share the same essence of cityness as Eridu: a fabric of people, things and the environment around them, woven into a life more complex that intersects with others to astound them. To provide more than what they need, to fulfil desires they never thought they'd see, to create ways of living that don't just exist, they exceed.

'And the urbanity that we analyse today; some say it's planetary, others say it's scary, most will say necessary, while the utopian dreamers will say it's visionary.

'One thing for sure is that change is a constant: the shifting sands of the concrete of the street beneath our feet can sometimes make us feel despondent, yearning for a stability in city-living that is nothing but an illusion, thrusting upon the urban citizen a vulnerability and permeability that negates any kind of durability.

'We see this change all around us, happening at breakneck speed; it's boundless. In recent times, this change has been relentless, with even the perceived strength and immutability of modernist tower blocks unable to prevent it. From the flats of Red Road in Glasgow, to, on the other side of the pond, the brownstones of Pruitt–Igoe: the utopian dream of a civic and idyllic life replaced with the shimmering and carbon-belching glass towers of capital, because, of course, they're far more palatable.

'The slums of Manila and the barrios of Mexico City, incandescent in their luminosity, growing and groaning without any official zoning, they are home to a vast, unknown number of new urban inhabitants that – according to the UN – make this world an urban habitat. From the luxurious heights of billion-dollar condominiums to the depths of the earth populated by worker drones and minions, cities spread up and down, east and west, can be sleepy market towns or bustling metropolises.

'The city is a place to rest, a base of capitalist practice, a space of cultural consumption, all with more than a trace of social dysfunction. A place where the powerless can become powerful, where the marginal – sometimes successfully – can amass an arsenal to attack those who try to disempower them.

'It's a collection of people and things all vying for a slice of vitality, more than a simple mix of mortar and bricks, it's a combustible tinderbox of ideological plurality.

'So, what is a city? I'm sorry but that's unanswerable because a city is uncapturable by any words we have at our disposal. We can only immerse ourselves in the glorious inconsistency of its existentiality. So, to understand what a city is, I can't tell you – get out there, and experience what is really is.'

Notes

Introduction: What's your perfect city?

1 See, among many, many others, the debate I had with Scott and Storper (2015) (Mould, 2016), as well as Lees *et al.* (2016) and Roy and Robinson (2016).
2 If that isn't convincing you, let's go with the fact that it made for a more interesting and ultimately survivable writing experience ...

3 Histories of resistance

1 This is sourced from the Bureau of Public Secrets, an archive created for the lesser-known documents, pamphlets, communiqués and leaflets of the Situationist International and the broader revolutionary movement of May 1968.

4 Situationism redux and the psychedelia of postcapitalism

1 Prefiguration is an important facet of anarchist thought, and is articulated in the next part of the book.
2 This will all sound very familiar to anyone who has been paying attention to how contemporary governments have been suppressing protestors in the UK, with new anti-protest laws designed specifically to curtail civil disobedience by climate and pro-Palestine activists.

6 From the care economy to the caring commons

1 Barcelona is also a city with a strong municipalist government (Bianchi, 2023) and has become somewhat of a model for progressive urbanism

in Europe, with Naples, Madrid, Grenoble and Zagreb all electing municipalist governments in the last few years (Thomson, 2021).

7 Urban commoning

1 This is a classic tactic of resistance used in many parts of the UK (and no doubt around the world). For example, in my dealings with the Long Live Southbank campaign that aimed to save the iconic concrete skate spot in the heart of London from demolition in 2014, the group applied to have the site deemed 'Village Green Status'. Clearly, the application was rejected, but it bought precious time to raise funds (Mould, 2015).

8 Prefigurative postcapitalist cities

1 It is worth noting, however, that Chongqing is a province that is also called a city. The only other 'city-provinces' in China are Beijing, Shanghai and Tianjin. So, many of the 30 million people of Chongqing live in quasi-rural areas but are governed by the Chongqing municipality.
2 Much of the information about the projects, the criteria for selection, and the results of the exhibition can be found here: https://www.degrondderdingen.be/ and https://www.vai.be/nieuws/the-neverending-park

9 Harvesting hope: Exploring solarpunk cities

1 I use the term 'resilient' here with caution, and note that it has been mobilised in neoliberal policy circles as a means to buttress the urban capitalist status quo (see Slater, 2021). A perhaps more progressive view of resilience can be found with MacKinnon and Derickson (2013), which critiques the neoliberalism inherent in the term and proffers 'resourceful-ness' instead.

Bibliography

Abu-Lughod, J. (2007) *Race, Space, and Riots in Chicago, New York, and Los Angeles*. Oxford: Oxford University Press.

Acuto, M. (2022) *How to Build a Global City*. New York: Cornell University Press.

Agee, S. (2023) 'A future dream: How solarpunk helped alleviate my existential dread', *Earth Island Journal*, https://www.earthisland.org/journal/index.php/magazine/entry/solarpunk-imagines-future-renewable-tech-socio-ecological-enlightenment (accessed 1 August 2024)

Akala (2018) *Natives: Race and Class in the Ruins of Empire*. London: Two Roads.

Alcarón, D. (2020) 'Chile at the barricades', *New Yorker*, https://www.newyorker.com/magazine/2020/10/12/chile-at-the-barricades (accessed 1 August 2024).

The Alternative (2022) 'A Lancashire village self-regenerating – via community centre, library, shop, pub – is good to see. But not every place has enough capital, human or financial, to succeed', *The Alternative*, https://www.thealternative.org.uk/dailyalternative/2022/1/9/village-self-determination-trawden-capital (accessed 1 August 2024).

American Civil Liberties Union (ACLU) (2020) 'A tale of two countries: Racially targeted arrests in the era of marijuana reform details millions of racially targeted marijuana arrests made between 2010–2018, https://www.aclu.org/press-releases/new-aclu-report-despite-marijuana-legalization-black-people-still-almost-four-times (accessed 1 August 2024).

Anderson, M. (2020) 'Racist housing practices from the 1930s linked to hotter neighborhoods today, *NPR*, https://www.npr.org/2020/01/14/795961381/racist-housing-practices-from-the-1930s-linked-to-hotter-neighborhoods-today (accessed 1 August 2024).

Andron, S. (2023) *Urban Surfaces, Graffiti, and the Right to the City*. London: Taylor & Francis.

Andrusz, G. (2019) *The Co-operative Alternative in Europe: The Case of Housing*. Abingdon: Routledge.

Anguiano, D. (2022) 'US prison workers produce $11bn worth of goods and services a year for pittance', *Guardian*, https://www.theguardian.com/us-news/2022/jun/15/us-prison-workers-low-wages-exploited (accessed 1 August 2024).

Apps, P. (2020) 'Designers and contractors knew Grenfell cladding system would fail in a fire, inquiry hears', *Inside Housing*, https://www.insidehousing.co.uk/news/designers-and-contractors-knew-grenfell-cladding-system-would-fail-in-a-fire-inquiry-hears-64866 (accessed 1 August 2024).

Architecture Workroom Brussels (2024) 'Garden of food', https://www.architectureworkroom.eu/en/projects/5227/tuin-van-eten-garden-of-food (accessed 1 August 2024).

Arteaga-Cruz, E., and Cuvi, J. (2021) 'Thinking outside the modern capitalist logic: Health-care systems based in other world views', *Lancet Global Health*, 9(10): 1355–6.

Atkins, J. (2018) '"Strangers in their own country": Epideictic rhetoric and communal definition in Enoch Powell's "Rivers of Blood" speech', *Political Quarterly*, 89(3): 362–9.

Atkinson, R. (2021) *Alpha city: How London was captured by the super-rich*. London: Verso.

Badiou, A. (2007 [1988]) *Being and Event*. New York: Continuum.

Badiou, A. (2012) *The Rebirth of History: Times of Riots and Uprisings*. London: Verso.

Bahaj, A., Blunden, L., Kanani, C., James, P., Kiva, I., Matthews, Z., Price, H., Essendi, H., Falkingham, J. and George, G. (2019) 'The impact of an electrical mini-grid on the development of a rural community in Kenya', *Energies*, 12(5), 778–9.

Basile, P., and Fidalgo, T. (2022) 'Community Land Trusts in contexts of informality: Process, politics, and challenges of implementation', *Radical Housing Journal*, vol. 4(1): 51–70.

Beck, B. (2020) 'Policing gentrification: Stops and low-level arrests during demographic change and real estate reinvestment', *City & Community*, 19(1): 245–72.

Becker, H., and Seddon, D. (2018) 'Africa's 1968: Protests and uprisings across the continent', *Review of African Political Economy*, https://roape.net/2018/05/31/africas-1968-protests-and-uprisings-across-the-continent/ (accessed 1 August 2024).

Beckert, S., and Rockman, S. (eds) (2016) *Slavery's Capitalism: A New History of American Economic Development*. University Park, PA: Penn State University Press.

Beebeejaun, Y. (2022) 'Race, gender, and positionality in urban planning research', *International Journal of Qualitative Methods*, 21: 1–10.

Beissinger, M. (2022) *The Revolutionary City: Urbanization and the Global Transformation of Rebellion*. New Jersey, NJ: Princeton University Press.

Bell, S. L., Foley, R., Houghton, F., Maddrell, A., and Williams, A. M. (2018) 'From therapeutic landscapes to healthy spaces, places and practices: A scoping review', *Social Science & Medicine*, 196: 123–30.

Berglund, O., and Schmidt, D. (2020) *Extinction Rebellion and Climate Change Activism: Breaking the Law to Change the World*. London: Springer Nature.

Bethea, C. (2022) 'The new fight over an old forest in Atlanta', *New Yorker*, https://www.newyorker.com/news/letter-from-the-south/the-new-fight-over-an-old-forest-in-atlanta (accessed 1 August 2024).

Bhatia, M., and Burnett, J. (2022) 'Immigration raids and racist state violence', *State Crime Journal*, 11(1): 33–51.

Bhattacharyya, G. (2018) *Rethinking Racial Capitalism: Questions of Reproduction and Survival*. Lanham, MD: Rowman & Littlefield.

Bianchi, I. (2023) 'The commonification of the public under new municipalism: Commons–state institutions in Naples and Barcelona', *Urban Studies*, 60(11): 2116–32.

Birchall, J. (1988) *Building Communities: The Co-operative Way*. Abingdon: Routledge.

Blakeley, G. (2024) *Vulture Capitalism: Corporate Crimes, Backdoor Bailouts, and the Death of Freedom*. New York: Simon and Schuster.

Boggs, C. (1977) 'Marxism, prefigurative communism, and the problem of workers' control', *Radical America*, 6: 99–122.

Bolstanki, L., and Chiapello, E. (2005) *The New Spirit of Capitalism*. London: Verso.

Booth, R. (2022) '"Every death was avoidable": Grenfell Tower inquiry closes after 400 days', *Guardian*, https://www.theguardian.com/uk-news/2022/nov/10/every-death-was-avoidable-grenfell-tower-inquiry-closes-after-400-days (accessed 1 August 2024).

Bourg, J. (2017) *From Revolution to Ethics: May 1968 and Contemporary French Thought*. Kingston, ON: McGill-Queen's University Press.

Boy, J., and Uitermark, J. (2017) 'Reassembling the city through Instagram', *Transactions of the Institute of British Geographers*, 42(4): 612–24.

Braidotti, R. (2008) 'The politics of radical immanence: May 1968 as an event', *New Formations*, 65: 19–33.

Bramwell, R. (2015) *UK Hip-hop, Grime and the City: The Aesthetics and Ethics of London's Rap Scenes*. Abingdon: Routledge.

Brenner, N., and Schmid, C. (2011) 'Planetary urbanization', in Gandy, M. (ed.) *Urban Constellations* (pp. 10–14). Berlin: Jovis Verlag.

Brenner, N., Madden, D. J., and Wachsmuth, D. (2012) 'Assemblages, actor-networks, and the challenges of critical urban theory', in Brenner, N., Marcuse, P., and Mayer, M. (eds) *Cities for People, Not for Profit* (pp 117–37). Abingdon: Routledge.

Bresnihan, P., and Byrne, M. (2015) 'Escape into the city: Everyday practices of commoning and the production of urban space in Dublin', *Antipode*, 47(1): 36–54.

Brooks, L. (2021) '"A special day": how a Glasgow community halted immigration raid', *Guardian*, https://www.theguardian.com/uk-news/2021/may/14/a-special-day-how-a-glasgow-community-halted-immigration-raid (accessed 24 July 2025).

Brown, M., and Jones, R. (2021) *Paint Your Town Red: How Preston Took Back Control and Your Town Can Too*. London: Repeater.

Brown, T. (2013) *West Germany and the Global Sixties: The Anti-authoritarian Revolt, 1962–1978*. Cambridge: Cambridge University Press.

Bruhn, K. (1997) *Taking on Goliath: The Emergence of a New Left Party and the Struggle for Democracy in Mexico*. University Park, PA: Penn State University Press.

Butler, J. (2015) *Notes Toward a Performative Theory of Assembly*. Boston, MA: Harvard University Press.

Cameron, R. (2019) 'In search of Afro-solarpunk, part 2: Social justice is survival technology', *Reactor Magazine*, https://reactormag.com/in-search-of-afro-solarpunk-part-2-social-justice-is-survival-technology/ (accessed 1 August 2024).

Candón-Mena, J., Domínguez, P., and MacFarlane, T. (2020) 'Self-build housing schemes in Marinaleda from the perspective of Ostrom's concept of self-governance in common-pool resource situations', *An International Journal for Critical Geographies*, 19(3): 684–706.

Care Collective. (2020) *The Care Manifesto: The Politics of Interdependence*. London: Verso.

Carod-Artal, F. (2015) 'Hallucinogenic drugs in pre-Columbian Mesoamerican cultures', *Neurología* (English edition), 30(1): 42–9.

Checker, M. (2011). 'Wiped out by the "greenwave": Environmental gentrification and the paradoxical politics of urban sustainability', *City & Society*, 23(2): 210–29.

Cheng, J. (2015). 'Introduction' in Cheng, J. (ed.) *The Use of Mao and the Chongqing Model*. Hong Kong: City University of Hong Kong Press.

Chenoweth, E. (2021) *Civil Resistance: What Everyone Needs to Know*. Oxford: Oxford University Press.

Christafore, D., and Leguizamon, S. (2018) 'Is "gaytrification" a real phenomenon?', *Urban Affairs Review*, 54(5): 994–1016.

Christophers, B. (2022) 'Mind the rent gap: Blackstone, housing investment and the reordering of urban rent surfaces', *Urban Studies*, 59(4): 698–716.

Christophers, B. (2023) *Our Lives in Their Portfolios: Why Asset Managers Own the World*. London: Verso.

Christophers, B., and Fine, B. (2020) 'The value of financialization and the financialization of value', in Christophers, B. & Fine, B. (eds) *The Routledge International Handbook of Financialization* (pp. 19–30). Abingdon: Routledge.

Clarence-Smith, S. (2023) *Prefiguring Utopia: The Auroville Experiment*. Bristol: Bristol University Press.

Coase, R., and Wang, N. (2016) *How China Became Capitalist*. New York: Springer.

Cobos, C. (2021) 'Disrupting normalcy: Artistic interventions and political mobilisation against the neoliberal city (Santiago, Chile, 2019)', *Social Identities*, 27(5): 538–54.

Coe, N., and Yeung, W.-C. (2015) *Global Production Networks: Theorizing Economic Development in an Interconnected World*. Oxford: Oxford University Press.

Coleman, A. (1985) *Utopia on Trial: Vision and Reality in Planned Housing*. London: Hilary Shipman Press.

Coleman, R. (2015) *Transforming Images: Screens, Affect, Futures*. Abingdon: Routledge.

Connolly, W. (2019) *Climate Machines, Fascist Drives, and Truth*. Durham, NC: Duke University Press.

Conroy, W. (2019) 'The (Im)mobilities of mutual aid: Occupy Sandy, racial liberalism, and the making of insurgent infrastructures', *ACME: An International Journal for Critical Geographies*, 18(4): 875–91.

Correia, D., and Wall, T. (2021) *Violent Order: Essays on the Nature of Police*. Chicago, IL: Haymarket Books.

Cronin, A. (2008) 'Calculative spaces: Cities, market relations, and the commercial vitalism of the outdoor advertising industry', *Environment and Planning A: Economy and Space*, 40(11): 2734–50.

Cross, G. (2015) *Consumed Nostalgia: Memory in the Age of Fast Capitalism*. New York: Columbia University Press.

Crossa, V. (2012) 'Relational positionality: Conceptualizing research, power, and the everyday politics of neoliberalization in Mexico City', *ACME: An International Journal for Critical Geographies*, 11(1): 110–32.

Cumi, K., Washington, A., and Daneshzadeh, A. (2017) 'Standing in solidarity with Black girls to dismantle the school-to-prison pipeline', *The Power of Resistance*, 12: 221–4.

Cummings, J. (2016) 'Confronting favela chic: The gentrification of informal settlements in Rio de Janeiro, Brazil', in Lees, L., Bang Shin, H., and

Lòpez-Morales, E. (eds) *Global Gentrifications* (pp. 81–100). Bristol: Bristol University Press.

Dagdeviren, H. (2024) 'Austerity urbanism, local government debt-drive, and post-COVID predicaments in Britain', *Journal of Economic Geography*, 24(1): 79–94.

Danewid, I. (2020) 'The fire this time: Grenfell, racial capitalism and the urbanisation of empire', *European Journal of International Relations*, 26(1): 289–313.

Danewid, I. (2023) *Resisting Racial Capitalism: An Antipolitical Theory of Refusal.* Cambridge: Cambridge University Press.

Dantzler, P. (2021) 'The urban process under racial capitalism: Race, anti-Blackness, and capital accumulation', *Journal of Race, Ethnicity and the City*, 2(2): 113–34.

Davies, J. (2021) *Sedated: How Modern Capitalism Created Our Mental Health Crisis.* London: Atlantic Books.

Davies, W. (2016) *The Limits of Neoliberalism: Authority, Sovereignty and the Logic of Competition.* London: Sage.

Davis, J., Jacobus, R., and Hickey, M. (2008) *Building Better City–CLT Partnerships: A Program Manual for Municipalities and Community Land Trusts.* Cambridge: Lincoln Institute of Land Policy.

Dawson, A. (2017) *Extreme Cities: The Peril and Promise of Urban Life in the Age of Climate Change.* London: Verso.

De Angelis, M. (2014) 'The commons: A brief life journey', *Community Development Journal*, 49: i68–i80.

Debord, G. (1967). *The Society of the Spectacle.* New York: Black and Red.

Dekeyser, T. (2021) 'Dismantling the advertising city: Subvertising and the urban commons to come', *Environment and Planning D: Society and Space*, 39(2): 309–27.

Deleuze, G., and Guattari, F. (1984) *Anti-Oedipus: Capitalism and Schizophrenia.* Minneapolis, MN: University of Minnesota.

Denvir, D. (2020) *All-American Nativism: How the Bipartisan War on Immigrants Explains Politics as We Know It.* London: Verso.

Derks, S., Koster, M., and Oosterbaan, M. (2020) 'Olympic legacies', *City & Society*, 32(1): 184–202.

Dhar, P. (2020). 'The carbon impact of artificial intelligence', *Nature, Machine, Intelligence*, 2(8): 423–5.

Diamond, A. (2018) 'Remembering Resurrection City and the Poor People's Campaign of 1968', *Smithsonian Magazine*, https://www.smithsonianmag.com/history/remembering-poor-peoples-campaign-180968742 (accessed 1 August 2024).

Dikeç, M. (2017). *Urban Rage: The Revolt of the Excluded.* London and New Haven, CT: Yale University Press.

Dorling, D. (2019). *Inequality and the 1%*. London: Verso.

Dorries, H., Henry, R., Hugill, D., McCreary, T., and Tomiak, J. (2019) 'Introduction', in Dorries, H., Henry, R., Hugill, D., McCreary, T., & Tomiak, J. (eds) *Settler City Limits: Indigenous Resurgence and Colonial Violence in the Urban Prairie West*. Winnipeg, MB: University of Manitoba Press.

Downey, C. (2013) 'Design with the blind in mind', TED Talk, https://www.ted.com/talks/chris_downey_design_with_the_blind_in_mind (accessed 23 July 2025).

Dudman, J. (2017) 'Belgian mayor wins world prize for work on integrating immigrants', *Guardian*, https://www.theguardian.com/public-leaders-network/2017/feb/16/belgian-mayor-wins-world-prize-for-work-on-integrating-immigrants (accessed 1 August 2024).

Edwards, F., Lee, H., & Esposito, M. (2019) 'Risk of being killed by police use of force in the United States by age, race-ethnicity, and sex', *Proceedings of the National Academy of Sciences*, 116(34): 16793–8.

Edwards, S. (2023). *The Chile Project: The Story of the Chicago Boys and the Downfall of Neoliberalism*. New Jersey, NJ: Princeton University Press.

Ehrenspreger, E. (2022) 'Cripping infrastructure', *Society and Space*, https://www.societyandspace.org/articles/cripping-infrastructure (accessed 1 August 2024).

Eiden-Offe, P. (2023). *The Poetry of Class: Romantic Anti-capitalism and the Invention of the Proletariat*. New York: Brill.

Eisenman, S. (2023) 'We need a working-class environmental movement', *CounterPunch*, https://www.counterpunch.org/2023/10/13/we-need-a-working-class-environmental-movement (accessed 1 August 2024).

Elkin, L. (2016) *Flâneuse: Women Walk the City in Paris, New York, Tokyo, Venice and London*. London: Chatto and Windus.

Elliott-Cooper, A. (2021). *Black Resistance to British Policing*. Manchester: Manchester University Press.

Ellis-Peterson, H. (2022) 'Bulldozers, violence and politics crack an Indian dream of utopia', *Guardian*, https://www.theguardian.com/world/2022/jan/16/bulldozers-violence-and-politics-crack-an-indian-dream-of-utopia (accessed 1 August 2024).

Engels, F. (2009 [1845]) *The Condition of the Working Class in England*. London: Cosimo.

Engelsman, U., Rowe, M., and Southern, A. (2018) 'Community Land Trusts, affordable housing and community organising in low-income neighbourhoods', *International Journal of Housing Policy*, 18(1): 103–23.

Essig, A., Leahy, M., and Shea, E. (2020) 'Redlining in South Side Chicago: A brief history and analysis', *ArcGIS Storymaps*, https://storymaps.arcgis.com/stories/6013968f316041879011fdc03857e146 (accessed 1 August 2024).

Estefania, J. (2018) '¡No queremos Olimpiada, queremos revolución!', *El Pais*, https://elpais.com/deportes/2018/10/01/actualidad/1538415487_180518.html (accessed 1 August 2024).

Ehwi, R., Maslova, S., and Burgess, G. (2022) 'Self-build and custom housebuilding in the UK: An evidence review', Cambridge Centre for Housing and Planning Research, https://thinkhouse.org.uk/site/assets/files/2593/cam0222.pdf (accessed 24 July 2025).

Faithfull, M. (2021) 'How the Marble Arch mound turned into "London's worst tourist attraction"', *Forbes*, https://www.forbes.com/sites/markfaithfull/2021/08/02/how-the-marble-arch-mound-turned-into-londons-worst-tourist-attraction (accessed 1 August 2024).

Fallon, K. (2021) 'Reproducing race in the gentrifying city: A critical analysis of race in gentrification scholarship', *Journal of Race, Ethnicity and the City*, 2(1): 1–28.

Federici, S. (2018) *Re-enchanting the World: Feminism and the Politics of the Commons*. London: Pm Press.

Ferreri, M. (2021) *The Permanence of Temporary Urbanism: Normalising Precarity in Austerity London*. Amsterdam: Amsterdam University Press.

Fick, C. (1990) *The Making of Haiti: The Saint Domingue Revolution from Below*. Knoxville, TN: University of Tennessee Press.

Fields, D. (2017a) 'Unwilling subjects of financialization', *International Journal of Urban and Regional Research*, 41(4), 588–603

Fields, D. (2017b) 'Urban struggles with financialization', *Geography Compass*, 11(11): 123–34.

Fincher, R., Pardy, M., and Shaw, K. (2016) 'Place-making or place-masking? The everyday political economy of "making place"', *Planning Theory & Practice*, 17(4): 516–36.

Firth, R. (2022). *Disaster Anarchy: Mutual Aid and Radical Action*. London: Pluto Press.

Fisher, M. (2017) *Acid Communism* (unfinished 'Introduction'), https://my-blackout.com/2019/04/25/mark-fisher-acid-communism-unfinished-introduction (accessed 1 August 2024).

Fisher, M. (2008). *Capitalist Realism: Is There No Alternative?* London: Zero Books.

Fisher, M. (2014) 'The slow cancellation of the future', talk at MaMa in Zagreb, https://archive.org/details/markfisher-theslowcancellationofthefuture (accessed 1 August 2024).

Flowers, D. (2005) 'The launching of the student sit-in movement: The role of Black women at Bennett College', *Journal of African American History*, 90(1–2): 52–63.

Forlano, L., Steenson, M., and Ananny, M. (eds) (2019) *Bauhaus Futures*. Cambridge, MA: MIT Press.

Fosters and Partners (n.d.) 'Projects/City Hall', https://www.fosterandpartners. com/projects/city-hall (accessed 1 August 2024).

Gentleman, A. (2017) 'Grenfell Tower MP highlights huge social divisions in London', *Guardian*, https://www.theguardian.com/inequality/2017/ nov/13/grenfell-tower-mp-highlights-huge-social-divisions-in-london (accessed 1 August 2024).

George, D., Hanson, R., Wilkinson, D., and Garcia-Romeu, A. (2022) 'Ancient roots of today's emerging renaissance in psychedelic medicine', *Culture, Medicine, and Psychiatry*, 46(4): 890–903.

Gerrard, J., Sriprakash, A., and Rudolph, S. (2022) 'Education and racial capitalism', *Race, Ethnicity and Education*, 25(3): 425–42.

Gibson-Graham, J. G. (2006) *A Post-Capitalist Politics*. Minneapolis, MN: University of Minnesota Press.

Gilbert, J. (2017) 'Psychedelic socialism', *openDemocracy*, https://www. opendemocracy.net/en/psychedelic-socialism (accessed 1 August 2024).

Gillam, W. (2023) 'A solarpunk manifesto: Turning imaginary into reality', *Philosophies*, 8(73), 1–12.

Gilmore, R. (2022) *Abolition Geography: Essays towards Liberation*. London: Verso.

Gilmore, R. (2020) *Geographies of Racial Capitalism with Ruth Wilson Gilmore: An Antipode Foundation Film*, https://www.youtube.com/ watch?v=2CS627aKrJI (accessed 1 August 2024).

Gilmore, R. (2007) *Golden Gulag: Prisons, Surplus, Crisis, and Opposition in Globalizing California*. Berkeley, CA: University of California Press.

Glass, R. (1964) 'Introduction', in Glass, R. (ed.) *London: Aspects of Change*. London: Macgibbon and Kee.

Gliddon, L. (2023) 'Black Panther', *Climate Lit*, https://www.climatelit.org/ literature/black-panther (accessed 1 August 2024).

Goh, K. (2021) *Form and Flow: The Spatial Politics of Urban Resilience and Climate Justice*. Minneapolis, MN: University of Minnesota Press.

Gold, J. (1984) 'The death of the urban vision?', *Futures*, 16(4): 372–81.

Gomez, A. (2023) 'Andalucía's communist mayor who ransacked supermarkets retires', *Sur in English*, https://www.surinenglish.com/andalucia/ andalucias-communist-mayor-who-ransacked-supermarkets-retires-20230406121538-nt.html (accessed 1 August 2024).

Gordon-Zolov, T. (2023) 'Chile's Estallido Social and the art of protest', *Sociologica*, 17(1): 41–55.

Gordon-Zolov, T., and Zolov, E. (2022) *The Walls of Santiago: Social Revolution and Political Aesthetics in Contemporary Chile*. New York: Berghahn Books.

Gourzis, K., Herod, A., and Gialis, S. (2019) 'Linking gentrification and labour market precarity in the contemporary city: A framework for analysis', *Antipode*, 51(5): 1436–55.

Graham, S. (2011). *Cities under Siege: The New Military Urbanism*. London: Verso.

Gramsci, A. (1999 [1926]). *Selections from the Prison Notebooks*. London: ElecBook.

Gramsci, A. (2017 [1927]) 'The Turin communist movement', *International Gramsci Journal*, 2(2): 40–51.

Gray, K. (2008) 'Community Land Trusts in the United States', *Journal of Community Practice*, 16(1): 65–78.

Greenberg, M. (2008) *Branding New York: How a City in Crisis Was Sold to the World*. Abingdon: Routledge.

Greenfield, A. (2024) *Lifehouse: Taking Care of Ourselves in a World on Fire*. London: Verso.

Grenfell Action Group (2016) 'KCTMO – Playing with Fire!', https://assets.grenfelltowerinquiry.org.uk/TMO00835660_GAG%20blog%20post%20-%20KCTMO%20Playing%20with%20fire..pdf (accessed 1 August 2024).

Guardian Editorial (2017) 'The *Guardian* view on Grenfell Tower: Theresa May's Hurricane Katrina', Guardian, https://www.theguardian.com/uk-news/commentisfree/2017/jun/15/the-guardian-view-on-grenfell-tower-theresa-may-hurricane-katrina (accessed 1 August 2024).

Guattari, F. (1992) 'Ecosophical practices and restoration of the subjective city', *Chimera: Review of Schizoanalyses*, 17: 95–115.

Guattari, F. (1989) *Les Trois Écologies*. Paris: Galilée.

Gudeman, S. (2001) *The Anthropology of Economy: Community, Market and Culture*. Oxford: Blackwell.

Guèye, O. (2018) 'May 1968 in Senegal', Verso blog, https://www.versobooks.com/en-gb/blogs/news/3880–may-1968–in-senegal (accessed 1 August 2024).

Hailey, C., and Wylie, D. (2019) *Slab City: 'Dispatches from the Last Free Place'*. Cambridge, MA: MIT Press.

Hamlett Films (2018) *Grenfell Tower and Social Murder*, https://hamlettfilms.com/work/grenfell-tower-and-social-murder (accessed 1 August 2024).

Hancox, D. (2013) *The Village against the World*. London: Verso.

Hanna, T., Guinan, J., and Bilsborough, J. (2018) 'The "Preston model" and the modern politics of municipal socialism', *openDemocracy*, https://neweconomics.opendemocracy.net/index.html%3Fp=3094.html (accessed 1 August 2024).

Haraway, D. (2016) *Staying with the Trouble: Making Kin in the Chthulucene*. Durham, NC: Duke University Press.

Harcourt, B. (2005) *Illusion of Order: The False Promise of Broken Windows Policing*. Cambridge, MA: Harvard University Press.

Harkness, R. (2011) 'Earthships: The homes that trash built', *Anthropology Now*, 3(1): 54–65.

Harlock, J. (2024) 'Rejecting dystopia: An introduction to solarpunk farming', *Offrange*, https://ambrook.com/research/sustainability/solarpunk-farming-regenerative-future (accessed 1 August 2024).

Hartnell, A. (2017) *After Katrina: Race, Neoliberalism, and the End of the American Century*. New York: SUNY Press.

Harvey, D. (1989) 'From managerialism to entrepreneurialism: The transformation in urban governance in late capitalism', *Geografiska Annaler. Series B: Human Geography*, 71(1): 3–17.

Harvey, D. (2012) *Rebel Cities: From the Right to the City to the Urban Revolution*. London: Verso.

Hatherley, O. (2014) 'Serried yuppiedromes', *London Review of Books*, https://www.lrb.co.uk/the-paper/v36/n16/owen-hatherley/serried-yuppiedromes (accessed 1 August 2024).

Hayes, K., and Kaba, M. (2023). *Let This Radicalize You: Organizing and the Revolution of Reciprocal Care*. New York: Haymarket Books.

Heiserová, S. (2021) 'The vertical order of the city: A gender perspective on the urban form', *Humanities Bulletin*, 4(1): 103–16.

Hendrickson, B. (2017) 'Finding Tunisia in the global 1960s', *Monde(s)*, 11(1): 61–78.

Herskind, M. (2022) 'Cop City and the prison industrial complex in Atlanta', Department of African American Studies, Princeton University, https://aas.princeton.edu/news/cop-city-and-prison-industrial-complex-atlanta (accessed 1 August 2024).

Heynen, N. (2010) 'Cooking up non-violent civil-disobedient direct action for the hungry: "Food Not Bombs" and the resurgence of radical democracy in the US', *Urban Studies*, 47(6), 1225–40.

Hickcox, A. (2018) 'White environmental subjectivity and the politics of belonging', *Social & Cultural Geography*, 19(4): 496–519.

Hill, A. (2023) 'Children raised under UK austerity shorter than European peers, study finds', *Guardian*, https://www.theguardian.com/business/2023/jun/21/children-raised-under-uk-austerity-shorter-than-european-peers-study (accessed 1 August 2024).

Hill, S. (2013) 'What did Bo Xilai's show trial tell us about China?', *Al Jazeera*, https://www.aljazeera.com/opinions/2013/8/29/what-did-bo-xilais-show-trial-tell-us-about-china (accessed 1 August 2024).

Hoffmann, C., and Matin, K. (2021) 'Beyond anarchy and capital? The geopolitics of the Rojava revolution in Syria', *Geopolitics*, 26(4): 967–72.

Hofmann, A. (1980) *LSD: My Problem Child*. New York: McGraw-Hill.

Holloway, J. (2010) *Crack Capitalism*. London: Pluto Press.

Hoole, C., Hincks, S., and Rae, A. (2019) 'The contours of a new urban world? Megacity population growth and density since 1975', *Town Planning Review*, 90(6), 653–78.

Hoyler, M., and Harrison, J. (2017) 'Global cities research and urban theory making', *Environment and Planning A: Economy and Space*, 49(12): 2853–8.

Hughes, S. (2020) 'On resistance in human geography', *Progress in Human Geography*, 44(6): 1141–60.

Hughey, M. (2023) '"Black people don't love nature": White environmentalist imaginations of cause, calling, and capacity', *Theory and Society*, 52(5): 831–63.

Huron, A. (2018) *Carving out the Commons: Tenant Organizing and Housing Cooperatives in Washington, DC.* Minneapolis, MN: University of Minnesota Press.

Huron, A. (2015) 'Working with strangers in saturated space: Reclaiming and maintaining the urban commons', *Antipode*, 47(4): 963–79.

IPCC (2021) 'IPCC sixth assessment report', https://www.ipcc.ch/report/ar6/wg1 (accessed 1 August 2024).

Irazábal-Zurita, C., Sosa, I., and Schlenker, L. (2020) 'The high-rise and the shack: Rhizomatic collisions in caracas' Torre David', *ACME: An International Journal for Critical Geographies*, 19(1): 1–34.

Jackson, T. (2007) *From Civil Rights to Human Rights: Martin Luther King, Jr., and the Struggle for Economic Justice.* University Park, PA: Penn State University Press.

Jaffe, R. (2021) 'Introduction: The disabling city', *International Journal of Urban and Regional Research*, https://www.ijurr.org/spotlight-on/disabling-city/introduction-the-disabling-city (accessed 1 August 2024).

James, C. L. R., (1938) *The Black Jacobins: Toussaint L'Ouverture and the San Domingo Revolution.* London: Penguin.

James, M. (2020) 'Racism, the media … and alternative (sonic) culture', *Ethnic and Racial Studies*, 43(13): 2372–8.

Jaros, K. (2023) 'The administrative structure and restructuring of cities in contemporary China', in Ergenc, C., and Goodman, D. (eds) *Handbook on Local Governance in China* (pp. 48–65). London: Edward Elgar.

Jaureguiberry-Mondion, J. (2023) 'Spatialising the collective: The spatial practices of two housing projects in Berlin', *Social & Cultural Geography*, 24(10): 1921–40.

Jay, M. (2019) *Mescaline: A global history of the first psychedelic.* London and New Haven, CT: Yale University Press.

Jencks, C. (1977) *The Language of Post-modern Architecture.* New York: Rizzoli.

Jens, B. (2023) 'Almere: The first solarpunk city?', *Blue Labyrinths*, https://bluelabyrinths.com/2023/02/13/almere-the-first-solarpunk-city (accessed 1 August 2024).

Jones, S. (2013) *Against Technology: From the Luddites to Neo-Luddism.* Abingdon: Routledge.

Jong, L. de, De Bruin, S., Knoop, J., and Vliet, J. van (2021) 'Understanding land-use change conflict: A systematic review of case studies', *Journal of Land Use Science*, 16(3): 223–39.

Jørgensen, C. (2012) 'Transurban interconnectivities: An essay on the interpretation of the revolutions of 1848', *European Review of History: Revue européenne d'histoire*, 19(2): 201–27.

Katz, Y. (2022) 'Intelligence under racial capitalism', *Monthly Review*, September 2022, 32–52.

Kaur, R. (2016) 'The innovative Indian: Common man and the politics of jugaad culture', *Contemporary South Asia*, 24(3): 313–27.

Kern, L. (2021) *Feminist City: Claiming Space in a Man-made World.* London: Verso.

Kim, W. (2024) 'A brief history of Silicon Valley's fascination with drugs', *Vox*, https://www.vox.com/2024/2/14/24067911/a-brief-history-of-silicon-valleys-fascination-with-drugs (accessed 1 August 2024).

Kirkland, E. (2008) 'What's race got to do with it? Looking for the racial dimensions of gentrification', *Western Journal of Black Studies*, 32(2): 18–30.

Klein, N. (2007) *The Shock Doctrine: The Rise of Disaster Capitalism.* New York: Macmillan.

Kline, B. (2022) *First Along the River: A Brief History of the US Environmental Movement.* Lanham, MD: Rowman & Littlefield.

Knikker, J. (2021) 'Almere Oosterwold, Netherlands: A Dutch utopia in the making', *African Journal of Landscape Architecture*, 2(9), https://www.ajlajournal.org/articles/almere-oosterwold-netherlands-a-dutch-utopia-in-the-making (accessed 1 August 2024).

Koekkoek, R. (2020) *The Citizenship Experiment.* New York: Brill.

Kramer, R., and Remster, B. (2022) 'The slow violence of contemporary policing', *Annual Review of Criminology*, 5(1): 43–66.

Kropotkin, P. (2022 [1902]) *Mutual Aid: A Factor of Evolution.* London: Penguin Classics.

Kurlansky, M. (2005) *1968: The Year That Rocked the World.* London: Vintage Books.

Lamont, T. (2024) '"Humanity's remaining timeline? It looks more like five years than 50": Meet the neo-Luddites warning of an AI apocalypse', *Guardian*, https://www.theguardian.com/technology/2024/feb/17/humanitys-remaining-timeline-it-looks-more-like-five-years-than-50–meet-the-neo-luddites-warning-of-an-ai-apocalypse (accessed 1 August 2024).

Laurent, S. (2019) *King and the Other America: The Poor People's Campaign and the Quest for Economic Equality.* Berkeley, CA: University of California Press.

Lees, L., and Philips, M. (2018) *Handbook of Gentrification Studies.* London: Edward Elgar.

Lees, L., Shin, H., and López-Morales, E. (2016) *Planetary Gentrification.* London: Polity.

Lefebvre, H. (1968) *Le Droit à la ville.* Paris: Anthropos.

Lefebvre, H. (1970) *La Révolution urbaine.* Paris: Editions Gallimard.

Lefèvre, C. (1998) 'Metropolitan government and governance in western countries: A critical review', *International Journal of Urban and Regional Research*, 22(1): 9–25.

Le Guin, U. (2014) National Book Foundation's Medal for Distinguished Contribution to American Letters Acceptance Speech, https://www.youtube.com/watch?v=Et9Nf-rsALk (accessed 1 August 2024).

Levy, P. (2018) *The Great Uprising: Race Riots in Urban America During the 1960s.* Cambridge: Cambridge University Press.

Li, S. (2014) *Understanding the Chinese City.* London: Sage.

Linebaugh, P. (2008) *The Magna Carta Manifesto: Liberties and Commons for All.* Berkeley, CA: University of California Press.

Lloyd, M., Peel, D., and Janssen-Jansen, L. (2015) 'Self-build in the UK and Netherlands: Mainstreaming self-development to address housing shortages?', *Urban, Planning and Transport Research*, 3(1): 19–31.

Lodi-Ribeiro, G., and Orsi, C. (2013) *Solarpunk: Ecological and Fantastical Stories in a Sustainable World.* Sãu Paulo: Word Weaver Press.

Loftin, T., Matisová, S., Yáñez Serreno, B., and Edwards, M. (2019) 'Viability: An accessibility guide', *Just Space*, https://justspace.org.uk/wp-content/uploads/2019/05/ucl-viability-group-report-2019.pdf (accessed 1 August 2024).

López-Morales, E. (2015) 'Gentrification in the Global South', *City*, 19(4): 564–73.

López-Morales, E. (2018) 'A rural gentrification theory debate for the Global South?', *Dialogues in Human Geography*, 8(1): 47–50.

Lourde, A. (2018 [1984]) *The Master's Tools Will Never Dismantle the Master's House.* London: Penguin Classics.

Löwy, M. (2007) *The Marxism of Che Guevara: Philosophy, Economics, Revolutionary Warfare.* Lanham, MD: Rowman & Littlefield.

Lyu, H. (2023) 'Seven days that ended the Prague Spring', The Nonviolence Project, https://thenonviolenceproject.wisc.edu/2023/03/24/seven-days-that-ended-the-prague-spring (accessed 1 August 2024).

Mackey, K., Ayers, C., Kondo, K., Saha, S., Advani, S., Young, S., Spencer, H., Rusek, M., Anderson, J., Veazie, S., Smith, M., and Kansagara, D.

(2021) 'Racial and ethnic disparities in COVID-19-related infections, hospitalizations, and deaths: A systematic review', *Annals of Internal Medicine*, 174(3): 362–73.

MacKinnon, D., and Derickson, K. D. (2013) 'From resilience to resourcefulness: A critique of resilience policy and activism', *Progress in Human Geography*, 37(2): 253–70.

MacLeod, G., and McFarlane, C. (2014) 'Introduction: Grammars of urban injustice', *Antipode*, 46(4): 857–73.

Madden, D., and Marcuse, P. (2016) *In Defense of Housing. The Politics of Crisis*. London: Verso.

Manzinger, K., and Wagner, P. (2020) 'Syrian Kurds, Rojava and alternative society building in Middle East', *Hungarian Defence Review*, 148(1): 15–40.

Marshall, A. (2023) 'Walking for revolution: From surrealism to the Situationist International', *New Readings*, 19: 19–42.

Martin, D., Pierce, J., DeFilippis, J., Williams, O., Kruger, R., and Hadizadeh Esfahani, A. (2024) '"I don't think anybody's ever been to scale": The imperative for growth and the implications of scale for Community Land Trusts in Minnesota, USA', *Urban Geography*, 1–19 (early online view).

Marx, K. (1998 [1894]) *Capital: Volume III*. London: Penguin Classics.

Mattar, D. (2020) 'Public space as border space: Social contention and street art in Santiago post-18/O', *Frame*, 33(1): 31–47.

Mauss, M. (1954) *The Gift*. London: Cohen & West.

Mazzucato, M. (2018) *The Value of Everything: Making and Taking in the Global Economy*, London: Allen Lane.

McAuliffe, C. (2012) 'Graffiti or street art? Negotiating the moral geographies of the creative city', *Journal of Urban Affairs*, 34(2): 189–206.

McDowell, M., and Fernandez, L. (2018) '"Disband, disempower, and disarm": Amplifying the theory and practice of police abolition', *Critical Criminology*, 26: 373–91.

McFarlane, C. (2021) *Fragments of the City: Making and Remaking Urban Worlds*. Berkeley, CA: University of California.

McGuire, L., Morris, S. L., and Pollard, T. M. (2022) 'Community gardening and wellbeing: The understandings of organisers and their implications for gardening for health'. *Health & Place*, 75: article no. 102773.

McGuirk, J. (2014) *Radical Cities: Across Latin America in Search of a New Architecture*. London: Verso.

McKittrick, K. (2006) *Demonic Grounds: Black Women and the Cartographies of Struggle*. Minneapolis, MN: University of Minnesota Press.

McMillan Cottom, T. (2020) 'Where platform capitalism and racial capitalism meet: The sociology of race and racism in the digital society', *Sociology of Race and Ethnicity*, 6(4): 441–9.

Medien, K. (2020) 'Foucault in Tunisia: The encounter with intolerable power', *Sociological Review*, 68(3): 492–507.

Medoff, P., and Sklar, H. (1994) *Streets of Hope: The Fall and Rise of an Urban Neighborhood*. Boston, MA: South End Press.

Medvedyuk, S., Govender, P., and Raphael, D. (2021) 'The reemergence of Engels' concept of social murder in response to growing social and health inequalities', *Social Science & Medicine*, 289: 1–13.

Mei, X. (2017) 'Why Chongqing's Red Culture campaign was not a real mass campaign', *International Journal of Politics, Culture, and Society*, 30(1): 63–81.

Meister, F. (2017) *Racism and Resistance: How the Black Panthers Challenged White Supremacy*. Berlin: Transcript Verlag.

Mezzadra, S., and Neilson, B. (2013) *Border as Method, or, the Multiplication of Labor*. New York: Duke University Press.

Mies van der Rohe, L. (1924) 'Architecture and the Times', available here: https://talhashahidarchitects.com/f/ludwig-mies-van-der-rohe%E2%80%9 9s-%E2%80%9Carchitecture-and-the-times%E2%80%9D-1924 (accessed 1 August 2024).

Minton, A. (2017) *Big Capital: Who Is London For?* London: Penguin.

Mollenkopf, J., and Castells, M. (1991) 'Introduction', in Mollenkopf, J., and Castells, M. (eds) *Dual City: Restructuring New York*. London: Russell Sage Foundation.

Molyneux, J. (2019) 'The environmental crisis and the new environmental revolt', *Irish Marxist Review*, 8(24): 38–42.

Montague, L. (1938) *The Black Jacobins: Toussaint L'Ouverture and the San Domingo Revolution*. New York: Dial Press.

Mouffe, C. (2005) *The Return of the Political*. London: Verso.

Mould, O. (2018). *Against Creativity*. London: Verso.

Mould, O. (2017) 'Brutalism redux: Relational monumentality and the urban politics of brutalist architecture', *Antipode*, 49(3): 701–20.

Mould, O. (2016) 'A limitless urban theory? A response to Scott and Storper's "The nature of cities: The scope and limits of urban theory"', *International Journal of Urban and Regional Research*, 40(1): 157–63.

Mould, O. (2020) 'Revolutionary ideals of the Paris Commune live on in Black Lives Matter autonomous zone in Seattle', *The Conversation*, https://theconversation.com/revolutionary-ideals-of-the-paris-commune-live-on-in-black-lives-matter-autonomous-zone-in-seattle-140673 (accessed 1 August 2024).

Mould, O. (2021) *Seven Ethics against Capitalism: Towards a Planetary Commons*. London: Polity.

Mould, O., Cole, J., Badger, A., and Brown, P. (2022) 'Solidarity, not charity: Learning the lessons of the COVID-19 pandemic to reconceptualise the radicality of mutual aid', *Transactions of the Institute of British Geographers*, 47(4): 866–79.

Mueller, G. (2021) *Breaking Things at Work: The Luddites Are Right about Why You Hate Your Job*. London: Verso.

Nahoum, B. (2013) 'Forty years of self-management in popular housing in Uruguay: The "FUCVAM model"', in Harnecker, C. (ed.) *Cooperatives and Socialism* (pp. 190–211). London: Palgrave Macmillan.

Nahoum, B., and Valles, R. (2014) 'Re-shaping the city by making urban land accessible: The case of housing cooperatives in Uruguay', in The Passerelle Collective (eds) *Take Back the Land! The Social Function of Land and Housing, Resistances & Alternatives* (pp. 177–81), https://www.coredem.info/IMG/pdf/takebackland.pdf (accessed 1 August 2024).

NASA (2016) '10 interesting things about energy', NASA Global Climate Change, https://climate.nasa.gov/news/2444/10–interesting-things-about-energy (accessed 1 August 2024).

National Audit Office (2020) 'Investigation into remediating dangerous cladding on high-rise buildings', https://www.nao.org.uk/reports/investigation-into-remediating-dangerous-cladding-from-high-rise-buildings (accessed 1 August 2024).

Navrátil, J., and Benčík, A. (1998) *The Prague Spring, 1968*. Budapest: Central European University Press.

Neate, R. (2018) 'Shard owners seek to ban protest by class war activist', *Guardian*, https://www.theguardian.com/world/2018/feb/06/shard-owners-seek-to-ban-protest-by-class-war-activist (accessed 1 August 2024).

NIHR (2024) 'Local green spaces and mental health', podcast, National Institute for Health and Care Research. https://evidence.nihr.ac.uk/alert/local-green-spaces-are-linked-with-better-mental-health/ (accessed 24 July 2025).

Nowicki, M. (2023) *Bringing Home the Housing Crisis: Politics, Precarity and Domicide in Austerity London*. London: Policy Press.

Ogundairo, T., Adegoke, D., Akinwumi, I., and Olofinnade, O. (2019) 'Sustainable use of recycled waste glass as an alternative material for building construction: A review', in IOP Conference Series, *Materials Science and Engineering*, 640(1): 1–12.

Ojeda, J. (2023) 'The Book of Revolt and the House of Rejection: On neoliberalism and the constitutional process in Chile, 2019–2022', *South Atlantic Quarterly*, 122(4): 827–36.

Oswin, N. (2015) 'World, city, queer', *Antipode*, 47(3): 557–65.

Ott, T. (1973) *The Haitian Revolution, 1789–1804*. Knoxville, TN: University of Tennessee Press.

Otte, H., and Gielen, P. (2020) 'Commoning art as political companion: On the issue of participatory democracy', in Négrier, E., and Dupin-Meynard,

F. (eds) *Cultural Policies in Europe: A Participatory Turn?* Toulouse: Éditions de l'Attribut.

Parson, S. (2018) *Cooking Up a Revolution: Food Not Bombs, Homes Not Jails, and Resistance to Gentrification.* Manchester: Manchester University Press.

Peck, J., and Theodore, N. (2015) *Fast Policy: Experimental Statecraft at the Thresholds of Neoliberalism.* Minneapolis, MN: University of Minnesota Press.

Peck, J., Theodore, N., and Brenner, N. (2013) 'Neoliberal urbanism redux?', *International Journal of Urban and Regional Research*, 37(3): 1091–9.

Perera, J. (2018) 'The politics of generation grime', *Race & Class*, 60(2): 82–93.

Pethokoukis, J. (2022) 'Why socialist "solarpunk" provides a poor vision of the future', American Enterprise Institute, https://www.aei.org/articles/why-socialist-solarpunk-provides-a-poor-vision-of-the-future/ (accessed 1 August 2024).

Phinney, S. (2020) 'Rethinking geographies of race and austerity urbanism', *Geography Compass*, 14(3): 1–12.

Piketty, T. (2014) *Capital in the Twenty-first Century.* Cambridge, MA: Harvard University Press.

Pidd, H. (2023) 'Plan to build over Salford riverside footpath dropped after outcry', *Guardian*, https://www.theguardian.com/uk-news/2023/feb/25/plan-to-build-over-salford-riverside-footpath-dropped-after-outcry (accessed 1 August 2024).

Pierson, E., Simoiu, C., Overgoor, J., Corbett-Davies, S., Jenson, D., Shoemaker, A., Ramachandran, V., Barghouty, P., Phillips, C., Shroff, R., and Goel, S. (2020) 'A large-scale analysis of racial disparities in police stops across the United States', *Nature*, 4(7): 736–45.

Pinder, D. (2002) 'In defence of utopian urbanism: Imagining cities after the "end of utopia"', *Geografiska Annaler. Series B: Human Geography*, 84(3–4): 229–41.

Pinder, D. (2015) 'Reconstituting the possible: Lefebvre, utopia and the urban question', *International Journal of Urban and Regional Research*, 39(1): 28–45.

Pinder, D. (2005) *Visions of the City: Utopianism, Power and Politics in Twentieth-century Urbanism.* Edinburgh: Edinburgh University Press.

Plant, S. (1992) *The Most Radical Gesture. The Situationist International in a Postmodern Age.* Abingdon: Routledge.

Poniatowska, E. (1975) *Massacre in Mexico.* London: Viking Press.

Potorti, M. (2017) '"Feeding the revolution": The Black Panther Party, hunger, and community survival', *Journal of African American Studies*, 21(1): 85–110.

Powell, C. (2020) 'The color and gender of COVID: Essential workers, not disposable people', *Think Global Health*, https://www.thinkglobalhealth.org/article/color-and-gender-covid-essential-workers-not-disposable-people (accessed 1 August 2024).

Pritchard-Jones, O. (2023) 'Tate Modern: Flat owners win viewing platform privacy case', BBC *News*, https://www.bbc.co.uk/news/uk-england-london-64481260 (accessed 1 August 2024).

Pruijt, H. (2013) 'The logic of urban squatting', *International Journal of Urban and Regional Research*, 37(1): 19–45.

Pulido, L. (2017) 'Geographies of race and ethnicity II: Environmental racism, racial capitalism and state-sanctioned violence', *Progress in Human Geography*, 41(4): 524–33.

Qatari Diar (2024) 'Citygate New Cairo', https://www.qataridiar.com/project/citygate-new-cairo (accessed 1 August 2024).

Raco, M. (2009) 'Governance, urban', in Kitchen, R., and Thrift, N. (eds) *International Encyclopaedia of Human Geography*. London: Elsevier.

Ramírez, M. (2020) 'City as borderland: Gentrification and the policing of Black and Latinx geographies in Oakland', *Environment and Planning D: Society and Space*, 38(1): 147–66.

Ramroth, R. (2007) *Planning for Disaster: How Natural and Man-made Disasters Shape the Built Environment*. New York: Kaplan.

Rast, J. (2019) *The Origins of the Dual City: Housing, Race, and Redevelopment in Twentieth-century Chicago*. Chicago, IL: University of Chicago Press.

Ray, L., Wylie, L., and Corrado, A. M. (2022) 'Shapeshifters, systems thinking and settler colonial logic: Expanding the framework of analysis of Indigenous health equity', *Social Science & Medicine*, 300: article no. 114422.

Re-Arrangements Collective (2023). 'On urban re-arrangements: A suite in five movements', *International Journal of Urban and Regional Research*, 47(3): 461–70.

Regenerative Design Collective (n.d.) 'A solarpunk manifesto', https://www.re-des.org/es/a-solarpunk-manifesto (accessed 1 August 2024).

Richards, B. (2006) *New Glass Architecture*. London and New Haven, CT: Yale University Press.

Roast, A. (2019a) 'A Letter from Chongqing', *Tribune Magazine*, https://tribunemag.co.uk/2019/05/a-letter-from-chongqing (accessed 1 August 2024).

Roast, A. (2019b) 'Peripheral modernities: Urban imaginaries, housing, and informality on the edge of Chongqing', PhD Thesis, University of Leeds.

Roast, A. (2024) 'Towards weird verticality: The spectacle of vertical spaces in Chongqing', *Urban Studies*, 61(4): 636–53.

Robertson, R., and Buhari-Gulmez, D. (2017) *Global Culture: Consciousness and Connectivity*. London: Taylor & Francis.

Robinson, C. (1983) *Black Marxism: The Making of the Black Radical Tradition*. Chapel Hill, NC: University of North Carolina Press.

Robinson, J., and Roy, A. (2016) 'Debate on global urbanisms and the nature of urban theory', *International Journal of Urban and Regional Research*, 40(1): 181–6.

Rodríguez, C. (2020) '"The whole damn system is guilty": Urban violence, the principal contradiction of racial capitalism, and the production of premature death in Oakland, California', *Critical Sociology*, 46(7–8): 1057–74.

Rojek, C. (2017) 'Paris, Wall Street: Reflections on the political crowd and labelling world historical events', *Sociological Review*, 65(2): 302–17.

Rose, M. (2025) *The Feminist Art of Walking*. London: Pluto Press.

Rose, M. (2021) 'Walking together, alone during the pandemic', *Geography*, 106(2): 101–4.

Ross, K. (2016) *Communal Luxury: The Political Imaginary of the Paris Commune*. London: Verso.

Rothstein, R. (2017) *The Color of Law: A Forgotten History of How Our Government Segregated America*. New York: Liveright Publishing.

Routhier, D. (2023) *With and Against: The Situationist International in the Age of Automation*. London: Verso.

Roy, A. (2011) 'Slumdog cities: Rethinking subaltern urbanism', *International Journal of Urban and Regional Research*, 35(2): 223–38.

Rubin, G. (2021) 'Lancashire village buys its own pub – to add to its shop and library', *Guardian*, https://www.theguardian.com/society/2021/nov/21/lancashire-village-buys-its-own-pub-to-add-to-its-shop-and-library (accessed 1 August 2024).

Rucks-Ahidiana, Z. (2022) 'Theorizing gentrification as a process of racial capitalism', *City & Community*, 21(3): 173–92.

Safransky, S. (2020) 'Geographies of algorithmic violence: Redlining the smart city', *International Journal of Urban and Regional Research*, 44(2): 200–18.

Salgado, A. (2019) 'During the 2019 Chilean protests, the walls of Santiago dreamed of a different world', *Jacobin*, https://jacobin.com/2023/08/walls-of-santiago-review-chile-2019–protests-art (accessed 1 August 2024).

Santoyo-Orozco, I. (2023) 'Future commoners', ee-flux Architecture, https://www.e-flux.com/architecture/in-common/529980/future-commoners (accessed 1 August 2024).

Sarkisian, N., and Gerstel, N. (2012). *Nuclear Family Values, Extended Family Lives: The Power of Race, Class, and Gender*. Abingdon: Routledge.

Sassen, S. (2001). *The Global City: New York, London, Tokyo*. New Jersey, NJ: Princeton University Press.

Sassen, S. (2011) 'The global street: Making the political', *Globalizations*, 8(5): 573–9.

Sassen, S. (2014) *Expulsions: Brutality and Complexity in the Global Economy*. Cambridge, MA: Harvard University Press.

Saunders, R. A. (2019) '(Profitable) imaginaries of Black Power: The popular and political geographies of *Black Panther*', *Political Geography*, 69: 139–49.

Schwartz, D. (2019) *Ghetto: The History of a Word*. Cambridge, MA: Harvard University Press.

Schwartz, S. (2022) 'Nekronology: The end of the future at the Hudson Yards', *Antipode*, 54(5): 1650–69.

Schwarz, L., Keler, A., and Krisp, J. M. (2022) 'Improving urban bicycle infrastructure: An exploratory study based on the effects from the COVID-19 Lockdown', *Journal of Urban Mobility*, 2: article no. 100013.

Schwiter, K., Berndt, C., and Truong, J. (2018) 'Neoliberal austerity and the marketisation of elderly care', *Social & Cultural Geography*, 19(3): 379–99.

Scott, A., and Storper, M. (2015) 'The nature of cities: The scope and limits of urban theory', *International Journal of Urban and Regional Research*, 39(1): 1–15.

Slater, T. (2011) 'Gentrification of the city', in Bridge, G., and Watson, S. (eds) *The New Blackwell Companion to the City*, Hoboken, NJ: Wiley-Blackwell: 571–85.

Slater, T. (2018) 'The invention of the "sink estate": Consequential categorisation and the UK housing crisis', *Sociological Review*, 66(4): 877–97.

Slater, T. (2021) *Shaking up the City: Ignorance, Inequality, and the Urban Question*. Berkeley, CA: University of California Press.

Smith, H. (2023) 'The Ronan Point scandal: Architecture, crisis, and possibility in British social democracy, 1968–93', *Twentieth Century British History*, 34(4): 805–34.

Smith, N. (1996) *The New Urban Frontier: Gentrification and the Revanchist City*. London: Routledge.

Smith, N. (1979) 'Toward a theory of gentrification: A back to the city movement by capital, not people', *Journal of the American Planning Association*, 45(4): 538–48.

So, R. (2021) *Redlining Culture: A Data History of Racial Inequality and Postwar Fiction*. New York: Columbia University Press.

Solomon, D., Maxwell, C., and Castro, A. (2019) 'Systemic inequality: Displacement, exclusion, and segregation', Center for American Progress, https://www.americanprogress.org/article/systemic-inequality-displacement-exclusion-segregation (accessed 1 August 2024).

Solomos, J. (2019) '"Strangers in their own land": Powellism's policy impact', *Patterns of Prejudice*, 53(2): 200–9.

Sousa Santos, B. de (1998) 'Participatory budgeting in Porto Alegre: Toward a redistributive democracy', *Politics & Society*, 26(4): 461–510.

Spade, D. (2020). *Mutual Aid: Building Solidarity During This Crisis (and the Next)*. London: Verso.

Sperber, J. (2005) *The European Revolutions, 1848–1851*. Cambridge: Cambridge University Press.

Springer, S. (2014) 'Why a radical geography must be anarchist', *Dialogues in Human Geography*, 4(3): 249–70.

Steinkopf-Frank, H. (2021) 'Solarpunk is not about pretty aesthetics. It's about the end of capitalism', *Vice*, https://www.vice.com/en/article/wx5aym/solarpunk-is-not-about-pretty-aesthetics-its-about-the-end-of-capitalism (accessed 1 August 2024).

Stone, Jr., B. (2024) *Radical Adaptation: Transforming Cities for a Climate Changed World*. Cambridge: Cambridge University Press.

Swyngedouw, E. (2002) The strange respectability of the situationist city in the society of the spectacle', *International Journal of Urban and Regional Research*, 26(1): 153–65.

Taub, M. (2020) 'These protest photos document life in "Resurrection City"', *Atlas Obscura*, https://www.atlasobscura.com/articles/jill-freedman-photos (accessed 1 August 2024).

Taylor, M., and Gayle, D. (2019) 'Battle of Waterloo Bridge: A week of Extinction Rebellion protests', *Guardian*, https://www.theguardian.com/environment/2019/apr/20/battle-of-waterloo-bridge-a-week-of-extinction-rebellion-protests (accessed 1 August 2024).

Taylor, P. J. (2013) *Extraordinary Cities: Millennia of Moral Syndromes, World-Systems and City/State Relations*. London: Edward Elgar.

Thomas, P. (2016) 'Youth, terrorism and education: Britain's Prevent programme', *International Journal of Lifelong Education*, 35(2): 171–87.

Thompson, M. (2021) 'What's so new about New Municipalism?' *Progress in Human Geography*, 45(2): 317–42.

Thornton, C. (2020) *The Hologram: Feminist, Peer-to-Peer Health for a Post-Pandemic Future*. London: Pluto Press.

Thorpe, A. (2014) 'Applying protest event analysis to architecture and design', *Social Movement Studies*, 13(2): 275–95.

Thorpe, J., Cannon, M., and Emili, S. (2019) '"Empresas Recuperadas": Argentina's recovered factory movement', Institute of Development Studies, Brighton, case summary no.4.

Ting, T. Y. (2020) 'From "be water" to "be fire": Nascent smart mob and networked protests in Hong Kong', *Social Movement Studies*, 19(3): 362–8.

Tombs, S. (2020) 'Home as a site of state-corporate violence: Grenfell Tower, aetiologies and aftermaths', *The Howard Journal of Crime and Justice*, 59(2): 120–42.

Torry, M. (2023) 'Introduction', in Torry, M. (ed.) *The Palgrave International Handbook of Basic Income*. London: Palgrave Macmillan.

Tronto, J. (2020) *Moral Boundaries: A Political Argument for an Ethic of Care*. Abingdon: Routledge.

Trouillot, M. (2015) *Silencing the Past: Power and the Production of History*. Boston, MA: Beacon Press.

Trujillo, S. (2021) 'Off-road, off-grid: The modern nomads wandering America's back country', *Guardian*, https://www.theguardian.com/lifeandstyle/2021/feb/04/modern-nomads-nomadland-van-life-us-public-lands (accessed 24 July 2025).

UK Parliament (2019) 'Government "far too slow" in Grenfell Tower fire response, says Committee', https://committees.parliament.uk/committee/17/housing-communities-and-local-government-committee/news/104461/government-far-too-slow-in-grenfell-tower-fire-response-says-committee (accessed 1 August 2024).

UN Habitat (2018) 'What is a city?', UN Habitat: For a Better Urban Future, https://unhabitat.org/sites/default/files/2020/06/city_definition_what_is_a_city.pdf (accessed 21 July 2025).

Van den Berg, M. (2018). 'The discursive uses of Jane Jacobs for the genderfying city: Understanding the productions of space for post-Fordist gender notions', *Urban Studies*, 55(4): 751–66.

Vasudevan, A. (2015) 'The makeshift city: Towards a global geography of squatting', *Progress in Human Geography*, 39(3): 338–59.

Vergara-Perucich, F., and Boano, C. (2021) 'The big bang of neoliberal urbanism: The gigantomachy of Santiago's urban development', *Environment and Planning C: Politics and Space*, 39(1): 184–203.

Vernet, A., Khayesi, J. N., George, V., George, G., and Bahaj, A. S. (2019) 'How does energy matter? Rural electrification, entrepreneurship, and community development in Kenya', *Energy Policy*, 126: 88–98.

Vidal, L. (2019) 'Cooperative Islands in capitalist waters: Limited-equity housing cooperatives, urban renewal and gentrification', *International Journal of Urban and Regional Research*, 43(1): 157–78.

Wacquant, L. (2008) *Urban Outcasts: A Comparative Sociology of Advanced Marginality*. London: Polity.

Wagner, P. (2023) 'Solarpunk spirituality: From the individual to community adaptation', *Solarpunk Station*, https://solarpunkstation.com/2023/06/22/solarpunk-spirituality-from-the-individual-to-community-adaptation (accessed 1 August 2024).

Wainwright, O. (2019) 'Marmalade Lane: The car-free, triple-glazed, 42–house oasis', *Guardian*, https://www.theguardian.com/artanddesign/2019/may/08/marmalade-lane-co-housing-cambridge (accessed 1 August 2024).

Wainwright, O. (2021) 'Mound zero: What is Marble Arch's new landmark all about?', *Guardian*, https://www.theguardian.com/artanddesign/2021/jul/23/marble-arch-hill-mound-london-oxford-street (accessed 1 August 2024).

Wall, T., and McClanahan, B. (2024). '"Little wars with the police": Aesthetic arsenals and intellects of insult', *Crime, Media, Culture*, https://journals.sagepub.com/doi/abs/10.1177/17416590241238952?af=R (accessed 28 July 2025).

Walsh, D., Dundas, R., McCartney, G., Gibson, M., and Seaman, R. (2022) 'Bearing the burden of austerity: How do changing mortality rates in the UK compare between men and women?', *Journal of Epidemiology and Community Health*, 76(12): 1027–33.

Wang, L. (2022) 'New data: Police use of force rising for Black, female, and older people; racial bias persists', Prison Policy Initiative, https://www.prisonpolicy.org/blog/2022/12/22/policing_survey (accessed 1 August 2024).

Ward, C., and Swyngedouw, E. (2018) 'Neoliberalisation from the ground up: Insurgent capital, regional struggle, and the assetisation of land', *Antipode*, 50(4): 1077–97.

Watt, P. (2017) 'Social housing and urban renewal: An introduction', in Watt, P., and Smets, P. (eds) *Social Housing and Urban Renewal* (pp. 1–36). Leeds: Emerald Publishing.

White, J. (2020) *Terraformed: Young Black Lives in the Inner City*. London: Repeater.

Wicks, M., Hampshire, C., Campbell, J., Graham, S., Maple-Brown, L., and Kirkham, R. (2024) 'Us and them: Colonialism and racism in remote Aboriginal healthcare discourse', *Ethnic and Racial Studies*, 1–25.

Willberg, E., Fink, C., and Toivonen, T. (2023) 'The 15–minute city for all? Measuring individual and temporal variations in walking accessibility', *Journal of Transport Geography*, 106: 1–11.

Wirth, L. (1928) *The Ghetto*. Chicago, IL: University of Chicago Press.

Woods, O. (2022) 'From roadman to royalties: Inter-representational value and the hypercapitalist impulses of grime', *Crime, Media, Culture*, 18(3): 412–29.

World-Habitat Awards, 2024 winners, https://world-habitat.org/world-habitat-awards/winners-and-finalists/?fwp_year=2024 (accessed 1 August 2024).

Yam, S. Y. S., and Ma, C. (2024) 'Being water: Protest zines and the politics of care in Hong Kong', *Cultural Studies*, 38(4): 668–96.

Yang, Q., and Ley, D. (2019) 'Residential relocation and the remaking of socialist workers through state-facilitated urban redevelopment in Chengdu, China', *Urban Studies*, 56(12): 2480–98.

Yates, L. (2015) 'Rethinking prefiguration: Alternatives, micropolitics and goals in social movements', *Social Movement Studies*, 14(1), 1–21.

Zhu, L., Goodman, L., Zhu, J. (2022) 'The Community Reinvestment Act meant to combat redlining's effects: 45 years later, Black homebuyers are still significantly underserved', Urban Institute, https://www.urban.org/urban-wire/community-reinvestment-act-meant-combat-redlinings-effects-45–years-later-black (accessed 1 August 2024).

Index

EU authorised representative for GPSR:
Easy Access System Europe, Mustamäe tee 50,
10621 Tallinn, Estonia
gpsr.requests@easproject.com